PERVERTING THE COURSE OF JUSTICE

PERVERTING THE COURSE OF JUSTICE

INSPECTOR GADGET

Monday Books

First published in Great Britain in 2008 by Monday Books

A CIP catalogue record for this title is available
from the British Library

ISBN : 978-1-906308-04-9

Printed and bound by Cox and Wyman
Typeset by Andrew Searle
Cover Design by Paul Hill at Kin Creative

www.mondaybooks.com
info@mondaybooks.com
http://mondaybooks.wordpress.com/
http://inspectorgadget.wordpress.com/

This book is dedicated to the wonderful Debbie, Vera, Chuck and Dave, to all those who protect and serve on the front line in F Division, Ruralshire Constabulary, and to the members of the Campester Terra Congregatio.

'Gentlemen, the Eagle has landed!'

CH-CH-CH-CHANGES

TWO years ago, a man calling himself PC David Copperfield wrote a groundbreaking book called *Wasting Police Time*. In it, he described the working life of an ordinary bobby, trying to do his job but frustrated at every turn by a strange bureaucracy which seemed almost entirely unrelated to his work, even counterproductive to it. At the time, people weren't talking much about paperwork and targets and 'detections', but Copperfield revealed to the wider world what most rank and file police officers already knew – that our Criminal Justice System was in severe danger of becoming a complete joke.

It was very funny book, I thought, and also very brave. (Declaration of interest: this book is from the same publisher.) He was exposing things that some senior officers and members of the Government didn't want exposing, and I don't know a single copper of my rank or below who didn't think every single word in it was true. Typically, the Police Minister Tony McNulty MP denounced it in the House of Commons as 'more of a fiction than Dickens', but he had to backtrack on this when interviewed for a BBC *Panorama* programme about the book and its author.

I'm sure there was something of a hunt on to discover Copperfield's true identity, but eventually he unmasked himself as PC Stuart Davidson. By then, a lot of what he had said had filtered through into the mainstream media, with newspapers across the political spectrum joining TV and radio journalists in asking questions about the form-filling and time-wasting that beset the police.

Although I had already agreed to write this book by then, I was confident that Stuart had said it all and that change might follow – the powers-that-be couldn't possibly ignore this media pressure, could they? Indeed, a variety of initiatives *have* since been launched and grand promises made. There's been Sir Ronnie Flanagan's Independent Review of Policing, pledges of hand-held computers to cut paperwork, the ongoing drive towards Neighbourhood Policing, more PCSOs than ever and even a Green Paper.

But all that's really happened is a few of the Titanic's deckchairs have been shifted around. Ronnie's report was a major missed opportunity, which skirts round the heart of the matter and will achieve nothing. Ditto, hand-held computers. Neighbourhood Policing and PCSOs are *part* of the problem, not the answers to it. The Green Paper was a rehash of old ideas and new nonsense that was rightly dismissed by the Police Federation as being full of empty promises. Despite recent 'spin' to the contrary, the situation with bureaucracy, political correctness and general target-driven baloney is now *worse* than it was before Copperfield, not better.

Lots of this stuff was brought in after scandals like the Guildford Four, the Birmingham Six and the bungled Stephen Lawrence murder investigation. Some of it was certainly needed, and no-one can say there is no corruption or racism in the police, but the pendulum has swung *far* too far the other way. The actions of a few bent or incompetent coppers working, in many cases, before most modern officers were even born are simply not a sensible justification for the current levels of regulation and mistrust we labour under, particularly as they now seriously hamper our ability to deliver a decent service to the public.

Thousands of officers who could and should be on the streets deterring and nicking criminals are employed behind desks 'auditing' crime reports and managing detection figures. I am concerned that our insane obsession with largely irrelevant targets will eventually cost lives. It probably already has.

It is not enough to tinker around the edges: major change is needed if you want us to be able to respond quickly to your burglary or assault or mugging – or maybe even stand a chance of preventing them from happening in the first place.

Like PC Copperfield, I'm a real police officer writing under a pseudonym about his job as a front line 'Response' officer. There are lots of other cops, some doing very worthwhile jobs, others sat in offices doing nothing in particular, but I'm writing about leading those who come out (eventually) when you call 999. The people Response police arrest are probably not much like you. We don't really deal with normal, law-abiding folks, we deal with seriously violent thugs who attack others for no reason, who viciously beat and rob old ladies, who pimp out their own children, who think first, last and always of themselves at the expense of others. Unlike Copperfield, I'm an Inspector, two ranks above him. This means that

I have a bit less of the day-to-day contact with members of the public than he had but more of a handle on the theory and practice of police bureaucracy*.

I work for a force I call 'Ruralshire Constabulary'. Without being too specific, it covers a population well into seven figures, across an area of hundreds of square miles and a number of towns, some large, some small. I'm based in 'F Division' – a couple of hundred square miles, a population of around 300,000 people and six or seven decent-sized conurbations.

I'm ex-Army, and ex a few other things that would really surprise you. I'm married, I have kids and a dog called Kibble Chops. I'm not trying to bring down the Government, or embarrass my Chief Constable, and I'm altering names and other details to avoid identifying myself, my colleagues or members of the public. If you think you recognise yourself in these pages, it's coincidental. I have to make these changes for obvious reasons, but I hope they won't detract from the essential message. If that message seems a bit repetitive at times, this only reflects the nature of my job.

Lots of the stories and views in here are controversial; you won't find members of the Association of Chief Police Officers queuing up to agree with me. It's my thoughts and experiences, from my perspective. I don't trust official crime figures or press releases personally, but to get the full, unbiased picture you probably need to read that sort of stuff, too, and be aware that there are others who see things differently from me.

---

*It would be impossible in a book of this size to do justice to the scale and lunacy of police bureaucracy – all I can do is hint at it. If you'd like to get really up to speed – perhaps you have some time on your hands or are having trouble sleeping – visit http://police.homeoffice.gov.uk and check out the slightly Stalinist-sounding 'National Policing Plan'. It's full of the usual meaningless buzzword bingo phrases like 'Key Milestones', 'Activity Based Costing' and 'National Strategic Assessment' – 'target' appears 34 times, 'prison' appears once and 'punish' and 'just desserts' don't rear their ugly heads at all. It contains the Home Secretary's key priorities for the police service and, according to the Home Office, 'should be seen in the wider context' of the 'Home Office Strategic Plan 2004-08' and the policy paper 'Building Communities, Beating Crime: A Better Police Service for the 21st Century'. It couldn't hurt to check out the National Community Safety Plan 2008-2011 while you're surfing.

It's not all about pens and form-filling – we still do get to help people, catch criminals and lock them up, and I wouldn't change my job, for all its frustrations, for anything. Every day can bring moments of fear, distress and jubilation, often within the same hour, and not many people can say that.

NANNY KNOWS BEST

ALL I want is a cup of tea. I have served this nation for the best part of two decades, both at home and abroad. I don't want medals and I don't want more money. I just want some tea.

Debbie has banned me from doughnuts and she can detect any offending behaviour faster than she would the perfume of another woman. Tea is just about the only indulgence I have left, come break time.

But I can't have a cuppa because electric kettles are prohibited in my workplace. Our Health and Safety department has banned them in case we kill ourselves or our colleagues by electrocution, burning or drowning.

Ah, well. It's hot today, anyway. I switch on my desk fan.

Ha ha… had you going there, didn't I? Of *course* I don't switch on my desk fan. I'm not allowed to use my desk fan until it has been checked and stickered as 'safe to use' by one of the highly-paid staff who descend upon Ruraltown nick every so often and examine everything in the place with beady eyes and subtle grins. It's August now; based on previous experience they will finally arrive to check the fans in early December.

Never mind. It's nearly time to clock off. Whoah! Almost caught *myself* out that time. The office clock's wrong. Of course it is, it's still showing GMT. We're not allowed to change the time, naturally. No, that would be dangerous and UNISON – the union of the official clock time changers – wouldn't like it, so we have to wait for one of those pesky engineers to come round from force HQ and set it for us. Last year I ignored this, got up on a chair and altered it myself. The next day, the nick's UNISON rep got up on a chair and *changed it back to the wrong time*. (This is not satire, or a joke, or a lie – this is

4

true.) The clock will start showing the right time around three weeks before we go back to GMT, and it will then show BST for the following 12 weeks before it's put right again.

Welcome to the public sector!

More than the tea, and the fan, and the clock, it's the trousers that get to me. A while back, we were issued combats which featured numerous and capacious pockets and, being a generally disorganised kind of person, I *loved* them. Instead of constantly having to remember where I'd last seen my pen/spare radio battery/Mars bar, I could simply load up those trews and crack on. Then they were withdrawn, at the behest of the Health and Safety Commissariat, in case bobbies injured themselves by falling over and pushing whatever was stuffed in their pockets into their thighs.

The weird thing is, when Saturday comes, and I'm facing a dozen drunken, violent and dangerous yobs outside the taxi rank in the High Street, with only three PCs and a guardian angel on my side, our Health and Safety officers are nowhere to be seen.

Kettles and trousers – too dangerous.

Tackling 250lbs of screaming, tattooed nightmare, armed only with a 50g tin of pepper spray which doesn't work and a weedy aluminium stick – you carry on, officer.

I climb two storeys to the top floor, where there's a newly-installed vending machine which dispenses quite vile hot-but-not-too-hot drinks for a price that verges on extortion. As I see the amount of takings in one week, I wonder if this isn't the real reason for banning kettles.

CRIME REPORTS

HOW we police is no different, really, to how we make tea or change the clocks; that is, it often makes no sense at all. If your knowledge of our ways of working is limited to having watched *The Bill* or *Inspector Morse*, you may not 'get' much of what follows in this book. If you remember how policing used to be, or you try to imagine how it might work in a sane world, you will probably have similar problems.

Thus, to help you appreciate how ridiculous it all is, and to understand why we do some of the mad things we do, here's a basic run-through of our processes.

If you've never reported a crime to us, you would be forgiven for thinking that what happens is this:

1. You call your local police station and speak to an officer.
2. You explain what has happened.
3. The police officer decides, based on his or her experience and the outline you give, how urgent the matter is, and sends other officers out to the scene to investigate.
4. When they get there, they use their experience and knowledge to assess what crime has actually been committed – if any – and what should happen next.

The first thing to note is that you are most unlikely, nowadays, to be calling your local police station. In an attempt to cut costs and be more efficient, most forces have moved to centrally-based call centres which may be a very long way away from where you are, local knowledge having been deemed surplus to requirements some time ago. After all, with A-Z map books and GPS, no-one could ever get lost, or confuse High Street North with North High Street, could they? The answer to that is, of course they could. Sometimes, we'll send multiple cars to one minor incident after the people calling us all give slightly different locations to different operators – whereas a local controller would have realised immediately that they were all going to the same job. Other times, we will be directed to a local landmark – the cinema, say, or Argos – where some disturbance is occurring, and get there to find it's not even in our town, but somewhere else on the other side of F division.

The second point is that you are very unlikely to speak to a police officer when you ring up. Most of the people who answer the phones for us are civilians. Often, they are agency staff, with little knowledge of the law, reading from checklists and ticking off boxes on our Command and Control computer system as you speak. They typically have no experience or understanding of police work to bring to bear, but despite this they are the ones who decide whether you are actually reporting a crime and what our response to your call will be.

You're probably thinking, *What do you mean… decide whether I am actually reporting a crime?*

I'm taking it as read that you are intelligent and have a bit of common sense, and will only report 'real' crimes to us. Lots of people, unfortunately, are either not very intelligent, or lack common sense, or have lost all perspective as to what the police are *for*.

What does this mean in practice? Well, we might get Mr Hughes ringing the call centre and complaining that his ex-girlfriend has just sent him a nasty text message. The police response to this ought to be: 'You are a grown man. Why not turn your phone off, or just ignore the texts? Because we do have fatal accidents, suicides, rapes, stabbings, battered old ladies and missing children to deal with, you see.'

But what is far more likely to happen is that an inexperienced call taker will create a crime report of 'harassment' and two officers will be sent around to Mr Hughes' house to take a statement from him. I'll talk later about the huge amount of paperwork generated and police time wasted by this, but you can take it from me that it could well soak up 10 or 20 hours and a small rainforest over the next few weeks and months. The girlfriend will be arrested and interviewed, and her phone seized and kept for three months while we go through the very lengthy and bureaucratic process of proving she sent the complained-of message (even if she admits she did). Then she will accept a caution, or the case will be dropped by the Crown Prosecution Service. (The following week, Mr Hughes will text his ex something unpleasant, and the whole charade will start again, only in reverse.)

In point 4 above, I said you might think that the two cops would be able to 'use their experience and knowledge to assess what crime has actually been committed and what should happen next'. Surely they can circumvent the nightmare created by the civvie call centre worker and tell Mr Hughes, politely, that this is not a police matter?

A nice idea, but sadly it's not as easy to do as it is to write.

We are all now working within a framework set up by the Home Office specifically to remove discretion and experience from the game. The National Crime Recording Standard (NCRS) was adopted with the aim of 'recording crime in a more victim-focused way' and 'maintaining greater consistency between police forces in the recording of crime'. The Home Office Counting Rules 'provide a national standard for the recording and counting of notifiable offences'. I'll talk a bit more about NCRS later, and you can read all about it on the Home Office website if you really want to, but what it means in practice is that once that crime report is generated on our computer system it is extremely hard to get it to go away, even if no crime has been committed. A PC can, in theory, 'no-crime' these jobs, but to do so takes a lot of time filling in forms to explain why.

Officially, I imagine the reasoning behind this is that we don't want bent, lazy or incompetent bobbies playing God with crime, because that ends up with the Birmingham Six. (Except that, no, it doesn't. For really serious cases, some important checks and balances have been brought in; no-one is going to beat up Mr Hughes' ex to get her to cough to phone abuse.)

Unofficially, the senior management team (SMT) don't like it – what they want is for this to remain a crime and for it to be 'detected' (solved) for our figures. Trivial stuff that we can actually get people to admit to is our bread and butter, because it balances out all the other stuff we can't clear up; any officers who no-crime too often will have to justify themselves to their bosses.

So, more often than not, we cross every 'T' and dot every 'I' and then employ a small army of back office police and civilian auditors to make sure we haven't missed any.

People say, 'But what happens if Hughes' ex stabs him to death a week later?'

Believe me, in 99.999% of cases she won't – and how much other crime, including real stabbings, has happened because we're chasing after her and a million other silly texters to prevent ones that never will?

Because that's the point – this is at least partly why you're left sitting at home for hours and hours wondering why we haven't turned up yet to your burglary/assault/mugging.

Rules and processes brought in to save time and money and make things fairer have ended up costing time and money and hampering us in our attempts to fight crime. This is about well-meaning idiocy, the usurping of front line professionals by managers and bureaucrats and the law of unintended consequences. All themes to which I will return throughout this book.

FAT DOGS

WE GET hundreds and thousands of jobs like that of Mr Hughes and his spiteful text messages.

We don't get too many like The Case of the Fat Dog, but it helps to amplify some of the points I've just made, about the loss of common sense and the police fear of no-criming stuff.

Mrs Kelly came back from her two weeks in Greece and went to collect her black Labrador, Samson, from the dog walker.

Unfortunately, she didn't think that old Samson was looking his best; in fact, she was convinced that he had put on weight during her time away. Only one conclusion could be drawn from this – the dog walker hadn't been exercising him properly.

Unsatisfied with his fitness levels, Mrs Kelly withheld payment. The dog sitter retaliated by refusing to hand over Samson.

There followed a sort of middle-class stand-off, at the end of which Mrs Kelly phoned the police.

She got through to a communications centre worker who listened for a while and then informed her that this was a case of blackmail and that a patrol would be sent out to 'take details for a crime report'.

The patrol duly arrived to find two middle aged women, each refusing to back down, and a fat dog sitting between them with his tongue out. A problem, yes, but wasn't there a time when these women would have sorted this out between themselves, or been advised to if they had called us?

I happened to overhear some of the traffic batting to and fro on the radio, and (after a risk assessment that things weren't going to get properly ugly) I intervened and instructed the two PCs to suggest to the two women that they resolve the matter in the civil courts, and then leave the address.

Later, I spoke to the two bobbies – both young in service.

'We would have crimed it if you hadn't got involved, sir,' they said.

They knew how barking this was, if you'll excuse the pun, but they wouldn't dare leave a 'blackmail' call without a crime report because it would look like they weren't doing anything about what looked, on paper, a serious matter. The Crime Audit Team from HQ would have seen this and sent threatening emails to them and their Sergeant, which would have required paperwork, time and embarrassment to sort out.

I can only listen to the radio so much of the time, and not all Inspectors would intervene like this – if you're looking for promotion, it's not very sensible. It's not hard to see how other 'Fat Dog' cases go a lot further.

KIBBLE CHOPS

TALKING of fat dogs, here's a great example of how we lost the support of the public in a completely unnecessary way to satisfy a few bean counters somewhere far from the front lines.

The subject might seem minor, but it represents a few drops from a free-flowing tap of similar rubbish.

We're a nation of dog lovers, right? Well, until recently, local people would occasionally bring in stray or lost dogs they had picked up wandering the streets near our nick.

We'd place these animals in the kennels in the back yard, feed and water them and enter the details of when and where they were discovered into a 'Found Property' book.

We'd give the RSPCA or the local kennels a bell and after a few hours someone would arrive and take them away. If the particular pooch was unwell or looked undernourished, the RSPCA would have it. If it was simply 'unclaimed', it went to the local kennels.

It didn't take much time or effort on our part – it was just one of those traditional non-crime things the police have always done, like helping grannies cross the road or telling you the time of day – but the public *really* appreciated us for it. We liked doing it, too. Most of *us* are dog lovers, after all, and simple things like this help us to build a rapport with our local residents, which is always good – tomorrow, they might be witnesses to a crime.

That was before SLAs.

I don't want to get too technical with the jargon (it's hard to avoid in the modern police), but these are 'Service Level

Agreements' which we now have to negotiate with other local agencies to agree responsibility for various things that need doing in our area. It's all part of the force's 'Best Value' strategy – which I think means providing a better service, year-on-year, for less money. Best Value is our current management religion, having just about superseded 'Citizen Focus' in the hierarchy of gobbledegook. This is ironic, as it's also the reason why we lost our *actual* citizen focus in the first place.

Looking after lost dogs 'had to go' under Best Value. In fact, a lot has had to go – usually the kind of things you can't really define, which local people value but accountants don't. Someone at Headquarters probably worked out that bobbies and front counter staff would have X more hours available each year if we didn't waste time with these dogs, and that we could cut the budget or the staff or deliver more for the same or offer more citizen focus or something utterly abstract like that. We were told to stop taking the animals in, and instead to agree new, formal SLAs about lost dogs with Ruralshire County Council, where – as before – the RSPCA would take responsibility for sick or ill-treated ones and the kennels for the lost or stray (only no longer on a goodwill basis).

Try explaining this to members of the public when they walk in with an animal they've just found.

'Sorry, madam, we don't take in lost dogs any more.'

'What do you mean, you don't take in lost dogs?'

'Yeah, sorry, it's our Service Level Agreements.'

'Your Service *what*?'

'You'll have to take it to the kennels, I'm afraid.'

'How far's that?'

'Oooh… five miles or so?'

'But I haven't got a car.'

'Well, I'm sorry but we can't take them in now. It's Citizen Focus, you see.'

'Can I just use your phone then? I'll call my husband and he…'

'Sorry, I'm afraid you can't use the police station phone any more, because of Best Value. Have you got a mobile?'

Eventually, an angry and upset and confused and resentful person storms out of the nick, muttering. Sometimes, they find a way to take the dog to the kennels. Quite often, they will leave it tied to the railings outside as they go. That makes the Chief Inspector very angry. 'What is wrong with these people?' he says. 'Don't they understand Service Level Agreements?'

And, as with any system devised by bureaucrats, there are unforeseens, loopholes and inconsistencies. Shortly after the introduction of the SLAs, this happened:

A local youth called Robbie was arrested for beating up his father and stealing his dole money for alcohol. This is, unfortunately, quite a common occurrence on some of our worst estates.

Robbie had a habit of bringing home various animals, then losing interest and leaving them for his parents to look after. The day he beat up his dad, he had come home with a dog and when he was arrested after running away from the house he still had it with him.

It was getting dark when he was nicked, and the dog was placed in the kennels at the police station (against the new policy) and looked after overnight.

At court the following morning, Robbie was remanded to prison. Now, what about the dog?

If it had been lost or stray, or maltreated, the local kennels or the RSPCA would have had responsibility for it. But it was neither: we knew who the owner was, he just couldn't look after it in jail.

In the old, pre-SLA days, we would have closed this loophole by ringing up the kennels and explaining the situation, and someone would have come down and collected it, as I say, out of goodwill.

Now, because we have these formal SLAs, with roles and responsibilities clearly delineated, that's no longer an option.

The kennels wanted £70 a day to take Robbie's dog for the period that he was on remand. The DI in charge of the investigation was not about to blow his overtime or equipment budget on kennel fees. What to do?

What actually happened is that Kibble Chops came to live at the Gadget household with me, Debbie and the kids. It was squared with Robbie, who didn't want him anyway, and, a couple of years on, he hasn't looked back. But there is a limit to how many dogs Mrs Gadget will let me bring home from work.

SCHOOL CROSSINGS

DOGS are only the half of it.

A headmaster rang up, extremely concerned because his lollipop lady had just quit after yet another near miss with a speeding motorist. Commuters in big German cars were roaring past the school gates, doing 40mph or more in a 20mph zone, and the head wanted something doing about it.

I came across the details of his call on our computer log. It's fairly quiet for us at that time on a school morning, so I decided to send a couple of bobbies up there the following week and put in some road checks, stop a few cars, hand out some tickets – the sort of stuff a Duty Inspector is expected to do, really.

I stuck this on our 'taskings list'. The next thing I knew, a more senior officer had come down to see me.

'You can't do this,' he said.

'Why not?'

'We have Service Level Agreements with the local authority about traffic outside schools – before we do anything, you need to get up there and find out what their safety, transport and roads policy is.'

'What?'

'Schools have to produce a policy about traffic calming, and safety, and school crossing patrols, and walking buses, and if having police up there is not in his policy we can't do it.'

I went over to see the headmaster with the traffic guy from Area. And we talked about signage and barriers and budget and length of time... all *I* wanted to do was take a patrol up there. It transpired that, officially, we couldn't do that because it wasn't in the various plans. The argument is, if we do that for one school, soon they'll *all* want it. Then it will become a demand, and then it will become a complaint if we can't fulfil it. And if we do that, we're not doing something else. Above all, it's about the letter of your agreements: it's the school's job in conjunction with the local authority and Highways to sort out their traffic issues. If the police do it for them they will abdicate their responsibility and spend the budget somewhere else. (Everyone in the public sector is at each others' throats like this now, though they will officially deny that.)

If I say all this to the head, and refuse to come out, what's going to happen? He's going to tell the parents that we don't give a toss about their kids at the next PTA meeting, or stick it in the school newsletter, and soon everyone will know, and they'll all tell 10 other people about it, and then our name is mud everywhere.

The public are not interested in SLAs; they expect the police to deal with motorists speeding outside schools.

Actually, I *also* expect us to do this, so I just sent my officers up there anyway. It's not illegal, after all, it's just against policy. Ironically enough, most of the cars we stopped and ticketed were driven by parents who were dropping their kids off and then racing off to work.

But this is where we're at now: much of the stuff people expect from us, culturally, traditionally, we no longer do. Once you start thinking about the police like a quasi-commercial operation, with customers and core business and auxiliary business, and using business management and accountancy models, you start to *run* it like a business. There's no money in what we do, but there are Home Office targets we can meet, which bring us funding and promotions and so on. Sadly, there are no targets for motorists outside schools and lost dogs.

LEFT HAND, RIGHT HAND

THE people at the top of the police are not necessarily bad people. Most of them are very good people. But the majority, to a greater or lesser degree, are out of touch with reality. Perhaps this is inevitable, given the distance between them and the streets, where real policing happens.

I used to know a very senior officer very well. He was a really good egg and, since he was now a long way from the front line, he would occasionally ring me – and other Sergeants and Inspectors whom he knew – to chew the fat about operational matters. He was an intelligent, thoughtful and highly experienced man, but some of the questions he would ask me were shocking.

He got on the blower one time about a bit of a situation they'd had in one of our big, rough towns.

A man who was on some ballistic drug that makes you virtually impervious to pain – crystal meth or PCP or crack or something – had broken into a pensioner's flat and gone absolutely berserk.

Two officers were called and when they arrived he *really* went ape.

He picked up an occasional table with one hand and a massive knife with the other and started fighting. The bobbies had their little lightweight aluminium sticks and tins of CS. After 20 minutes or so, the officers had all-but collapsed with exhaustion. Drug boy had a broken arm, a fractured skull, he was blind in one eye and he had stabbed himself in the leg. But he was still raring to go.

A dog team was called: he picked up the dog and threw it out of the window.

Firearms arrived and asked for permission to arm. Permission was refused, so they self-armed and fired a baton round at him. When he got back up, he picked up the baton round and used it as a weapon on them.

Eventually he jumped out of a window and knocked himself unconscious. He was then wrapped up in ERBs (emergency restraint belts) and taken away.

He was really seriously injured by now. The two officers originally involved were suspended pending an investigation – clothing seized, interviews, the works – despite the fact that they were pretty badly hurt themselves.

It was during this big internal investigation that the very senior officer phoned me.

'Gadget,' he said, 'why didn't they get the shields out of the back of the vehicle? Why didn't they get the big Arnold batons out, rather than those silly little sticks?'

I said to him, 'We don't *have* shields and Arnold batons in the back of the vehicles any more. They were withdrawn by the Diversity Department eight months ago because they made ethnic minority teenagers feel uncomfortable.'

'*What?*' he said.

'But you must know about this,' I said. 'It was done in your name. ACPO* signed up for it.'

---

*ACPO – Association of Chief Police Officers, which speaks on behalf of Chief Constables, Deputy Chief Constables, Assistant Chief Constables and their equivalents in the 44 forces of England, Wales and Northern Ireland.

He didn't know it had happened, or that it had been signed off in his name; to his credit, he overturned the policy. Now we have proper batons in our vehicles again.

No-one wants to make innocent kids feel uncomfortable, but sometimes you really do need a big stick to defend yourself with.

A DEAD MUM

THE main reason I wrote this book is because I am worried about the gulf that has opened up between us and our core supporters – law-abiding, tax-paying folks living ordinary lives – and I'd like to try to bring us closer together again. This is important, because we police with consent and without the support of the majority we are lost.

We can try to change the things that prevent us giving you a decent service vis-à-vis crime, but we could also do a better job of getting across all the other stuff we do. If you understood some of that, maybe your appreciation of us would be better. That's my hope, anyway.

I'm lucky that my service in the Army came before today's dangerous, high tempo tours in Iraq and Afghanistan, but I still saw death three times when I was in the forces. One guy was killed in Northern Ireland, another drowned on a training run and the third was a good friend of mine who was crushed between two armoured vehicles; I went to his funeral, sat with his girlfriend, all very emotional and difficult.

Things like that stay with you forever, and I've had far more of them in the police.

You're never far from death in the police. Well, *some* police officers are never far from death. One in every ten things a Response PC goes to is a death or a serious injury – a suicide, a road accident, a nasty assault. As a Response Inspector, *everything* I go to is serious – otherwise, why would I go? Hangings, people who have thrown themselves off motorway bridges, people who've jumped in front of trains, people who have blown their own heads off, or been stabbed to death, or been crushed in industrial accidents, or just died of natural causes... in a patch as big as ours, there are unpleasant jobs to visit, all day every day, and almost all of them have a dead body or a seriously injured person on the end of them. As I write this, in the last fortnight I've dealt with five.

Seeing bodies is something that takes a bit of getting used to, even though, mostly, they're not too gruesome, there are no suspicious circumstances and they just look like they are asleep.

My first road death came on the day I was sent to a school where a 14-year-old boy was threatening his French teacher with a pair of scissors and refusing to let him leave a classroom. As we pulled up in the school carpark, the headmaster came running out.

'It's alright,' he said. 'He's let the teacher go, he's dropped the scissors and his mother is on the way.'

The boy was crying and remorseful, other teachers were talking to him and the French master was none the worse for it.

Those were the days – and I'm only talking a few years ago – when you said, 'Fine, thanks very much, we're out of here.' If it happened now we would have to get a detection out of it – the boy would have to be arrested, there would have to be statements from everyone, DNA and other forensics taken, CCTV examined, the lot, when actually the head teacher had things under control and further involvement from us was unnecessary.

Just then, a call came over the radio. There had been a serious accident about two miles away. We jumped back in the car, stuck the lights and sirens on and were there within two or three minutes.

The smash had happened on a bend under a railway bridge on a narrow and winding road.

The first thing we saw was a white Transit van parked at an odd angle, with three or four other cars stopped nearby and people running about. We stuck our car behind the van with the lights on, and went round to the front.

I was obviously nervous about what I was about to see. What I saw was a green estate car, smashed up and half buried in the Transit's grill. Both vehicles were now hard up against the brick of the bridge. The van was on the correct side of the road: you didn't need to be an expert accident investigator to work out that the estate had been straddling the white lines as it had come round the bend and had hit the Ford head on.

There were children's clothes and toys everywhere; a kid's car seat was even hanging from a tree above us. But we couldn't see any children. People often fly out of vehicles in collisions, so we spent five minutes out of our minds with panic and worry, looking under the car, under the van, everywhere, until we finally worked out that, thank God, there had been no kids in the vehicle.

The driver, a woman in her mid 30s, was in the front. My colleague Paul tried to wrench open the passenger door to get to her while I went round the back and squeezed myself along the wall, grazing and scratching myself to pieces on the rough old bricks to get to her door. Her window was down. She was sitting in the driver's seat, not a scratch on her, eyes open, staring ahead but unconscious. Silent, but alive. I leaned in and held her hand, as Paul put his hand on her shoulder.

I looked into her eyes and said, 'It's OK, we're going to get you out.' At that moment, she died.

Seconds later, the paramedics appeared, and a fire crew with all the cutting gear, so I got out of the way.

The ambulance crew tried very hard to resuscitate her, but she was gone: it turned out that she had been hit very hard by the steering wheel and had died from internal injuries. It took three hours to cut her free. Eventually, she was lifted gently from the vehicle and laid out on the road by undertakers.

She had two children, and she'd been on her way to pick them up from swimming; I thought about them waiting for a mum who was never going to arrive.

About three months later, I had a message that the woman's husband had called to speak to me so I phoned him and asked him how I could help.

He said that something was troubling him. 'I've been thinking about it all,' he said. 'How she was still alive when you got there, and that she died with you by her side?'

'Yes, that's right,' I said.

'I can't get it out of my head,' he said. 'I just want to know, did she say anything about me or the children?'

This is really hard. Part of me wanted to say she'd asked me to tell them all she loved them. It's a natural human instinct – you want to comfort the grieving. But we're taught never to play God like that: the implications are unknown.

'I'm sorry, but she didn't say anything,' I said. 'She was unconscious, and she didn't regain consciousness.'

He said, 'If she had been conscious, what was going on? What would she have seen and heard when she died?'

I said, 'I was holding her hand and my colleague was holding her shoulder, and we were saying to her, *"It's going to be OK. We'll get you out of here."* That's the last thing that she would have heard.'

He was grateful for that and I'm sure it would have been of some small comfort.

It was an emotional experience for me, obviously. Despite the fact that you're in uniform, you can't help thinking, *This could be my family*. You try not to let it spill beyond those fleeting thoughts and, ultimately, we have to remain professional, but it can be hard.

I felt sorry for the van driver. A young lad, he'd just got his licence, the skid marks showed he'd been doing less than 30mph.

Accidents happen, it wasn't his fault, but he'll never forget it.

A NUMBERS GAME

THE other Friday, someone said to me, 'In my day, there was an Inspector, two Sergeants and 16 PCs at my nick.'

I said, 'We haven't got that many on duty in the whole *division* tonight.'

As I say, F Division covers around 200 square miles. It has a population of very close to 300,000 spread across several major conurbations. We have motorways and major A roads, main railway lines between cities, an awful lot of villages and winding rural B roads... the number and variety of potential issues, and the travelling time between them, can be huge. It's tough to provide people with what I would regard as a decent service with the strength we have on *paper* – with the strength we have in *reality*, it's near enough impossible.

I think most really senior police officers don't appreciate how few people we have physically out there every night, and I'm sure the media and politicians are equally unaware. I do think the public are starting to cotton on, but who cares about them?

Part of the problem, I think, is that the majority of officers of Superintendent rank and above come from a time when a much bigger proportion of the total police strength actually *was* on the ground, doing the job. Even if they're told that we're stretched, they look at the number of staff the force employs and it just doesn't make sense to them. So they don't believe it.

As PC Copperfield always said, there may well be enough police – there may well be more than there ever *have* been – it's just that a huge number of them are working 9-5, Monday to Friday on Neighbourhood Policing or in offices, auditing and managing. We need them out on the streets, at night, at weekends, able to respond when crime actually happens.

I sit in our morning meetings, and I listen to the tactical plans being discussed, and I think, *Where are they getting the bodies from for all this?*

You can quite often find yourself on your own policing a sizeable town. You will start with your team on a Saturday night, and you're immediately nicking people for criminal damage, smashing shop windows, drink driving, fighting. Within an hour, everyone else is tied up and there's only you still out and about. One evening a while ago, I remember standing in the High Street on my own, with hundreds of people around me, thinking, 'That's it. All my people are gone, back in Central Custody, nine miles away. I am the only police officer left.'

Just then, my radio went, calling me to a heroin-wracked shoplifter who was threatening to stick needles into a member of staff at a late-night chemists she was trying to steal drugs from.

And no sooner had that call come in than there was another, to go to a pub where the management were asking for urgent assistance because one of their people had been bottled and the guy was still there.

I stood there, literally thinking, *Who is most likely to die?*

I decided that I had to go to the chemists, on the basis that there were bouncers at the pub and none at the shop. Luckily, as soon as I got there the offender was compliant. But I had to nick her – and that was me gone as well. In the end, I managed to get officers down from another town to transport her to custody, though they didn't want to come because that meant *their* town was empty. This stuff is going on day after day, but if you talk to people at Headquarters, where the car park is rammed during normal office hours, they don't seem to get it.

Recently, the trainers from force HQ came down to work through our procedures for a major crime scene – something we practise fairly often.

They put up a huge map of a fictional town. Then they turned to me. 'Right,' said one of them. 'It's 1am on a Saturday, Gadget. Your division, you're the Duty Inspector. The call comes in that there's a male dead in the street with a knife in his back. What are you going to do?'

I ran through our standard actions – securing the scene, protecting the public, starting the investigation and keeping the rest of the county running.

Eventually, one of the trainers stood up. 'That's all very well,' he said. 'But you're missing a few things, here. What you need to do with this scene is have uniformed cordons here, here, here and here. You then need to place two separate uniforms at the scene. There's a prisoner to be conveyed by one unit in a separate vehicle, and the victim's family in another to avoid cross-contamination. As part of our custody strategy, you'd then look to use other officers to…'

I stuck my hand up. 'Hang about a sec,' I said. 'Where are all these people *coming* from? You're talking about 15 or 20 officers here.'

'Well, that's not a problem,' he said. 'When we get a murder scene, we just get the bodies in.'

They do for the investigation, sure. But for all these cordons?

'There is no point in building SOPs around a fantasy that doesn't exist,' I said. 'It's not right. We need to be looking at things in terms of the practicalities.'

'We cannot compromise the National Core Investigation Model,' said the trainer.

'But your National Core Investigation Model *is* compromised,' I said. 'It's compromised by the fact that there are actually only eight of us on duty and most of them are tied up with prisoners.'

He looked at me for a moment. Then he said, 'Talk to control and they'll send you more people.'

'From *where*?' I said. 'From a magic box somewhere inside Headquarters? And you're assuming that we only get one incident at a time. We get a dozen incidents at a time.'

'What are you saying?'

'I'm saying that we will deal with bodies with knives in them, and we'll do it professionally and properly, but that we need a bit of reality regarding cordons and the custody strategy and so on.'

'I am not prepared to compromise the National Core…'

I said, 'Look, I'm sorry about this, but can I just ask, when was the last time you actually *policed*?'

The answer was 12 years ago, in a big town where there were (then) far more cops on the street than we have now.

There should be tenure at training school – work there for two years at a time, and then back to the street. That way, they would stay in touch. As it is, some of them are like Hitler in his bunker, pushing fantasy battalions around the map as the Soviet troops pour into the streets of Berlin.

I can't do that, much as I might like to: I have to work with reality.

REALITY

SO what is reality?

When I come on as the Duty Inspector on a Thursday, Friday or Saturday night – in these times of 24/7 licensing and all that brings with it – I will have something like three Sergeants and 20 PCs on Response, plus a couple of Custody Sergeants and a few gaolers. Available to me from the centre will be one dog unit, as long as it's not employed elsewhere. I also have the ability to get firearms units in, if necessary.

Neighbourhood Policing have all gone home, because they work Monday to Friday, 9-5 – you know, when all the crime happens. All the squads – Domestic Violence, Car Crime, Burglary etc etc – have gone home, too, for the same reason. As have all the PCSOs, because they're not allowed to work after dark in case they get attacked.

I've explained how big my area is. I have 20 PCs, split around six different reporting stations (most of which are closed to the public) to cover it.

Only I don't.

The moment I start work, one of the Central Custody Sergeants will be on the phone saying that his oppo is sick so he needs a Sergeant down there – and he does need one, because they will be turning over a lot of prisoners during the night. So I'll have to pull one of the skippers (Sergeants) off the street and send him to custody, replacing him with a PC as an acting Sergeant (so that's a PC out of a crew.)

Then we'll discover that two of the gaolers are off – one is sick and the other is on a course. So I'll have to provide a couple of PCs for custody, too.

From the shift itself, with colds and flu and sickness bugs and busted noses and courses and secondments, there will always be two or three people missing from the 20 down on paper. Let's say one Sergeant and two PCs (that means another PC is acting-up as a Sergeant).

Another will be on annual leave. Two more will be working on MISPER enquires (of which, more later).

Then, as sure as eggs are eggs, I will have two officers out making an arrest and the suspect will 'collapse' and claim he has taken an overdose. This will obviously be a lie, but we can't be too careful, can we, so my guys will have to take him to hospital and wait with him until he is given the all-clear. (We have to use two officers to transport prisoners now, in case allegations are made against us and for Health and Safety reasons – a lone officer concentrating on driving is too vulnerable to attack from the kind of nutters we deal with.) By the time he's been seen by a doctor and admitted as a precaution, five or six hours have gone by and those two officers will therefore be out of action for the entire shift. As soon as he is judged fit to be released, he will be brought to the station. As soon as he gets to the station, he will claim he has 'chest pains'. Two different officers will then convey him back to hospital and wait with him again. This is a game, and it is happening all over Britain, all the time; I don't think that senior officers, politicians and the media really appreciate that.

Now, the main nick's front counter will need covering later on; civvies don't like working there at night, because all the lunatics come in ranting and raving and trying try to take them out across the desk, so I'll lose another bobby there.

Where does that leave me, an hour into the evening?

I'm down 10 PCs and two Sergeants.

I haven't even mentioned my own sickness and leave and courses, yet.

So even the 23 bodies I've got on paper, with which to cover 300,000 people across our vast area, isn't reality.

When we start arresting people, the very thin blue line we have shrinks further still. I'll talk in a bit about the length of time it takes to nick people and book them in but, for now, suffice it to say that having someone in for a simple criminal damage can easily take an officer out of the game for four hours, even when the suspect admits it.

There is Late Turn*, yes, which overlaps until the early hours, but these guys have been taking emergency calls, solid, since the afternoon. They are in custody with prisoners, or waiting for solicitors or interpreters or appropriate adults, or interviewing, or calling CPS Direct**, or writing, photocopying and faxing reams of paperwork, or transporting people to mental hospitals, or at cordons at road crashes, or at people's houses taking statements, or trying to get something to eat. They may have gone off duty sick or injured, or they may be up at the hospital getting details from a road crash victim or waiting with another 'overdoser', or they may be doing breathalysers, but the one thing they are not doing is waiting for me to click my fingers so they can come running. Trust me, they are fully soaked up.

We get 3,000 calls a day in my force, spread across a number of divisions. In my patch, I have a dozen or fewer people to cover our end of it; I don't care what the stats say, or *anyone* says, that is reality, that is the bottom line.

---

*Late Turn is one of our three shifts. Early Turn runs from breakfast time to mid-afternoon. Late turn is mid-afternoon until the middle of the night. Nights is the middle of the evening until breakfast time. There's an overlap of about two hours between Late Turn and Nights.
**CPS Direct is part of the Crown Prosecution Service – more detail about this later.

I have *never* seen Tony McNulty or the Area Commander, or anyone from 'Human Resources' or the Press Office or Training, down on the streets with me on a Saturday night, physically counting heads (or cracking them). They have *no* idea *at all* what it is like.

You do, occasionally, see an ACPO rank out. But when a Chief comes down on the street there are more uniformed police out than there would be for England vs Germany in the World Cup final. Neighbourhood are out, Specials are out, anyone with arms, legs and a functioning pelvis is out; why the Chiefs can't see what's going on I do not know, because it must have happened in their day. But apparently they can't – they walk around, nodding and grinning and surrounded by blue serge tunics and hi-vis jackets, and they think it's all hunky dory.

In the Army, an infantry battalion of 500 men will consist of 75% front line soldiers – people with rifles, there to deal with the enemy – and 25% in HQ support roles. In the police, 10% are on the front line and everyone else is back at base, drinking tea and making plans. It's quite mad.

You can still be reassured, I think, that our ability to respond to level two criminality – what would be classified as serious crime like rapes, stabbings and murders – is and will remain very good, because we find ways of dealing with that sort of stuff. But in terms of keeping the lid on day-to-day 'volume crime' – the anti-social behaviour, the criminal damage, the assaults, the drunkenness, the violence, the car theft, the problems that you're most likely to suffer from… Being ex-Army, I've learned the hard way to make the most of what I have in front of me. We get on and do our jobs, whatever the manning levels. Somehow, we have made it happen without major outbreaks of live anarchy. How much longer we can continue along this road, I really don't know.

The frustrating thing is, the answer is reasonably simple. Get police officers out of cushy offices and 9-5 jobs, onto the streets. Spend the money wasted on PCSOs on more proper cops. Cut paperwork and stop massaging figures. Stop chasing targets and trying to socially engineer a new country. Concentrate on criminals, missing kids and road accidents.

But maybe that's all too revolutionary for modern tastes.

CENTRAL CUSTODY

I MENTIONED Central Custody earlier and it's probably worth explaining what it means because I know that a lot of members of the public assume we have cells in all our police stations.

This isn't the case – in my force, we now have one custody suite per division and it can be 30 minutes' drive or more from where you make your arrest.

When that's full, as it often is, we have to drive our prisoner over to another division.

But, by the time we arrive, that's also full, because, in the 30 minutes it takes to travel *there*, their own patrols have nicked more people.

Then we hear that our *own* custody now has a space (some drunk has been ticketed and booted out) so we go all the way back over.

Eventually, we arrive back at our own Central Custody, to be told that four illegal immigrants have come in from the motorway with the Immigration people and all the cells are now full again.

So it's up to Metro City, our neighbouring force, for a two-hour wait to get into *their* cells.

Don't forget, our prisoner may now have been in custody, without seeing a Custody Sergeant, for three hours or more. No phone call, no medical check, no solicitor. He might be innocent. He might have mental health problems. He might also be violent, which presents problems because we're using up all the vans. (Why do I say, 'All the vans', like we have a huge fleet of them on the road in my division?) He might be you, or your kid.

In the morning, Ruralshire officers will have to go up to Metro City to bring him back – more cars needed, more fuel burned, more PACE* time used up etc etc.

---

*PACE: The Police and Criminal Evidence Act (PACE) and the accompanying Codes of Practice define our powers and your safeguards in respect of things like stop and search, arrest, detention, investigation, identification and interviewing detainees. PACE sets out to strike the right balance between police powers and the rights and freedoms of the public. It appears, largely, to have been produced by people whose experience of the streets comes from old episodes of *Juliet Bravo*.

Not to mention, the policemen and women driving these people around for half the night and then back again are not on the streets, preventing, deterring or arresting.

Why on earth *did* we go over to a system of having one Central Custody Unit?

There are probably a number of official reasons, like:

1. Health and Safety standards for police officers dealing with prisoners are important and expensive, so we can only afford one per division.
    Like being in the car with a mad, drunk and violent prisoner for three hours is safe?

2. We should be doing more street bail/home cautions and Penalty Notices For Disorder* nowadays – ie, deal with minor offences outside the custody area – so we don't need as many cells.
    Yep – when you're dealing with juveniles and generally compliant people, during the day, this works. But the night/weekend/violent/abusive/drunk/criminal prisoners? No chance. They just do not stand there and play along while you explain the benefits to all parties of a Home Caution. Not practical. Dreamed up by people in offices who have never rolled their sleeves up and nicked anyone who didn't want to be nicked.

3. So officers can't fit up prisoners and get them to admit stuff they haven't done.
    Except that the most celebrated cases happened at central nicks.

4. Because it seemed like a good idea at the time and saved loads of money?
    Bingo!

---

*Street bail: custody is full, and we're swamped with work, so for minor offences we can give you a piece of paper which tells you when to turn up at the police station to be dealt with. Home cautions – if you're suspected of a minor offence, we can deal with this by coming to your house, having you admit it on tape and administering a caution. Penalty Notice for Disorder – an on-the-spot fine by way of a ticket, usually for £80; more on these shortly.

This is the point where someone from ACPO or the Government says, 'Aha! But lots of these cases will involve people arrested for relatively trivial matters. As Gadget knows, where a prisoner can be processed within six hours, officers are allowed to use non-designated police stations.'

A 'Designated Police Station' is defined in PACE, which requires that they contain certain features including:

– specific numbers and types of staff (a Custody Nurse, Custody Sergeants, Detention Officers and senior officers available for various PACE authorisations [mostly now an Inspector or above])
– an independent CCTV system, inside and out
– facilities to provide food
– beds
– showers
– special cell facilities for juveniles
– a female cell block (separate from the males)
– interview rooms with tape and video machines
– medical facilities
– an Intoximeter room for dealing with drunk drivers

Naturally, our Designated Police Station is the one that contains our Central Custody Unit.

As our friend from ACPO says, you can, indeed, deal with some prisoners at outlying nicks.

But are we likely to?

That CCTV and all the rest of the gubbins is there to protect us as much as the prisoner, you know. No police force in its right mind will sanction use of any other custody space in case the prisoner dies, is injured or there's some complaint (justified or not) about treatment or process. These things can get *extremely* expensive in terms of compensation and they can also wreck careers.

I don't like many of the people we detain, but there is no way on earth I would ever hit one of them, or deny him his rights, or anything like that – even assuming I wanted to, how barmy would I have to be to risk my job and my pension and a year in the clink for these oxygen thieves? I don't think anyone I work with would behave like this, either. But because some stupid officers *have* occasionally done bad things, mostly a long time ago, the great mass of us are, apparently, no longer to be relied on to treat our prisoners properly and must labour under a whole host of belt-and-braces conditions brought in with PACE.

That's fine, just so as you know we're not the only ones labouring under them. Prisoners can be arrested literally on the steps of one police station and have to wait two, three or four hours before they're even through the doors of the one they'll be charged at. And while we're doing all that, we're not answering your 999 call. If that's what people want, OK. But is it? Has anyone asked them?

SWIVEL

DEAD dogs, mentally ill people, angry sheep and now – swivel chairs.

It has been a difficult few days for Inspector Gadget of F Division, Ruralshire County Constabulary.

The Senior Admin Support Clerk spins around in the aforementioned chair when I enter, casts a suspicious eye over me and points a carefully-manicured fingernail in my direction, all in one immaculately choreographed movement.

'You haven't got an appointment.'

I can see her wrinkling her nose up at the sight of my boots on her carpet.

'Not unless you count the one given to me by the Sovereign, her heirs and successors,' I say.

Straight over her head. I can tell we're going to get along just fine. Down to business.

'Can I take your teenage daughter out for dinner?' I ask, respectfully.

Actually, I don't say that, I just ask for some stationery. But it receives the same sort of reaction.

Once she's calmed down, she says, 'Have you typed both parts of the requisition form and added the cost centre code?'

'Yes,' I say, casting the form on to her desk. Feast your eyes on that, sweetheart.

'Sorry,' she says, with a smile. 'That's not properly completed. I'm afraid I need your signature at the foot of the form.'

'I can't sign it.'

'Why not?'

'Because it's a requisition form for a new pen. I haven't got one, so I can't sign it. But I can't have a pen without signing. What shall I do?'

Twenty minutes later, down in the custody block where it's unusually quiet, I'm collecting my winnings, in cakes. We have an ongoing reward system for the best piece of organisational terrorism of the week.

My mobile rings. It's Debbie.

The Senior Admin Support Clerk was at school with Debbie, and they sometimes walk the dogs together. How was I to know?

More worryingly, she also knows about the cakes. The Sergeants are suddenly very quiet. Debbie knows all of their wives and girlfriends. In typical police fashion, my support suddenly evaporates.

An unholy alliance of wives and clerks: best we get back out on the streets and do something safer and less frightening.

THE WEEK IN KNIFE CRIME

SO where are we with knife crime *this* week?

Monday.

Oh, how we sigh in the nick when we hear the Prime Minister demand that youngsters found with knives should be charged and sent to court instead of being cautioned*.

In Ruraltown, this will impress only those with no knowledge of the generosity of the Ruralshire Bench.

I recently managed the execution of a warrant for the arrest of a local man with 250 previous convictions, many for violence.

*Where I talk about juveniles being 'cautioned', I'm using this in the colloquial sense: juveniles are actually 'reprimanded' or 'warned'.

He had breached his Drug Testing and Treatment Order* and failed to appear (for the eleventh time in his criminal career) at Ruraltown Magistrates Court in a criminal damage case.

In the last two years, this man has been sentenced to, and breached, four Community Sentences of one description or another.

A late afternoon telephone call from the court informed me that (after all our efforts) he had just been sentenced to a fifth after a guilty plea. The 'Failure to Appear' was dealt with concurrently (that is, he received no additional punishment for it). If a man like this, with a record of almost continual violent offending since the age of 12, walks away every time, what exactly does Mr Brown think will happen to the odd knife-wielding youngster?

Meanwhile, at the 'Bite the Bullet' conference in Brixton, leading youth worker the Rev Les Isaac ('himself a former gang member and street fighter') says young people involved in knife gangs are 'angry' and 'confused'. 'They feel a tremendous sense of hopelessness,' he says. 'Drug dealers are using their entrepreneurial skills. Some of them are controlling three mobile phones at once.'

Tuesday.

A huge amnesty is announced. Bins are installed in police stations around the country. A few hundred Swiss Army penknives are handed in, along with one paperknife, one WWI bayonet and a plastic pirate dagger from Woolies.

New figures show that police stop-and-searches were up in the last 12 months. There's lots of handwringing about this from liberals, not so much from victims and people who actually live in the areas where knife crime is rife.

---

*Addicts can escape jail by promising they will stop using, and agreeing to a DTTO which checks they are clean. Of course, they often test positive, or don't turn up for their tests, and nothing happens. I mean, *eventually* some of them may get recalled to prison, but it's not a case of, *Breach your DTTO and you're back in, matey*. Even better than this, in the way that criminals are often one step ahead of the system, we now get *non-addicts* asking for DTTOs. At court, they're all downcast and talking in hushed tones about the huge habit they don't really have – they'll have swallowed a small amount of heroin, just enough to show up in their system, in case they're tested. They come out, get tested and are, obviously, completely clear. As a bonus, they can sell the methadone prescribed to them on the black market.

Wednesday.

The Met's Deputy Commissioner Sir Paul Stephenson publicises the formation of a special knife-crime unit to address the recent spate of fatal stabbings in London.

The unit will have 75 officers in it. Perhaps these are brand new bobbies from a box under his desk? If not, that means other teams are going short. Unless I missed it, he doesn't mention this – nor the fact that only 20 of them will be on duty at any one time, and that this means there is one of them for every 500,000 Londoners. Still, good headlines all round.

Sir Paul says, 'We need to broadcast the message quite simply: if you carry a knife, you are likely to be caught, you will be charged and you will be likely to go to prison.'

In the nick, there's a lot of choking on doughnuts and coffee spluttered everywhere. Likely to go to prison for carrying a knife? See 'Monday' and repeat after me: Almost *no-one* goes inside for just 'carrying a knife'.

I wonder to myself why we're happy to shred what credibility we have left by making statements like this? The kids know damn well they won't go to jail for anything far short of murder. Can it possibly be that Sir Paul is less well informed than they are?

Thursday.

Gordon Brown tells *The Times* that, contrary to what Sir Paul says, 'jail or young offender institutions are not always the right approach'.

Sir Ian Blair says everyone should 'pull together' on this.

In the van, Sergeant Dan and I are trying to pin down what the last pop song was. He claims that it was probably *Everything She Wants* by Wham! I'm thinking *Motorcycle Daydream* by Bedroom Eyes.

Twenty minutes later, we're at Ruraltown General Hospital A&E looking like extras from a particularly gory horror movie. Blood and phlegm, probably infected with something, cover our faces and arms. We were called to the middle of one of our estates by a terrified member of the public. We turned up and found two lunatics armed with one knife, one broken bottle and two lumps of wood with nails hammered through. They were trying to kill each other, and then they tried to kill us. People like this can take any amount of CS gas or PAVA* and keep coming right at you. It took six of us quite a while to get the pair of them under control.

Later, Sergeant Dan says to me, 'Have these people not been listening to Gordon Brown or Sir Paul Stephenson, or what?'

There is silence for a few minutes. Then we vote. The Last Pop Song? *Motorcycle Daydream*.

Friday.

On the *Guardian*'s 'Comment is Free' website, Sunny Hundal writes a piece called *What Knife Crime Epidemic?* He demands a 'sense of perspective' and says 'the figures don't bear out the reality of a crisis'. As his article is published, 19 teenagers have already been stabbed to death in London this year. In the 32-hour period following its publication, no less than seven people lose their lives in stabbings in Britain. Sunny Hundal is not among them, as far as I know. That's his perspective. In the paper itself, Michael White calls for 'tough love'. On the streets, they're not too interested in love of any sort.

Meanwhile, the number of youngsters caught with knives in school has risen more than sevenfold in a decade. In 1996, 902 children were dealt with for this offence; by 2006, the figure was 6,334.

Home Secretary Jacqui Smith, a former teacher who used to smoke cannabis and has never arrested a youth with a foot-long bread knife who's screaming that he wants to take her head off, unveils new plans for dealing with such people. A TV reporter asks, 'One of those proposals is that people caught carrying knives should be taken to see people in hospital who have been stabbed, or to meet the families of victims, is that correct?'

'It is,' Ms Smith replies.

Saturday.

Whoops! Doctors and victims' groups react with horror at Ms Smith's suggestion. She explains that we're all mistaken and she didn't really mean it. 'We are not, and I have never said we are, proposing to bring young people into wards to see patients,' she says. This is not a u-turn, she emphasises.

---

*PAVA – Pelargonic Acid Vanillylamide, a synthetic pepper spray which works on old ladies and vicars but not violent drunks.

Luckily, Mr Brown has another trick up his sleeve: 20,000 families will be subject to 'intervention projects' and, under a 'community payback' scheme, young offenders will spend up to 300 hours cleaning streets or doing other menial tasks. 'Too many people do not feel safe in the streets, and sometimes even in their homes, as a result of the behaviour of a minority,' he says.

In *The Times*, columnist Alice Miles tells us that 'Amazing progress is being made in tackling the hard-core problems behind violence. More talk of jail won't help.' As far as I know, Alice's experience of wrestling in the gutter with tooled-up street thugs is zero. Thank goodness she doesn't let this get in the way of her opinions.

Sunday.

The jails are full. Prisoners are being paid to leave early.

In Suffolk, Derek Burns is set free after serving just over two weeks of a 16-week sentence for assaulting his mother-in-law. He goes straight round to his pregnant girlfriend's house and, in front of their four screaming kids, he *stabs* her, later telling paramedics, 'I can't believe they let me out. I told them I would do it.'

This is joined-up thinking in the modern Criminal Justice System at its very best!

So where *are* we with knife crime?

The total number of people stabbed in Britain this year is... well, we don't know. The *Sunday Telegraph*, collating figures from 33 of the 44 police forces in England and Wales, found that 20,803 'serious knife crimes' were recorded in the year to March – that's 56 per day. If you add in the other 11 forces and Scotland, the figure is obviously going to be higher than that. And then it will be higher again, because not everyone who gets stabbed calls the police, and there's no requirement on A&E departments to report injuries to us, either.

Mike Walsh, a consultant trauma vascular surgeon at The Royal London Hospital, tells the media, 'Our experience is that the number of people suffering knife injuries is increasing year-on-year. If we took the figures for 2007, we had a total of 185 injuries in the year; so far in the first half of this year we've had 140.'

Nationally, researchers for the *Journal of Epidemiology and Community Health* reveal that hospital admissions for serious violent assaults have risen by 30 per cent in four years. Around

30,000 people were admitted to hospital in England last year as a direct result of violence, and ten times that number attended A&E.

A survey of 1,200 police officers by the think tank Policy Exchange suggests that they think the problem is getting worse.

But *The Guardian* reports that the latest British Crime Survey figures show violent crime is 'down by 12%'.

You can believe the cops and the doctors and the nurses, or you can believe *The Guardian* and the official figures: that's up to you.

THAT LAST IDEA OF GORDON'S...

I LIKE it, in principle, though naturally he's as short on the detail as he always seems to be.

He says the Government is going to identify 110,000 families 'in need of support', where children are 'at risk of becoming prolific offenders'. Of those, 20,000 families will be identified as requiring 'early intervention'. These will be cases where 'it's clear that the mother or father have lost control of their children and their whole life is actually in difficulty'.

These people would face the threat of eviction if they failed to respond positively to 'support'.

Kids who are caught carrying knives will be made to do up to 300 hours unpaid work in the community, such as cleaning graffiti and tending parks on Friday and Saturday nights.

To be honest, I'd prefer it if he said: 'We'll be speaking to CID and Response officers in all the police forces and asking them who their worst scum are. Then we're going to nail them.'

Still, it's a step in the right direction.

That is, if you ignore the holes: as with most Government announcements, it contains more of those that the average Ruralshire burglar's defence.

How will the 110,000 families be 'identified' (and why not 120,000, or 100,000)?

What does the Prime Minister mean by 'at risk of' becoming prolific offenders? Is he saying prolific offending is something that just *happens* to you, like the weather?

What does he mean by people having 'lost control of their children'? You 'lose control' of a car on unseen black ice: the people he's on about never had control of their kids and never wanted it.

How will the Government narrow down the 20,000 apparently more urgent cases?

What 'support' are they 'in need of'? How much will it all cost?

How will the Government go about evicting them when they don't use this 'support' if they own their homes or rent privately?

If they live in council housing, will the local authorities play ball? Surely they will just be rehoused somewhere else? Which set of evicted lowlife will take the first state-funded legal case to the European Court of Human Rights, and what will happen then?

What will be done to force kids to carry out these 300 hours of community service that isn't already being done? And why should we believe that it will be any more effective?

Yes, it bears the traditional hallmark of Government policy: produced with today's headlines in mind and no thought given to tomorrow's practicalities.

The thing is, Gordon Brown may be streets ahead of our feral Ruraltown criminals when it comes to the theory of PFI projects or monetary policy, but real life? They're far more switched on than he is.

Here's what will happen when Ruralshire's finest 'parents' are told they face sanctions for the behaviour of their kids: they'll simply report them 'missing' every night.

Once the child's a MISPER, the responsibility transfers to others. People like me.

We are talking here about a small number of Britons, two or more generations of them, who are completely detached from morality, concepts of right and wrong, personal responsibility, maternal or paternal feelings and respect for the law. Gordon Brown, like all of them, is just shadow boxing around the problems.

24 HOUR PARTY PEOPLE

WE HEAR a lot about 'booze Britain' these days, but it's not the booze which is the problem, it's the people.

Most of us like a drink now and then. As a younger man, particularly when I was in the Army, I had a few beers and rolled back home drunk more than once, but I never smashed all the car mirrors off in the streets on the way back, or attacked anyone with a baseball bat, or told the police to f**k off. I still enjoy a pint from time to time, but I don't get absolutely slaughtered and I don't go out and smack people in the face and puke all over the pavement. I don't drink-drive and I don't beat up my wife or kids or neighbours. I don't smash shop windows, or urinate in doorways, or use foul language at the top of my voice.

I'm nothing special: there are millions of people who don't do any of these things, and you're probably among them.

The problem is, there are also quite a lot of Britons who don't feel like they've had a decent night out until they've ticked several of the above boxes, *and* had a kebab/KFC.

Of course, their behaviour is often appalling when they're sober, but it's far worse when they're drunk, as whatever inhibitions or social polish they might have had are swept away on a tide of Stella Artois and blue, vodka-based pop.

There are people who say that it was ever thus, and point to Hogarth's Gin Lane and the back streets of our port cities where sailors would get tanked up and fighting drunk after months at sea. But this new phenomenon is happening on our High Streets, at least three or four nights a week.

The protagonists are often young, and they have a lot of disposable income: they can't afford to buy houses anymore so they all live with their parents way beyond when they used to. With no responsibilities, and with discount drink far cheaper than it ever was, why not go out and get hammered every night?

Into this poisonous cocktail the Government recently threw another ingredient – 24 hour licensing.

Not many places are open 24 hours, it's true, but lots are now open much later than they were. I don't care what the figures say, this has caused us huge problems. When the nightclubs used to shut at the same time, we could gear everything to that point. We would have a flurry of issues – the town centre fights, the robbing or bilking of taxi drivers, the drink-driving accidents, the people falling over and smacking their heads on the concrete etc – but at about 2.30am it would all start to die off. Now it carries on all the way through to 6am. Ask any front line cop, and they'll tell you: broad daylight on a Sunday morning, getting towards the end of the shift, and they are *still* going to fights in the High Street. What's going on?

The Government calls it the 'Night Time Economy' (NTE). This Orwellian phrase refers to those bars, clubs and other such venues operating at night in town centres. It is a nightmare of vomit, urine, chips and police officers being punched in the face, but that doesn't square with the official vision of longer licensing and the NTE – where everyone meets up in cafés to share polenta and vine-ripened tomatoes, sips their five units of alcohol and chats about the issues of the day.

Again, I may have missed it but I don't think any minister has gone on telly and admitted that the NTE licensing experiment has been a disaster. They don't like to admit they're wrong about much, do they? Instead, the pressure is on the police to find ways to deal with NTE crime and anti-social behaviour.

Launching an advertising campaign recently, Jacqui Smith said, 'I am not prepared to tolerate alcohol-fuelled crime and disorder on our streets and this new campaign will challenge people to think twice about the serious consequences of losing control. It reinforces Government action already underway to deal with excessive drinking, including tougher sanctions for licensees who sell to young people, new powers for the police to disperse disruptive drinkers and better education and information for everyone.'

The Government's input, then, is an advert, some 'better education and information' and the *wildly* misguided hope that the lunatics we arrest each weekend will somehow start to 'think twice about the serious consequences of losing control'.

As for actually sorting it out, that's down to us. Luckily, they are legislating to give us 'new powers'.

The problem with politicians these days is that very few of them have actually ever *done* anything in the real world. They go from university, to jobs as MPs' research assistants, to themselves becoming MPs and then Ministers. Being law-abiding types (save for the odd run-in with cannabis), they actually believe that a ton of extra verbage on the statute books is all it takes. If only it were that simple.

The Government says irresponsible landlords who serve drunk people should be prosecuted, and that we should also identify the bar staff who served these idiots their booze. Which sounds great when you announce it at the despatch box in the House of Commons, or on Richard and Judy's sofa, or in an exclusive interview with some newspaper political editor. It's not so easy at midnight in our towns, when the streets are full of paralytically drunk yobs who are kicking off, smashing windows and fighting with us. We don't have the time or the personnel to start checking CCTV to find out where they just came out of. Even if we *did*, and we went to speak to the manager of the venue, what's he going to say? He's going to say, no, we didn't serve them, they came in pissed so we kicked them back out. So we spend however many hours reviewing the tapes to find all the previous venues they went to, and the managers in those places say, no, we didn't serve them either, they were pissed when they came in here, too.

OK, so we grill the bar staff instead. We push our way into a club we think a given bozo has come from. There are 300 people in there, the 'music' is at about 140 decibels, the five barmaids are all Polish and hardly speak a word of English. Shouting to be heard, we're trying to ask them if they served a man in a striped shirt with tattooed forearms and a gold earring, in a club containing about 200 men in striped shirts with tattooed forearms and gold earrings. Back on the street, meanwhile, a whole different group of drunks is now kicking the living s**t out of my officers.

This is the stuff of fantasy. It is ludicrous. It is dreamed up by people sitting in air conditioned rooms whose experience of modern drinking, I can only think, must be limited to nights out in country inns in the Cotswolds or metropolitan bars in London. In a trendy pub in Islington, there might be three dozen people sitting listening to jazz all night and if one of them later goes mad outside the 24 hour Tesco *possibly* you can pin something on the people who served him his last quart of pinot grigio. But these are not the places from which the trouble emanates.

The police can shut problem pubs, says the Government. Yep, we can. But it's not quite as easy as it sounds when you say it to Andrew Marr and he's nodding in agreement. I *have* shut a pub down. Once. But it was a *really* difficult thing to do, it took days of police time and it wasn't easy to get it through at court. The licensees don't just roll over, they put up a vigorous defence because it's their livelihood you're taking away. Plus, all it does is displace the problem. People don't stop drinking and brawling just because their favourite bar has closed, after all.

I don't know the full answer to the problem. I suspect no-one does. It probably involves all sorts of things, from improving attitudes to civility and behaviour from a very young age, to changing our drinking culture, to making booze harder and more expensive to buy (though this would penalise non-problem drinkers), to tougher enforcement of the basic laws against public drunkenness and violence.

This latter element of a wider solution is the one thing the police actually *could* do something about – after all, Ms Smith says that she has given us new powers to 'disperse disruptive drinkers'. But this is another one straight from the la-la land school of public order: 'Excuse me sir, can you put that bottle down and stop trying to blind that other man? We have new powers to disperse you, you see.'

Disperse them with *who*, Jacqui?

I know the Home Secretary says we have more police than ever, but how many of them are working Response? I know, too, that we have PCSOs now, and that they look a bit like police, but very few of them work beyond 9pm because it's too dangerous (it's not too dangerous for the public, note, but it *is* too dangerous for PCSOs, despite their stab vests and their radios). In the first few months of 24 hour licensing, we were given enormous amounts of centrally-funded extra money to put more bodies on the street – the overtime was great for the Sergeants and PCs. As a result, everywhere you turned there were police. Once that dried up, we were back to normal – and we really don't have the numbers to do much more than control things to a just-about acceptable level.

So, what if we could do something to the *figures*, to make it *look* like things are better? If it's not within our gift to stop the nations' youth getting drunk and fighting, and it's not, the only place left for us to go to, to get the reductions we need, is our bureaucrats.

If we arrest lots of people for relatively minor things, so we get lots of 'detections', we at least have some ammunition to use in our defence when people start squealing about NTE crime. Or if police statisticians start to look at *definitions* of crime, maybe we can shift things that *would* have been counted into areas that *wouldn't* be?

For instance, someone is being aggressive and drunk in the street. We have two options. We can arrest him for being 'drunk and disorderly' or for one of the offences under the Public Order Act 1986 – sections 3, 4 and 5 of which are more commonly known as 'Affray', 'Threatening Behaviour' and 'Disorderly Conduct'.

What's the difference? The difference is that 'drunk and disorderly' is not a notifiable crime. You are found in that state by a police officer, arrested and bound over to keep the peace at court the next day (or, more often, given a Penalty Notice for Disorder and sent on your way). *It doesn't show up on the national crime figures.* S5 POA is notifiable, and does.

There is widespread anecdotal evidence of PCs being put under pressure to arrest for drunk and disorderly. Even if they arrest for S5 POA, it can later be changed to d&d – this is perfectly legitimate, no-one is doing anything technically wrong or illegal, but it does have the added benefit of making the NTE figures look a lot better than they actually are, doesn't it?

I don't even really blame senior officers if they are creating this pressure: the Government has said it wants to see reductions, so we have to provide them.

Whether it actually makes things better... well, who in authority really cares? As long as they aren't getting stabbed in the kebab house, or having their car walked over at 3am, or being woken up by people fighting in their front garden – and they aren't – then is there really a problem?

ORDINARY KIDS

ANOTHER night, another body.

Four teenaged girls are heading home from a restaurant where one of them has just celebrated her 18th birthday.

It's a little hatchback, full of joking and gossip and laughter.

The driver is sober.

The passengers in the back are not wearing seatbelts.

The car clips the kerb and comes back across the road, at speed. Later, when we see it, we can't work it out: somehow, one of the girls in the back has been thrown out of the car, between driver and front passenger and through the windscreen. Then she has accelerated beyond the vehicle, impacting with a telegraph pole. Finally, the car has landed on top of her and cut her in half, before rolling away and coming to a stop. The only good thing about this is that she died instantly.

It doesn't seem to make any sense. I say to one of my blokes, 'The driver must have been going at a hell of a lick.'

But then we look at her little motor with its puny engine, and we look at the road, and there's no way she could have got any speed up. And how did the poor dead girl get out ahead of the car like that?

It's weird, but then car accidents often are.

My mind goes back to another strange job. An open-topped sports car has blasted down one of our notorious blackspot roads, in the small hours at about 90mph, and met a truck coming the other way. Head on, in the middle of nowhere. I get a call from the scene. 'Guv… the car is absolutely mashed under the front of the lorry. Fire have jacked the lorry up but there's no sign of the driver.'

Which is a problem. I go up there, with plans to launch a major search for the missing person.

By the time I get there they've found him: he's *in a tree above them*. Draped over the branches, looking down but smashed to pieces.

With our dead girl, I arrive as the scene is being secured, but before the crash investigation team get there. I go up to the vehicle, but I don't go around to the front. I know she's dead, and I know how she's died and, to be honest, I don't want to see it. Two other officers who have seen it are white-faced nearby, badly shaken-up.

I look down the road, to the restaurant the four girls left not half an hour earlier. Now, three of them are back inside, with my officers trying to console them. Often, people are numbed and shocked into quietness at times like this. Not these girls. They've seen everything, and they're in a terrible state, weeping and screaming and rocking about.

Just ordinary kids who forgot about seatbelts.

STRANGE DAYS

THERE are some strange lives being led behind Britain's net curtains.

Being a Response Inspector opens doors to you – literally – that other people never get to look behind. Being in the job, you see so much of it that you actually kind of forget how odd some of it is. Then you come home, stick the telly on and start talking about work to a normal person like your wife, and the expression of horrified bemusement on her face brings you back to reality.

Here's one we recently dealt with.

An 18-year-old female, Mandy, came in to report a sexual assault.

The investigation revealed the following:

Mandy had slept with her best friend's boyfriend.

The best friend had discovered this and, by way of revenge, she had broken into Mandy's flat, smashed the place up and set fire to all her clothes.

Mandy, now having nothing to wear and nowhere to live, had then ended up sleeping round at her best friend's house (the best friend is the offender, remember).

While she was there, her best friend's stepfather came into her bedroom and began touching her up.

In the middle of this, the best friend came home and caught him at it – but got *completely* the wrong end of the stick. She thought Mandy was trying it on with her 'dad' as payback for burning the flat, so later that night, in a fury and to get back at Mandy, she slept with her own stepfather.

The stepfather, by the way, is not George Clooney. He's about 60 and smells strongly of stale urine, beer and fags.

We ended up with crime reports for burglary and arson (the flat), criminal damage (the clothes), sexual assault (the stepfather on Mandy) and ABH... when the best friend's mother got home and found her daughter in bed with stepdad.

I know it's confusing and it sounds weird and mad, but it's honestly fairly normal stuff for us. I only wish I was making it up.

Here's a slightly bloodier, but no less odd, case.

A few weeks ago, the paramedics called us to an horrendous flat inhabited by two heroin addicts. It was the kind of place we see a lot of, where you struggle to get inside for all the mess and detritus, and then immediately regret making the effort.

Two of our young officers had initially been sent in response to the ambo crew's call for assistance. When they got there, they found that one of the junkies was dead. The other was standing in the hallway, waving a bloodied knife and covered in puncture marks. He was also off his head, yelling, virtually frothing at the mouth and very dangerous.

The two lads – they were only 19 or 20 years old – went in and nicked him on suspicion of murder, seizing the knife and securing the scene. This is when relatively inexperienced police officers are at their best, though sadly it's largely ignored: we hear the phrase 'a man was arrested' and we switch off – it doesn't occur to us that the man might have been armed with a carving knife, eyes bulging, threatening to cut the throat of anyone who went near him.

I attended after all the hard work was done.

All was not as it had first seemed.

The guy with the knife was a self-harmer, hence the puncture marks and the blood, and the dead man had simply pumped too much heroin into himself. It turned out that they were father and son. Imagine that – though I suppose it's not all that different from following your dad into his trade.

Perhaps the oddest call I've been to was when I was a new-ish PC. A landlord had been going round to collect the rent on one of his flats for weeks and had been getting no answer. Finally, fearing the worst, he had gone in. He'd found the bathroom door locked and, unable to get any response from within, had called us. We smashed through the door, banging it against the tenant's head and back in the process. He was lying on the floor with his wrists slashed and blood everywhere. Next to him was an empty whisky bottle, and empty blister packs for 60 or more aspirin were lying loose on the floorboards. There were suicide notes all over the place saying he couldn't go on: it looked pretty open-and-shut to me. But still, I dropped down to have a look at him and did a quick check of his pulse and breathing – yep, he was gone. The ambulance was on its way, so we radioed to tell them the man was dead so that they could turn the blue lights off and slow down. Then I radioed my Inspector and told him we had a sudden death, and we started gathering the evidence, putting the suicide notes in bags, seizing the whisky bottle, counting the empty blister packs. With everything secured, I walked off into the living room to see if there was anything else we needed. Suddenly my colleague Nick shouted from the bathroom, 'He's just moved!'

'No way,' I said, and rushed back in there.

'He just blinked,' said Nick. 'Look.'

I knelt down by the body and prodded him in the face. No response. I lifted his arm and dropped it. Nothing.

At that moment the ambulance crew arrived.

'Bit odd, this,' I said. 'I've checked his pulse and stuff and he's dead... but then my colleague says he saw him blink.'

One of the paramedics knelt down by the side of the man, took out a pen and jabbed him in the eye with it. He yelped. He was faking it.

'Nothing wrong with him at all,' said the paramedic.

'But look at the state of the wounds on his arms,' I said. 'And what about the Scotch and pills?'

'Nah, those wounds are all superficial,' he said. 'The aspirins are probably flushed down the bog, along with most of the whisky. He's just a drama queen. There's something wrong with him *mentally*, yes. But physically he's fine.'

I watched them strap the guy up and walk him to their ambulance, thinking, *But we couldn't get any signs out of him... he was bloody dead!*

Then I called my Inspector and broke the good news that our corpse was in the rudest of good health. He was fuming with me; I learned a major lesson that day.

In the movies, people confirm death with a quick grasp of the wrist. But a pulse is a notoriously bad indicator – you're stressed, there's often a lot of noise and movement, it's hard to find, your own pulse intervenes. A thorough check starts with opening the mouth and checking the airway for obvious obstructions. Then you check for breathing – if it's quiet you listen, if not you place the back of your hand in front of the 'dead' man's mouth and feel. You shout and stick your fingers in his nostrils to see what happens. Finally, as the paramedic did, you prod him with a sharp object – few people can maintain an act with a pen in their eye.

I knew all of this, of course, but what had fooled me was the evidence. It looked overwhelming – the empty aspirin packets everywhere, a whole bottle of spirits gone, and he stank of it, his wrists cut and blood everywhere. We'd kicked the door in against him without him moving an inch, which is pretty good going. He was a brilliant faker, I had to admit that.

We have another regular offender who often goes into a 'coma' in custody: her heart rate is almost flat, she's hardly breathing, she's unresponsive – even when you jab her with a sharp object. She gets carted off in an ambulance, they get her on to a ward, plug her in to all the life-saving machines… and the next thing is, if you're not careful she's upped and gone. It sounds crazy, but she always gets a cell near to the custody exit because we know what's going to happen.

Some people seem to have no concept of what we are for. I attended a nice house in an expensive suburb of one of our towns after the elderly man who lives there – a retired Colonel – set off a residential panic alarm. We raced over on blues and twos from several miles away, risking God knows how many lives to get there, to find him standing on his porch with a stop-watch. It turned out he had triggered the alarm deliberately to find out how long we'd take to get there if he ever was in trouble.

We summonsed him for wasting police time, to which he pleaded guilty, but the magistrates let him off with a conditional discharge on the basis that he had a right to be protected by the state under Article whatever of the Human Rights Act, and a further right to determine whether that protection is in place.

DOMESTIC VIOLENCE

YESTERDAY I sat in our fortnightly 'tasking and coordinating' meeting with our partners in the local 'Community Safety Partnership' – the people from agencies like housing, education and health.

We were discussing domestic violence.

We have targets to increase reporting of domestic violence offences and, simultaneously, targets to reduce the number of domestic violence offences in our area.

The woman responsible for domestic violence on the CSP stood up and reported that she had managed to achieve a 3% increase in DV reporting. Then our DV Detective Inspector, whose job it is to reduce these crimes, stood up and – obviously – revealed that there had been a 3% increase in crimes, too.

When we left the meeting, one public servant walked away happy and the other walked away sad. There is no way that both of them can ever walk away happy: one is employed to make the situation look worse, and the other is employed to make it look better.

This would almost be funny if you weren't paying for it, and if there weren't real victims nearby who were probably being beaten up and abused while we sat there talking about our targets and counting statistics and worrying about a couple of percentage points' rise here and fall there.

It might surprise you, but I care about domestic violence. I'm a basically normal human being. Plus I'm married, I have a sister and a mother and two grannies and female friends: the idea of someone physically attacking any of them is horrifying – the idea of *any* woman trapped in her home and being beaten up by a bigger, stronger man is horrifying.

I'm just not convinced that the way the police now deal with this problem is actually the best way: I think it might even be counterproductive.

Domestic violence is, along with racism and diversity/multiculturalism generally, the biggest and hottest of the hot potatoes we currently have to handle – the media and the pressure groups and the politicians and the senior officers are all extremely vocal about the problem, and that has led to changes in police policy and, thus, how we respond to it on the streets.

And it *is* a serious problem. There are studies showing a horrendous percentage of women are physically attacked in their homes, and that many DV victims only call the police after they have been assaulted a horrible number of times before.

Everyone sensible wants to do everything possible to prevent this.

The question is: how do we define 'everything possible'?

Currently, what it means in my force, and I believe in most other forces, is a Positive Arrest Policy. If Response officers now go to a reported domestic violence incident, there is a very good chance that any man in that house will be arrested. On our DV forms, it says: *Was an arrest made? If not, why not?* We used to come from a world where you explained why you *had* arrested people. Here there is no paragraph for that – just one for why you haven't.

Let's make one thing clear: if the woman has called us herself, I have no problem arresting the man. If the call has come in from a concerned neighbour, and when we arrive the woman looks hurt or distressed, or she seems evasive, or the man is threatening or violent to us, or if any one of a number of other danger signals are present, ditto.

The problem comes when we are forced to arrest *irrespective* of whether there is *any* real evidence at all – and even when the woman is denying there's any problem and is practically hanging on to his ankles as we drag him out of the house.

I'll look at the consequences of this in a moment. First, how and why has this policy arisen?

Partly, it comes out of the prevalent theory of domestic violence, which is that when the police are called, women hide the truth. When they say, *He's done nothing*, they are lying, out of fear of what the husband or partner will do to them if we do arrest him, or out of loyalty or even love. Women lie out of shame, or to protect their children, or because they have nowhere to go and no money coming in if the man is locked up. I have no doubt that this is true in some cases. However, in others it isn't true – there really *is* no problem and what the neighbour has heard is just a run-of-the-mill row of the type that we all have from time to time (or he has heard nothing at all and is only calling us in revenge for when next door called us on *him* last week: this happens a lot).

It's also about the need to protect the backsides of the police and politicians if the worst happens. If we take a woman at her word and leave the house, what happens if the man *does* lose it later on that evening and batters her to death? Quite apart from this being an appalling tragedy and a serious crime, police officers will be suspended, the Independent Police Complaints Commission* will get involved and the media will be all over it like a rash – and the Chief Constable doesn't want any of that.

What was once a matter of the discretion of the bobbies who attended a given property and decided how to act on the evidence they saw with their own eyes has mutated into an exercise in ticking boxes and following pre-determined courses of action, laid down in offices miles away by nine-to-fivers who haven't seen the front line in years (if ever) and have no idea as to what the job is really like now.

The key point to bear in mind here is that if you allow a PC any discretion, he or she will – being human – occasionally get it wrong.

The answer to this is to arrest everyone – then at least you can't be blamed.

What are the consequences of this?

Well, in many cases we are nicking entirely innocent men, upsetting their wives or partners and children, potentially destroying families and driving another wedge between ourselves and the public. I can't count the number of times I have handcuffed blokes and led them to a panda with their wives walking behind me asking what I'm doing. I can't count the number of times my colleagues and I have said, 'Christ, I've had worse rows than that with my missus… thank God *my* neighbours haven't called anyone.'

Here's a typical case. I was a new Sergeant sent to arrest a 45-year-old scaffolder called Wayne for domestic violence that he hadn't committed. It was the usual story: we had been rung by the neighbours, who told us that next door were shouting at each other, really giving it hammer and tongues. Then the female had started screaming, before she suddenly stopped.

Fair enough: we need to go to calls like that, and no-one would argue that we shouldn't.

We banged on the door. No reply. Net curtains on the windows, we couldn't see anything. So, under S17 of PACE, acting to preserve life and limb, we kicked the door down (which doesn't tend to endear us to householders).

---

*The Independent Police Complaints Commission (IPCC) investigates complaints against the police, fatal road accidents involving police vehicles, deaths in custody and so on.

We found them in their living room, with loud music playing. They hadn't heard the door and were surprised, to say the least, to see two uniformed cops suddenly burst in.

'What's going on?' said the wife, Tracey. She wasn't hurt, or tearful, though she did have her arms folded a bit defensively. They both looked slightly on edge, but then wouldn't you if the police had just battered their way into your house, unannounced?

'We've had reports of screaming and shouting,' I said. I pointed to the kitchen. 'Can I just take you in here so I can have a word with you, madam?'

The idea, obviously, is to speak to them individually.

'No, you can't,' she said. 'I don't know what you're on about. We were arguing because he went to the pub after work and he's only just got in. Is that illegal, now, is it? Who rang you, anyway?'

'I'm afraid I can't tell you that.' Often, the people who call us to report DV incidents will start off by saying they don't want to be identified or make a statement, and our domestic violence people say we can't compromise DV sources at any cost.

'Well, I don't want you here,' said Tracey. 'He's done nothing. Can you get out of my house, please?'

It didn't look to me as though there'd been anything serious going on. No evidence of any injuries, and a wife who doesn't seem to need or want us there. But on the other hand, why won't she go into the kitchen with me? Maybe she just doesn't want to? Perhaps she's telling the truth? Then your mind goes back to the various domestic violence courses you've attended, and experts you've spoken to: the fact that a woman refuses our help and won't make a statement is irrelevant… she can yell at the top of her voice that the man is innocent if she likes, it doesn't mean he is.

'They all do that,' say the experts. 'They won't support because they're frightened.'

'But she wasn't injured.'

'They beat them where the marks don't show.'

'She said it was just a normal row, and I really think it was.'

'You don't know what goes on behind closed doors.' (Whereas they do, obviously.)

If I walk out of there without a body, I will have to justify that decision in writing, reams and reams of it, and it will be on my head, too. I can't rely on support from above, because our policy is to arrest.

'Wayne,' I said. 'If Tracey won't let me speak to her in the kitchen, I need you to come outside with me so my colleague can have a word with her in here.'

'Get lost,' he said. 'This is my house, mate. Who do you think you are?'

I reached out for his arm, and he pushed me away.

'Right, Wayne,' I said. 'I'm sorry, but we're going to have to arrest you.'

At which point he went ballistic. A 45-year-old man who spends his working life shifting scaffold poles about is a serious proposition, and I honestly thought he was going to take our heads off. He trashed half of the house before we got him under control, with Tracey screaming at us to let him go and telling us he'd never touched her. We dragged him, cuffed but still thrashing and fighting, out of there, with his kids out of bed and crying and wailing and all the neighbours watching.

Imagine that. He'd had a bit of a row with his wife. We *all* have them. Now he's had his door kicked in and he's got a criminal record for resisting arrest and assaulting the police (nothing ever happened in respect of the DV, because there was no DV). How can this be right?

Well, there is a line of reasoning in favour of the policy – the 'if it saves one life' argument.

This is a very difficult argument to counter, but I'm going to try.

Firstly, if you even attempt to raise objections to it, this will be construed in some quarters as a sign that you don't actually care about battered and murdered women. As I say above, I most certainly *do* care about them. I can't prove this: you'll just have to take it on trust.

Secondly, while we *do* collate figures on domestic violence, as we should, we *don't* (because it's impossible) collate figures on crime that we don't prevent or detect while we're tied up following our rigid, must-arrest DV policy. For instance, if we send two officers out to arrest Wayne the Scaffolder, bring him back to custody and book him in, they will be off the streets and out of the game for, conservatively, three or four hours each. If this happens on a Friday night, it's by no means impossible that a drunken fight is erupting outside a pub in the High Street at the same time. If this fight might have been prevented by the presence of those two officers in the High Street, and if their absence results in one of the participants being kicked to death, then in fact our DV policy has not *saved* a life but *cost* one. I appreciate that this is an extreme example, but it is essentially entirely plausible: there are a limited number of us, and if we spend time arresting people who don't actually need arresting, we can't arrest other people who do. (Ironically, some of these may be serious DV perpetrators – we can only be dragging one man out of one house at a time. What happens if a particularly nasty call comes in 30 seconds after one which isn't serious, and we only have one crew available?)

The third argument against our current policy is that it doesn't work. I looked at our own DV figures for January 2008, expecting to see a reduction, year-on-year (this policy having been in place for five years now). There was none. The experts say that if we arrest everyone immediately, we can stop 'escalation'. But while this might help in some cases, there are others where the bloke either doesn't need nicking at all or is a really violent bastard for whom a night in the cells is just time to stew. These *real* nasty scumbags, who regularly threaten and abuse and beat and torture and rape their wives and partners, we aren't going to change their behaviour *at all* with this policy. Serious domestic violence recidivists are virtually mentally unstable: they are serial offenders, and they don't stop, ever, at least until they are physically too weak to raise their fists any more. Court orders make no difference. Banging them up for 24 hours looks good, because we're doing something, and a 'no arrest' on a report of domestic violence is like cancer, but it just enrages them further.

If we could just step back and look at this problem without all the surrounding noise and controversy, we would see, I think, that we need to be targeting more time and effort on these offenders and their victims, not Wayne and his missus.

EVIL, VIOLENT, NASTY MEN

HERE'S an example of the sort of guy we *should* focus on.

One night, CCTV came up on the radio and said that they were watching a male around the back of one of the main supermarkets on the edge of the town centre. He was dragging a female along the pavement by her hair. Every few steps, he would stop and punch her in the face.

We went down there, hell for leather, blue lights on but no sirens, a silent approach. I screamed into the street and saw the assault happening with my own eyes, just as the operator had described it: a long-haired woman with shiny hoop earrings being pulled down the street by a man. As I looked on, he stooped down and slapped her hard, twice, with the back of his hand.

I pulled up next to him, just as another crew arrived.

The other two officers grabbed the man (Tony), bundled him over to a low wall and sat him down on it, firmly. As they started talking to him, I helped the woman (Mary) to my car.

Cameras came back to me on my earpiece as I did so. 'We've got the whole thing on tape,' they said. 'Quite clear and very nasty... we're willing to make a statement immediately.'

Mary was a real mess – puffy-eyed, cut and bleeding. A female officer got there, sat with her in the back of my car and started taking details. Except that she was refusing to *give* any details. The first words out of her mouth were, 'I'm not saying anything. I've just had too much to drink, I fell over and Tony was helping me up.' She wouldn't go beyond this plainly nonsensical story of a drunken fall.

All is not lost, though. We've got CCTV and some good forensics – Tony's knuckles and clothing were thoroughly spattered with her blood.

'Can we just swab your face?' asked the female officer. If we get her DNA from her cuts, we can match it with that in the blood on his hands.

'No,' said Mary.

We can't force victims to let us take their DNA or swab their injuries, so this ruled forensics out; even though we could and would swab Tony, without a matching sample from her it was evidentially worthless.

I walked over to the wall. Tony was a thick-set bruiser who looked as though he could do a fair bit of damage to a 6ft bloke, never mind a 5ft woman. He was sullen and angry into the bargain. 'We've got his account,' said one of my blokes. 'He says she fell over and he was just helping her up.'

I looked at him. 'That's rubbish,' I said. 'I've just spoken to CCTV, plus I saw it with my own eyes. You're nicked.'

He kicked off at this, obviously, and was cuffed and put in the back of the van, where he started shouting and swearing and threatening all and sundry.

By the time we'd got him to the custody desk, he was thoroughly wound up – it took three of us to control him.

Mary's injuries were clearer in the station's strip lighting; there were lots of cuts and bruises and her face was smeared in blood and dirt, from where he'd repeatedly thrown her into the gutter.

The PC who had arrested Tony explained to the Custody Sergeant what had happened, and the Custody Sergeant gave him the spiel. 'You have heard what the officer has said… is there anything you want to say to me?'

'Yeah,' he said. 'She's my wife. It's none of your f**king business.'

He was genuinely aggrieved – bewildered, even – to have been arrested; it was as though she was his property.

We stuck him in a cell, put the case together and charged him after discussions with the CPS. Although Mary wouldn't make a statement, or allow photographs of her injuries to be taken, or turn up to any of our subsequent meetings, or let anyone in to see her at home, we are empowered to take DV offenders to court without the victim's support. It's a sensible recognition of the fact that the victims are vulnerable to further attack and are often terrified to assist, as Mary was.

That's a nice policy and a good headline, but in reality? It doesn't mean it's easy to get convictions.

At court, Mary wouldn't give evidence about what had happened – we can compel victims to do so, but this is very rare.

We had a description of her injuries in a notebook, but that doesn't carry quite the same impact as the photo we hadn't been able to take.

We couldn't prove that the blood on his knuckles came from her face.

When we showed the CCTV pictures, Tony's lawyer said, *Yes? And? He told you, she just fell over and you can see, there he is, helping her up.* Suddenly, the punches aren't that clear... maybe he *was* just wiping the blood away?

My evidence? Irrelevant. Yep, I've seen it happen, but so what? I'm just a copper, my word against Tony's.

He walked out of court, and as he passed me he raised his *digitus impudicus* and stuck it in my face with a wide grin.

So what is the answer?

I think we have to accept, collectively, that there are limits on what the police can do. We cannot cure the ills of society. Without CCTV cameras installed in every home, we cannot stop all domestic violence. Pretending we can – or that this is a realistic goal – is a lie and a fraud perpetrated on the public.

I also think we have to return to trusting our officers. Yes, mistakes will be made. But mistakes are being made anyway.

If we don't have two officers tied up for six hours with Wayne the Scaffolder, we can put those resources into other areas. If we concentrate on people like Tony – remanding him in custody with support from the courts, working with other agencies to help Mary get away, encouraging Mary to support us on the basis that he will get a guaranteed five years if convicted and she will be helped to establish a new life – maybe that would make a difference.

Meanwhile, we sit in our police stations and count statistics.

Two cases and, actually, two detections. Wayne and Tony, both arrested and charged (though only Wayne gets a criminal record out of it.) Because we can't nail men like Tony, we make damn sure we get men like Wayne. We concentrate on picking the low-hanging fruit, hauling people in for drunken shouting matches and angry squabbles so that our backsides are covered and our figures look good and we can be seen to be doing 'everything possible' about domestic violence.

DETECTIONS

LET'S go back to basics for a moment.

Lots of people probably don't quite understand the words 'crime' and 'detection', and the role they play in modern policing.

That's not surprising, because what they mean in *reality* and what they mean in *surreality* – ie modern policing – are often two completely different things.

In real life, a crime means something which we would all agree is against the law – theft, assault, burglary – and has an actual victim who has really suffered some harm.

In *policing*, a 'crime' – because of the 'victim-focused' National Crime Recording Standard I mentioned earlier – can mean, in practice, almost anything which half sounds like it might possibly be a bit like a crime and which is reported to us. (Because who are we to tell Mr Hughes that his ex's nasty text message isn't a crime?)

Here is one example of a non-crime taken seriously by us.

It's late one afternoon in the middle of last December. The Christmas lights are ablaze on every house in Bigtown, and the concrete walkway outside the local Spar is covered in fresh white litter. Inside, there's a queue of people waiting to pay for their groceries. Halfway down the line, a little girl and her mum are chatting about Santa Claus, and the presents he will be delivering in a fortnight.

In front of them is a typical Bigtown youth – Burberry scarf, Nike trainers, NY Yankees cap and a ton of bling.

Overhearing their conversation, he turns round, looks at the girl and says, 'You don't believe in Father Christmas, do ya? Your mum's telling you lies... he ain't real.'

The little girl bursts into tears and the angry mum storms out of the shop.

I like to think that, if that happened to me, I'd tell my daughter that the nasty man was talking rubbish, and chalk it up to experience.

But modern life being what it is, mum doesn't do this; instead, she phones us on her mobile from the street outside, like it's a police matter.

OK, so we get a call from a lady wanting to report a Santa denier. We just tell her we're awfully sorry but it's not really one for us, right?

Wrong. The call-taker logs it on the system as a harassment offence. We all know that if the woman had been calling to report a criminal damage that had happened the night before she'd have got someone out a week next Tuesday. But because certain triggers are hit – there's a child involved, this area happens to be a crime hot spot and the man is still at the scene – a patrol is despatched immediately, to speak to the mum and little girl and, if possible, grab the 'offender' and even seize the CCTV to see if they can ID him.

To me, that's just about as mad as it gets. Is it, even at the edges of abstract technicality, a crime? Harassment is about causing alarm or distress to another. As a senior officer asked in the SMT morning meeting, 'How can it be harassment to tell someone Santa doesn't exist? I mean, he doesn't. Does he?'

He's got a point. Short of producing Santa himself at an ID parade and proving he's real, the case is going nowhere. But time and resources have been wasted in a fairly ludicrous way.

Here's another one.

Two young lads outside a newsagent. One, a 10-year-old, goes in and buys a packet of crisps. Walkers, salt and vinegar I believe. When he comes back out and opens the packet, his 11-year-old chum swoops on him, sticks a fist into the bag and legs it down the road, cackling in glee with a handful of crisps.

The first boy tells his mum and, yes, she calls us. The 'thief' is questioned but – horror of horrors – he denies it. This causes our whole system to collapse, because we're all about getting people to cough to minor offences and accept cautions for them to make detections. Where do we go from here? Forensics? ID parades with witnesses from the scene who saw the boy make off with the crisps? Thankfully, there is some residual common sense in the police, and the case eventually got 'no-crimed' – but not before hours of police time was wasted, and only after submissions in triplicate to the crime auditors to get them to wipe it off the computer.

These aren't isolated cases. Here are a few others from the papers recently:

– A man 'found in possession of an egg with intent to throw'.

– A child who removed a slice of cucumber from a sandwich and threw it at another youngster.

– A woman arrested (on her wedding day) for criminal damage after her foot slipped on the accelerator and her vehicle damaged a car park barrier.

– Another child who threw cream buns at a bus.

– A 70-year-old pensioner arrested for criminal damage after cutting back a neighbour's conifer trees.

– A man who threw a glass of water over his girlfriend.

I didn't make any of these up. Anti-social, yes, and in some cases maybe we ought to have a quiet word with the people involved. But are they really 'crimes'?

Once someone reports them to us as such, and the call-taker enters them onto our computer databases as such, then, yes, they are.

So that's 'crime'. What's a 'detection'?

You perhaps think this refers to a mechanism whereby the person responsible for a crime, real or surreal, is caught and punished for it.

In fact, it may just mean that a suspect has been charged* – he doesn't have to be found guilty. Equally, he may have been cautioned, or reported for summons, or been issued with a Penalty Notice for Disorder, or the offence may have been taken into consideration when he is sentenced for other matters.

What are the implications of all of this?

They are many and varied.

Firstly, all of a sudden anyone who has been looked at a bit funny can ring the police and demand a response.

Secondly, this will mean one extra recorded crime on the force's figures (eg 'harassment' for looking at someone funny).

Thirdly, we can't just ignore them. Under NCRS, we mostly have to take them seriously, which is just one reason why it takes us three days to show up for your burglary. Plus lots of undetected 'crimes'

---

*The reason we're judged on 'detections' and not the outcome of a case at court is that the police have no real influence over what some crazy buffoon of a magistrate decides to do, and no control over a jury in Crown Court. All we can really do is influence the investigation. Though in many cases we *can't* really do that either – witnesses decide not to give evidence because they are a friend of the accused, or victims (often women in DV cases) are frightened to assist in prosecutions.

make Chief Constables look bad, and worry the Home Secretary, so they have to be detected with a response that is bureaucratic and slow and will take officers off the street for hours.

Fourthly, a boy who throws a piece of cucumber at a classmate may feel under pressure to accept a caution – and a permanent entry on his criminal record. This may affect his chances of employment later in life. (Though at the rate we're criminalising the population, it won't be long before pretty much everyone has a record, and it's weird if you haven't.)

Finally, in many forces, each officer now has an individual 'Detection Target'. If he or she does not hit this target, he or she will end up with an 'Action Plan' on his or her Annual Appraisal. This is essentially a negative statement on your file, which can exclude you from an interview for a specialisation or promotion at the 'paper-sift' stage. Helping old ladies across the road, diving into swollen rivers to rescue drowning people and preventing or deterring crime from happening in the first place – none of these count against your individual target.

Of the above implications, the only one that really matters is our figures for undetected crimes. That's because these are the only ones that affect senior police officers and politicians.

It doesn't matter that bobbies might be so tied up looking for youths who don't believe in Father Christmas that they can't come out when you're assaulted, because senior cops and MPs don't very often get assaulted. If the young salt and vinegar crisps thief gets a criminal record, that doesn't matter either, because who cares? And neither does the systematic degradation of what was once a force into a 'service' that often only seems to serve the non-contributory members of society, because if the Chief Constable or the Lord Chief Justice or The Right Honourable Jacqui Smith MP has a gang of rowdy youths hanging around outside late at night, you can bet there'll be a rapid and forceful response to that. (Though remember, Jacqui, that you were once a humble schoolteacher, and you won't be Home Secretary for ever.)

PC David Copperfield was the first to break ranks and tell people about this nonsense. Since then, there have been lots of noises about how it's all going to change, and they're going to slash bureaucracy and cut targets. Well, it hasn't happened yet, and I'll believe it when I see it.

Incidentally, the crisps theft was not a lone incident. There were 500 similar thefts, of 'nominal value under £1', across my force in the past six months. What are these £1 thefts? Well, this might explain some of them: If your credit card is nicked and used, and the guy who stole it is later arrested with it still on him, this presents us with an opportunity. How about if the police crime this twice? Once for the deception involved in using it to buy alloy rims for his Vauxhall Corsa, and once for the theft of the *actual piece of plastic, nominal value under £1.*

So some copper calls you up. 'Mr Smith, isn't it great? We got the guy who nicked your card. We're talking to the bank about the loss of the money, and we also want to deal with him for the card itself. Can we just come and take a quick statement from you?'

This is called a 'Loser's Statement' – it's designed to head off a defence in court that you are the thief's best mate and you always let him use your card.

You say, 'Yep, no problem', and the Old Bill nip round. Result: the theft of the credit card *itself* is detected and the crime figures for theft look a little better. I'll leave it to you to decide whether we'd bother criming the theft of the card if we hadn't actually already recovered it.

COULDN'T PROSECUTE SATAN

ON TELLY, there's a murder at 8.05pm and it's wrapped up by John Nettles just before the nine o'clock news.

You might catch a glimpse of a defence lawyer and sometimes there are two or three minutes of courtroom action, but no-one ever seems to mention the CPS.

Until recently, the police decided whether suspects would be charged, and with which offences. Now, the people who usually* do

*There are occasions where Inspectors can charge, and I can tell you that *everyone* gets charged when I do it. Additionally, the SMT can appeal CPS charging decisions, but this comes with a procedural nightmare all of its own for the officers involved, often bigger than the original file, and is very rare, not least because we know that it is extremely unlikely that the offender will receive any meaningful sanction if convicted anyway.

this are the 9,000 staff of the Crown Prosecution Service, or CPS – jokingly referred to in some circles as the 'Criminal Protection Service', or 'Can't Prosecute, Sorry', or 'Couldn't Prosecute Satan'.

It ought to be fairly clear, then, that it's no good complaining to or about the police when it is decided that John Smith will be done for ABH and not attempted murder after he stabs you in the kebab house one Friday night.

Somehow, though, we *do* still get the complaints. I suppose we're standing there in recognisable uniforms, whereas the CPS people all wear suits (M&S or Gieves and Hawkes, depending on pay grade), but I think it's more because of all that unrealistic TV. In real life, when we don't live up to that small screen ideal, people get very cross.

One school of thought is that a return to the old days might mean less paperwork and bureaucracy and that things would be processed faster*. That said, I don't know of any major groundswell of support among officers for a return to police charging; I think what we really want is for the *existing* system to work more quickly and simply, for the CPS to back us up a bit more than it does and for its lawyers to show more consistency.

It would also be nice if they were not subjected to the same sort of targets we are. With us, it's arrests and detections – with them, it's convictions. In order that they don't lose too many cases and end up

---

*It can take months and months for decisions to be made on charging, with suspects on bail all the time – enabling them, potentially, to intimidate witnesses or for witnesses to move away or forget details. The Government, to be fair, is aware of this problem, and recently introduced a thing called CJSSS – Simple Speedy Summary Justice. This is a 'quick fix' introduced to speed up the court process and cut down on paperwork. It's complicated, but essentially it requires the police to look for 'early guilty pleas' from alleged offenders, and produce a certain kind of file to reflect this. Naturally, there are all sorts of claims that this is making a big difference, and that the courts system in England and Wales will soon be a model of efficiency. Again, I'll believe it when I see it; there is already anecdotal evidence that defence solicitors in the custody area are advising their clients' *not* to indicate whether they are likely to plead guilty or not as a tactical ploy to confuse us into not knowing which type of file to produce, in the hope that the wrong kind of file is submitted and some technical grounds for the case being dismissed might later emerge.

looking bad, they have to consider whether there is a 'realistic prospect of a conviction' before deciding whether to charge a suspect.

This sounds reasonably sensible until you think it through.

Firstly, of course there's a realistic prospect of a conviction – he's guilty as sin, we've just faxed over 50 pages of evidence to prove it which took us six hours to put together... and you're saying *No*?

Secondly, I thought guilt or innocence in criminal cases was supposed to rest with magistrates or a jury, who convict if a case is proved 'beyond all reasonable doubt'. Introducing the CPS into the mix gives an extra layer of protection that the criminals we arrest (and they really are usually as guilty as sin, irrespective of whether they get convicted) neither need nor deserve.

Thirdly, there's that danger of inconsistency: where most cops would charge and let the courts decide, different CPS lawyers in different parts of the country – or even in the same building – will make entirely different decisions as to whether there's a realistic prospect of conviction, given identical sets of facts. Most big police stations have a permanent CPS presence in an office on the top floor. If the in-house lawyer is weak or defence-minded, police officers can, quite legitimately, play the system by using CPS Direct. This is an out-of-office hours telephone service staffed by on-call lawyers all over the country; you ring a central line and the next brief in line picks up. So if the in-house guy has gone home, you can always try them and see what you get. Moreover, if the first CPS Direct lawyer you talk to isn't interested in charging, and you accidentally drop a file on the phone and cut him off, the next one might be. You've done nothing wrong – just managed to find one Government lawyer who disagrees with another. (Our permanent bloke was off on leave the other week and we got a woman in who was *brilliant* – yep, we'll charge this, you should arrest him for that, I'll run with conspiracy here. Everyone loved her, word got round and the queue outside her door was halfway round the block.)

Worst of all, though, is that the CPS's own target culture leads to ridiculous, almost impossible burdens being placed on us to produce an enormous quantity and quality of evidence for even the most basic job. Again, best of motives and all that – but it has grown out of all proportion and is one of the things that, indirectly, causes the most grief between the public and us.

An example: You hear a noise outside at midnight. You rush to your bedroom window, throw the curtains open and see a group of youths walking down the road, smashing car windows and giggling.

They have their hoods up, but as they draw level with your car you shout down at them, 'Oi, what do you think you're doing?'

They look up at you, and you recognise two of them in the conveniently-placed street lighting because you run the corner shop, you've been serving them pop and sweets for the last decade and you know their parents.

They smash your window and leg it.

You hurry downstairs in your dressing gown, but by the time you're outside they've gone. You call the police. We arrive quickly, because criminal damage is a Control Strategy Crime* and it's in progress in the middle of an otherwise quiet night. One of the PCs gets out of his car and runs over. 'Officer,' you say. 'They went that way, they're wearing hoods and tracky bottoms, and I know them… Jimmy Jones and Paul Potts.'

The police, knowing that most criminals are stupid, go straight around to their houses and wait. Sure enough, they turn up 15 minutes later and get nicked for criminal damage. They get stuck in the bin and the next morning are interviewed on tape. They deny it, but so what? We have control samples of broken glass from two of the cars collected from the pavements and matched to glass found on the youths' sleeves. We know this was the clothing they were wearing at the time, because they were in it when the police arrested them a quarter of an hour after the 999 call. Chuck in a bit of house-to-house confirming that the windows were not broken earlier in the evening. Finally, we have you – you saw them do it and you even know who they are.

Result!

Except, not really. I have seen CPS decide not to charge on cases exactly like this because there is 'insufficient evidence'. I've seen them decide not to charge on *more* evidence.

What will happen is the defence brief will slide a prepared statement across the desk to us and say, 'This is all we're saying.'

---

*Control Strategy Crime is crime which, though sometimes apparently minor, is high on our list of priorities. More on this later.

What they're saying is, yes, sure you saw them. They were there. But they know you – you're always shouting at them and giving them grief over nothing. They were walking along, minding their own business, when a brick suddenly flew through the air, probably thrown by you, and hit the car, showering them with the glass. Then you started yelling abuse at them. They might add in that you then came downstairs and touched one of them inappropriately, on the inner thigh. So now, from being our eyewitness, you are suddenly someone we have to arrest on suspicion of sexual assault.

Remember, we'll never be able to tell the magistrates or a jury that they each have six previous convictions for criminal damage, and you are spotless. The waters are muddied: your sexual assault is going nowhere, but neither is their criminal damage. And next time it will be your living room window, not your car. (I'm not saying we like this, because we don't, though if it puts people off calling the police it does have the effect of lowering crime figures.)

Later, you ring us up and want to know what's going on. Why are they not going to court? We say we're awfully sorry but it's a CPS decision, claim on your insurance. As soon as we say CPS, your eyes glaze over. As far as you're concerned, the police haven't done their job properly.

The bottom line is, the CPS are reluctant to charge in many cases unless we have absolutely everything and there is literally no wiggle room for the other side.

Here are some real-life examples.

Friday night in Ruraltown. An off-duty Othershire police officer gets drunk and starts swearing at a patrol led by me. He gets arrested, after an initial warning, for disorderly conduct under Section 5 of the Public Order Act and taken to custody. He accepts a Penalty Notice for Disorder and is released. There are witnesses, pocket notebooks, statements and CCTV from custody of him making comments admitting the offence. Later on, he refuses to pay the PND and opts for a court hearing. The CPS then drop the charge due to lack of evidence, without consulting me. He walks away.

Saturday night in Ruraltown. Response go to a house to arrest a man for wife-beating. They go in to the front room and he jumps up from the chair and lunges at one officer's face/neck with a kitchen knife. The officer puts his hands up in a defensive posture and gets stabbed in his palm. Both officers take him down and disarm him. He gets arrested for GBH, the knife (with the police officer's blood on) is seized and the room is made a Crime Scene. CSI (Crime Scene Investigation) arrive and take various forensic samples proving the suspect's presence in the room, the officer's blood on the floor and so on. A few weeks later, the CPS authorise a charge for actual bodily harm – relatively speaking, a minor offence. Yes, the injuries, though requiring stitching, were, thankfully, not too serious – but if the officer had not raised his hands in time the knife could easily have gone into his neck and we could have been looking at a dead colleague. Surely we need something tougher than ABH here?

Sunday night in Ruraltown, a bloke is nicked for smashing a phone box up with a hammer.

'Have you viewed the CCTV?'

'No, but we just spoke to the operator and it's on it, in real time.'

'You must view it.'

'But we have to download it in the morning and then it goes on to a CD and then we have to...'

'I don't care. It has to be viewed.'

'But he is in custody, we've got the hammer, we've got witnesses, there is the broken window and he is even admitting it.'

'It says on my threshold test that it has to be viewed.'

For goodness' sake, we're talking about *charging* him, not setting up a rope on the nearest tree.

PENALTY NOTICES FOR DISORDER

IT COMES to something when *defence* solicitors start complaining that criminals are getting off too lightly because police are chasing performance targets, but that's what has lately been happening.

The lawyers are worried that Penalty Notices for Disorder and cautions are being overused to increase our detection rates and avoid court cases.

How cynical can you get?

The thing is, they may have a point.

You get detections by charging people with crimes. But, as I've explained, you also get them by getting people to agree to PNDs or cautions, and they count for the same on our crime figures at the end of the year. And which are easier to obtain? Getting someone charged these days takes forever; if you can write them out a little ticket and tick the same box, why not do it?

The latest Home Office figures for PNDs do show a 37% increase in 2006. There was a 17% rise in cautions.

The Ministry of Justice says that it's not always necessary for crimes to be dealt with in court. This is fair enough, most people would say, if you're talking about minor offences. But some of these were dished out to sex offenders, burglars, robbers and those who had committed acts of violence against others.

One of those angry solicitors, Digby Johnson of the Johnson Partnership in Nottingham, told the BBC: 'Offenders who would normally face court and serious sentences are walking away with a ticket in their back pocket. I've known a caution for a serious offence of actual bodily harm where the victim required stitches. A caution was issued for having a house full of cannabis plants. A 20-year-old man who had unlawful sex with a 15-year-old was cautioned.'

Other solicitors were equally worried. One defence brief in Leicester said the city's court had seen its workload drop by almost half since Christmas. Another, who works with the Ministry of Justice, described the system as 'staggering and deranged' (welcome to my world). 'The bottom is falling out of the criminal justice system,' he said. 'Workload in London courts is easily down by half.'

Worse still, the lawyers point out, where PNDs are issued, half of the tickets aren't paid. I can't say that surprises me. People routinely give the wrong addresses, or use a number of other ruses which I won't repeat here, and there's not much we can do about that. And therein lies the problem with the PND system. Fine, for speeding offences and very minor public order matters. Fine, also, if they are followed up and people are made to pay their £80. But when they're levied over much more serious issues and no-one really bothers to enforce them, this is getting close to farcical.

The Police Federation told the BBC that pressure on forces to improve crime detection rates was to blame. A spokesman said officers were being 'encouraged to dispense instant justice where at all possible'.

(He didn't address the question of whether it's really 'justice'.) 'It's a dumbing down of the criminal justice system. Persistent offenders, like shoplifters for example, can pick up £80 fines and never pay them.'

The Police Superintendents' Association of England and Wales blamed the Crown Prosecution Service for making it harder to charge (ironic, that, since I'd say most of the pressure for PNDs and cautions comes from Superintendents) and a spokesman for the Association of Chief Police Officers disagreed that the system is failing and claimed record numbers of people are being brought to justice. Er, if you say so, sir.

POLITICS AND PROMOTION

I WAS recently unfortunate enough to attend a seminar on the new appraisal system for all staff in my force, the Personal Development Review.

The PDR system is designed to allow us all to monitor and record the professional achievements of our officers, set diversity objectives and list our skills and 'competencies'.

It requires supervisors and line managers (Sergeants and Inspectors in plain English) to complete an extensive form for each PC, fill out a supervisor's check list and then send it to personnel with a covering memo. This is a considerable task which takes a lot of time, particularly when you have a shift of officers to appraise.

The Headquarters disciple of political correctness who delivered this piece of news to us made the mistake of asking for comments at the end of the session.

I couldn't resist this opportunity to get revenge for the last 60 mind-numbing minutes of complete nonsense, and raised my hand. 'Why are we doing this?' I asked. 'Where have all these new objectives come from, and who decides on these competencies?'

'The Home Office requires us to complete the PDR forms and compliance will be inspected by HMIC*,' he said.

---

*HMIC – Her Majesty's Inspectorate of Constabulary. A body set up to check police efficiency. How you define 'efficiency' is key here: your definition might be different to theirs.

'What I don't understand,' I said, in my most innocent voice, 'is that the Home Office also requires us to cut down on the amount of paperwork we have to complete, doesn't it?'

I was briskly informed that this was not very helpful.

We'll leave aside the minor issue of a chap just out of college with little experience of life and none of front line policing telling Inspectors that they are not being helpful: I think I made a valid point. What exactly *do* the Home Office want? Do they really want us to continue to adopt ever more complex and weighty procedures for the way we manage our staff, or could they not just trust us to get on with it?

The answer is that they don't know *what* they want.

It doesn't just apply to PCs, of course.

You don't get promoted in the police by being red-hot and nicking lots of villains. The only way you can now be promoted is by 'evidencing' 'competencies' in line with something called the National Competency Framework.

The competencies are things like 'Respect for Diversity', 'Teamworking', 'Honesty and Integrity' and 'Openness to Change'. Within these areas there are sub-categories, like: 'The officer can demonstrate that he is prepared to embed himself in a particular diverse community for a year', or 'The officer can show that he is happy to talk to the Professional Standards Department* about colleagues and will challenge inappropriate behaviour'.

Without evidence that has been signed off by a senior officer, you cannot get promoted. In fact, you can't really exist, because you have to renew these things every year.

In order to get signed off, you have to provide an enormous amount of practical evidence.

That can be tougher to provide than you might think. Say you're a Sergeant on a rural patch, looking to make Inspector, and you're really good and there are no complaints and you deliver an excellent service. That's all well and good, but how do you evidence your ability to deal with racially aggravated crime? You have to go looking for it, so you get ridiculous scenarios where people will hang around their one Asian shop in the area desperate for a theft or a criminal damage that they can deal with and put down in their PDR.

---

*PSD are the internal police who police us – who polices them I don't know.

The more senior you get, the more sophisticated these competencies are and the more they are arranged around things like:

Is able to identify and reduce Control Strategy Crime in line with Government guidelines

Is able to identify, understand and implement Home Office initiatives regarding gender and race equality

Is able to contribute to the creation of local policies around public space management

You think, *What on earth is 'public space management'?* You look it up and find that it is about 'encouraging ethnic minorities into diverse interacting' (or some similar jargon), and you think, *But we don't have a very large ethnic minority population on our patch. That's not my fault, we just don't.*

So you end up inviting a Jamaican steel band in from three towns away to play in the town centre, and you police it and you evidence it and your PDR gets signed. Or you go on courses. At the end of the year, when once again there have been no race riots, we all stop policing and some guy comes down and tells us what happened in Bradford and we go away and work up some scenarios, do some role play. On *my* evidence it says there haven't been any race riots in Ruraltown, but we can confirm that the officer is trained in this scenario.

I know what you're thinking, or what you *should* be thinking: *What has this got to do with the police? When did the police become the major arm of social engineering enforcement?* Because meanwhile, Gladys down the road has been burgled and there is no-one to go to it.

The Government sets these national competency framework requirements, changing them with the shifting political agenda. The effect of this is that the Government decides who gets promoted – or even gets to join up in the first place.

We have Respect for Diversity forms – the RFD1 and RFD2. I haven't come across an RFD2 yet but an RFD1 is used to report on selection and promotion candidates for inappropriate language and behaviour. If anyone was stupid enough to say anything genuinely racist, obviously you wouldn't want them in the force. But people get binned for using the word 'he' when answering questions about hypothetical situations involving senior officers; after all, not all senior officers are male, and using the masculine pronoun indicates a worrying failure to appreciate the input of women.

This is not how it's meant to be. This is not Germany in the 1930s. We are supposed to be able to nick Government ministers for wrong-doing. You start reading about how the Soviets ran things in the 1950s, and you wonder: how long before each shift has a Political Officer attached to it?

PRISON WORKS

I SAW a very nasty man crumble and turn into a small child in front of my very eyes yesterday.

Why? Prison.

Criminologists, sociologists and human rights activists believe that prison doesn't work.

When they say that, I think what they mean is that the *current* system doesn't work. Ironically, these are the same people who tend to be against the one thing which would ensure jail time did some good: longer sentences (or current sentences which are served in full).

The theory of prisons is that they have a variety of purposes: crime prevention, rehabilitation, punishment and deterrent.

Prison certainly *does* work as a means of crime prevention. Any sensible police officer will tell you that the burglary rate in a given area will drop by a huge amount when the right person is locked up. For me, this is the most important job of jail: it is now a public protection issue, more than anything else.

In 21st century Britain, it's true that prison doesn't really work as a rehabilitative tool. Yes, it would be nice if a few of our customers got the chance to learn to read and be trained in some work skills, but they're never inside long enough. What good is a six-month literacy course with a three-month waiting list to a bloke doing 18 weeks? He'll hardly start it, let alone see it through to the end.

Is prison a punishment? (Are we even allowed to think of it in those terms now?) To some, it is. Although I've not seen any, I suppose some of the people we deal with must be ordinary folk like you or me who have gone off the straight and narrow and can be brought back on it. For them, jail would be no fun at all. But the overwhelming majority of convicts are people who were never on the straight and narrow in the first place: they don't even know what it is. They end up doing lots of very short sentences in a comfortable environment, bills paid, drugs and booze and porn (and even hookers, we lately read) available, with their mates. Does prison punish these people? Not really.

It follows from that that it doesn't deter them, either.

However – and here's where we came in – soft as it is, it does deter all but the truly serious, professional career criminals if they're looking at a really long stretch.

If you have someone in custody who is facing a proper sentence, they change.

Suddenly, they want to talk to you and grass their mates up, suddenly they want a lawyer, suddenly they need consultations for hours, suddenly they are in tears and want to see their family, suddenly they are asking their missus to bring in their favourite pictures of the kids. They are calling you Sir and smoking 20 fags an hour. When you have the same men in for a summary-only offence (only triable before the magistrates, with no custodial sentences beyond six months and terms that long an extreme rarity), they're sneering and swaggering and hoping the police officers and their families all die of cancer.

This tells me more than any number of academic studies or papers or surveys; a mountain of statistics can't change what you see with your own eyes.

Let me give you an example.

Mickey, the guy I mentioned at the start.

He is a big bloke and a deeply violent individual – what we call a 'five-hander'. In the past, when we've gone to arrest him, he's pulled a shovel out of the boot of his car and it's game on... we've had to use dogs, CS gas, lots of officers, and it's still very dangerous stuff.

Despite this, and despite the fact that he has around 130 previous convictions, he has never done more than 12 weeks in prison at a stretch.

He's always out on an early release scheme, or because it's Christmas, or because he's got a tag, or because his wife has given birth to a new baby. (She's a thief too, a prolific shoplifter.)

One of those 130 convictions came after a row in the street with a neighbour, some time ago when I was a PC. The police were called and I was among those who attended. I found Mickey shouting and swearing and gesticulating in the street, and went over. 'What's going on, Mickey?' I said.

He started shouting at me, eyes bulging with hate.

'Look,' I said. 'You need to calm down, stop threatening people and go back into your house.'

He started swearing at me and telling me that I knew what he was capable of, I'd better back off or I was f**ked. And so on.

'Right,' I said. 'You're nicked.'

He messed me about a bit, but not too much for once, and I cuffed him and got him into the van. On the way to the police station, he was full of it: 'I know where you live, you w****r. I'm going to get you. I know which school your kids go to. You want to watch they don't all get run over by a f**king lorry tomorrow.'

A thoroughly charming man.

(Interestingly, as soon as we got to the police station and he got in front of the Custody Sergeant, his demeanour changed. These people learn from an early age to divide and rule. To the Custody Sergeant they are nice as pie, very respectful and compliant; to the arresting officer, horrendously violent, overreacting to everything they say. The idea is to create tension between the PC and the Custody Sergeant, to the point where the Custody Sergeant begins to doubt the word of the bobby as to the suspect's earlier behaviour.)

After the usual rigmarole, he accepted a Penalty Notice for Disorder for being drunk and disorderly and went on his way. I let him out of the nick, and as he went he spat on the ground and looked into my eyes. 'You can f**k off you pig b*****d,' he said. 'You were lucky… if I'd wanted to I could have taken your head off.'

So that's how Mickey behaves when he knows there's nothing serious coming to him, which is pretty much every time he has ever been arrested.

I saw a different side to him yesterday.

He has recently turned his hand to commercial premises burglary. These people like to steal a 4x4 and tour our villages and towns on reconnaissance with a mate or two, driving round offices and shops and industrial units and farms, probing for weaknesses, looking for anything they can move through their network of handlers and fences. It varies from riding tack – this stuff can be worth thousands of pounds, and there's a huge market for it in southern Ireland – to agricultural plant and machinery and, more recently, diesel fuel. Then, in the dead of night, 2am or 3am, they'll put on their balaclavas and ram their way into their target building, stuff the vehicle full of whatever they can and get out of there.

Sometimes they get away and we find the stolen Jeep or Landrover burned out 10 miles away. Other times, we get on to them very quickly. These are serious people: they are quite prepared to ram our cars and seriously injure our officers to get away. We have had examples of what I would regard as really serious attempt-murders – though they are never charged with that, naturally.

Last night, we had a pursuit with one of these burglars, and it turned out to be Mickey. He'd stolen a van and we caught him on the plot, breaking into an antiques shop. We followed him for 15 or 20 miles until he lost control, rolled the vehicle and legged it on foot. The dog team got him shortly afterwards – there was a fight, but we pinned him to the ground and nicked him.

All the way back to the station with the dog handler, not a squeak.

He gets into custody, and he stands in front of the Custody Sergeant, quiet as a church mouse, all *Yes, Sir, No, Sir*.

The Custody Sergeant listens to the dog handler's version of events: 'We saw this man climbing out of a window with an antique carriage clock under his arm, get into this stolen vehicle and drive off at 90mph away from us. The vehicle crashed, he got out and I arrested him. We have the antique clock, we have forensics, we have the car, we have witnesses, CCTV and three other officers. I arrested him for burglary, theft of a vehicle, dangerous driving, failing to stop and assault-police.'

This is a bit like producing a Royal Flush in a game of poker.

The Custody Sergeant puts his pen down and exhales, a soft, low whistle. 'Blimey, Mickey,' he says. 'You're on licence for burglary, you're disqualified from driving, you've got a history of assaulting the police. You know you're going down for three or four years for this?'

Mickey, white as a sheet, says, 'Are we on tape?'

'Yes.'

'I want to see a solicitor and I want my phone call. I can tell you whose been knocking off the factories on the industrial estate and I know who did that big farm job where the farmer got battered last year.'

All of a sudden, now he *doesn't* want all our children to get leukaemia or be murdered, and he's not going to rape our wives when we're at work.

Off he goes to his cell, as meek as the proverbial lamb. Down come Intel, and he is in there for half an hour with them, telling them everything he can about handlers, other burglars, recent jobs.

All his 'F**k off, pig, I'm going to kill your mother' bravado is gone, because he knows now that the only chance he has is for us to write out a nice little report for the judge which says that he co-operated and gave us loads of info.

And they're all the same. You catch a hardened criminal bang to rights in someone's house with a weapon, doing a burglary, and they are totally different people because they are generally (though not always) going away for a long while.

What does that say? It says that prison works. All we need to do is use it properly.

AND ON THE SUBJECT OF PRISON

YOU have *got* to love Anne Owers, Chief Inspector of Prisons.

A recent report by HM Inspectorate of Prisons found that some prisoners at Doncaster jail are living and sleeping 'in toilets' because of overcrowding.

That's not strictly true – they have loos in their cells, and extra beds had been put in 'the toilet area' of some cells to turn two-man cells into three.

Leaving aside that the kind of people who end up behind bars live in worse conditions at home, who cares?

Anne Owers does. She said it was 'unacceptable'.

Unacceptable to whom? Does it keep *you* awake at night? Does it keep the victims of these people awake at night? Are taxpayers marching through the streets of your local towns complaining that they need to give even more money to the Government so that *all* our prisons can be turned into Hilton hotels, instead of just some of them?

Anne Owers is paid by the public, but I would hazard a guess that she does not represent public opinion. This is not an unusual trait in our bureaucrats; they tend to think they know better than us.

Here are ten things you may not know about Anne unless you read *The Times* (which carried a nice profile of her recently).

1. She is 'usually woken at 7am by the *Today* programme'. She breakfasts on porridge or muesli and coffee, and wears 'reasonably smartish' clothes, 'usually from John Lewis or the Army & Navy'. How civilised.

2. She leaves the house at 8am and takes a 10-minute bus journey to the Home Office. Her predecessor had a driver, 'but I don't need that'.

3. On inspections she meets 'young men' in prison who are 'very lonely and depressed'.

4. For her, 'meeting the prisoners is a privilege' because you are 'introduced to a parallel world where people haven't been to school working out what GCSEs they'll do or what university they're going to'.

5. When she sees some of the conditions in prison, she 'feels quite angry'.

6. She thinks it's 'important not to lose the capacity to be shocked'. 'I was actually in a young offenders' institution when a man was screaming because three prison officers were holding him down as he forcibly had his clothes removed,' she says. 'I expressed my concern, and now force isn't used to strip-search in juvenile prisons.' How do they search them then, Anne? Just ask them, I guess. And... er... what if they say No?

7. Women prisoners exercise her greatly. 'We need more alternatives to prison for women,' she says, because often they lose their children and homes when they go inside. 'Women in prison have very low self-esteem, which is why they end up where they are.' Well, that and being criminals, Anne. Incidentally, some of the prisoners she meets are 'lovely women'.

8.   When people hear what she does they ask, 'Aren't you
      scared?' 'I say: "I'm more scared walking home from the
      Tube alone in the evening than in prison.""

9.   She is a 'reasonable cook', as is her husband. They have
      nice evenings together, eating dinner and drinking wine
      'going to concerts or the theatre'.

10.   She goes to bed 'about 11, and has no trouble getting to
      sleep'.

What a nice woman. Naive, but very nice.

Perhaps it never occurs to her that the 'depressed young men' and
'lovely women' are the same people who con war veterans out of
their savings, batter elderly ladies half to death for a few quid and
generally burgle, steal, rob and threaten their way through life.

It couldn't be that, when they tell her tales of how hard it is
inside, and talk about their contrition, they're lying to her, could it?
No, they're paragons of honesty – it's what got them there in the first
place, after all.

She says it's a 'privilege' meeting these people. So why not move
to live on a rough estate, Anne, so you can experience the richness
of life amongst them when they aren't being watched like hawks by
prison officers?

Anne Owers is 'more scared walking home from the Tube alone
in the evening than in prison'. She apparently lacks the curiosity to
consider why that might be.

COURTS

I FIND myself increasingly exhausted and depressed by the
continual, deliberate and almost smug way in which the courts
protect the guilty and spit on the decency of the rest of us.

I could fill a book with the mad sentencing decisions that they
come up with.

Every day, people who should be sent to jail are treated with
extreme leniency. I'm not talking about, *He stole a car and he only
got a month*, I mean seriously dangerous animals who walk away
with nothing.

Government sentencing guidelines and bursting prisons and modern doctrines about punishment are all part of the problem, but I think the main issue is that magistrates and judges (and journalists, and academics, and nice, liberal people generally) don't – literally – see our end product the way we do.

We see them when they are shouting and swearing and threatening and kicking and screaming and stabbing and gobbing and jumping on heads.

The courts see people who have sobered up, are on their best behaviour and have been advised to dress in decent clothes. No tattoos, no hatred, no bile and no drunkenness. And no victims, either, because if there is a serious victim the defendant will almost always plead just to avoid getting that person in the witness box.

The magistrates and judges do watch the CCTV, but they look at the person in front of them and don't seem to connect the two. They think the man in the dock charged with beating and stabbing and mugging is someone who leads a normal, everyday life but who just happened to 'make the wrong choice' this time. That isn't the case, as I've said.

The result of all of this is that the courts hand out joke sentences. I'm not sure members of the public appreciate how bad it's got.

Late one night a while ago, a burglar broke into a house in our town. When the householder came downstairs and challenged him, he threatened the man with a firearm and ran off. The householder called the police, and two of my Response team guys were on the scene very quickly. As they approached the house on blues and twos, they saw another vehicle coming the other way at high speed. He was all over the road, swerving from side to side, so they took a punt (correctly) that it was the offender, handbrake-turned their car and chased him all the way over to Oldtown.

He crashed and burned, leapt out of his vehicle and ran off into a block of flats. They chased him inside and up the stairs. On the landing, he turned and pointed an automatic weapon directly at the head of the first officer. The officer ignored the gun and barrelled straight into him... massive fight... on the decks... splayed, handcuffed... job's a good 'un.

The guy on the other end of it turned out to be Barry. Barry is one of our local persistent burglars: he is well-known to us, he is very violent and he was absolutely off his face.

77

They got him into the nick and he was charged with the following offences:

Aggravated burglary
Possession of a firearm
Disqualified driving
Drink driving
Theft of a motor vehicle
Failing to stop
Possession of Class A drugs
Assaulting a police officer

That is a pretty serious list in anyone's book; to make matters worse, he was also out on licence from a three-year sentence imposed for an earlier series of burglaries.

You'd like to think he'd get a serious stretch for all of that. After all, the mandatory minimum sentence for possessing a firearm illegally is *five years*.

He was let go with 120 hours' community service.

He pleaded to the lot, they bailed him for reports and the reports came back with all the usual tall tales – he's just had a baby by some errant female and he's really making a go of being a father, he's trying to get his life back together and is on drug and alcohol counselling and doing some nonsense course at college, his probation officer says he's actually a really nice guy blah blah bloody blah.

This is a nasty, dangerous, druggie burglar who threatens householders and police officers, and he walks, despite the fact that he's on licence for other similar offences. The PC who had charged past his pistol to make the arrest got a bravery award; so, on the one hand, this was so serious an incident that the police officer involved needs decorating, on the other, it merited a few hours not bothering to turn up and paint some walls.

Every time I use my blog (http://Inspectorgadget.wordpress.com/) to complain about weak sentencing by magistrates and judges, two things happen. One is that other police officers and members of the public post up examples of even more ludicrously rubbish sentences than I had previously thought possible. The other is that the legal brigade post comments accusing me of 'failing to understand' and pointing out that judges and magistrates are bound by sentencing guidelines.

What about that mandatory five years for firearms, then? Never mind Barry, some recent figures revealed that the average sentence handed down for the crime in the last year for which data was available was three years and nine months. Only 40% of offenders were given the five-year minimum. So much for being 'bound by sentencing guidelines'.

The BBC's website carried an example of a case where the minimum had not been applied. A judge at Manchester Crown Court jailed Natasha Peniston for three years for possession of a gun which accidentally killed her daughter Kamilah as her son Kasha played with it. Mr Justice Holland said there were 'exceptional circumstances' to justify her not receiving the mandatory term, as she had been 'prevailed upon' by a boyfriend to look after the weapon.

Oh, her *boyfriend* told her to do it. Well, that's OK, then.

A spokesman for the Ministry of Injustice responded that 'the mandatory five-year term for possession of a firearm is a starting point... judges must then take aggravating and mitigating factors into consideration when determining the final sentence.'

I don't know about you, but I'm not sure he understands the word 'mandatory'.

The criminal underclass are not clever. Trust me, they aren't. But even they can understand 'cause and effect'. They are waging violent and random hate campaigns against the rest of the world. To encourage this by making it consequence-free is dangerous. In fact, the decisions made by magistrates and judges are a major part of why these people offend. I used to believe that they committed crimes because they thought they wouldn't get caught; now I realise many of them do it because they know that nothing will happen to them if they do.

A FEW MORE EXAMPLES

OFFICERS were called to a house where a teenager had gone nuts, beaten someone up and was rampaging round his house with a knife. By the time they arrived, he had locked himself in the bathroom and was shouting that he was going to kill himself. A Police Support Unit was called, and they kicked their way in with shields. The youth tried to stab the officers six times, was nicked and charged with assault, possession of an offensive weapon and attempted murder.

He walked from court with a conditional discharge. 'You've got a lucky face,' the judge told him.

You can say that again, Your Honour. Here's hoping the next time you see it he isn't climbing through your drawing room window, eh?

The problem for the police – apart from the fact that these nutters are back out on the streets with their knives and guns, trying to kill us (and you) – is that people blame us for it.

One of our prolific local criminals was found guilty and sentenced to three months. Unfortunately, he'd been inside on remand so he walked out of court that day. Irritating, but that's the way it goes. Half his estate phoned me to complain over the next day or two.

I told them it was bad, sure, but that it was down to the court, not us.

'Well, that's just typical. You police always just blame everyone else.'

'But we spent a *fortune* in overtime on this case. We wanted him to go down as much as you did.'

'So why's he out, then?'

'Because the judge has let him out. What do you want me to do about it?'

I was told that was just an excuse, and that the police were useless.

In March this year, the *Daily Telegraph* carried a story about one Joanne Jones. The introductory paragraph ran as follows: *"A serial petty thief convicted for the 175th time, at a total cost to the taxpayer of more than £700,000, has been spared jail despite carrying out her latest crime while on bail."*

I'll bet her local Inspector got similar calls. I hope he pointed out the phrase 'convicted for the 175th time' – what that tells you is that the police did their jobs. They got her to court, with the evidence to convict; the rest was up to the bench.

That doesn't stop politicians claiming that we can deal with crime more effectively if we can just somehow reorganise the police, with a 'Safer Neighbourhoods' programme or more 'Citizen Focus'.

Next time you hear any of this rubbish, give a thought to Carl from Ruraltown.

Last week, Carl was on bail for punching his elderly mother in the face. He went back to the house (breaching his bail conditions) and pushed his elderly father down the stairs. He was drunk at the time and had gone round to 'persuade' his mother to drop the charges against him.

He was quickly arrested by police from F Division and remanded in custody. He went to court the next day... and was released on bail again.

This time, they gave him a curfew as well as the usual 'not to contact named witnesses' stipulation. Thing is, these offences were committed *during the day* and he is *bound* to contact the witnesses (and threaten them). Never mind. Curfew it is.

Naturally, his behaviour reinforced several times by the court's apparent acceptance of it, Carl got drunk and went back round to his parents' address again. We attended, and he was arrested – this time, at the back of the house with a can of petrol and a lighter.

Three arrests, a 'home safety package', two Remand Applications, three taped interviews and two court appearances.

Someone tell me where the rank-and-file *police* have failed here? Someone tell me how Citizen Focus is going to stop Carl burning his mother to death?

Weak sentencing creates *actual* victims, too, not just potential ones.

In 1995, Roy Whiting snatched a young girl from the street in broad daylight, bundled her into his car and drove her to some woods. There, he threatened her with a knife and carried out a serious sexual assault as she sobbed in terror. It's plain to me that any man who can carry out so brazen and revolting an attack as this will reoffend: paedophiles don't just suddenly stop one day. If only for public protection, he needed to go to jail for a very long time – a minimum of 10 years, served. The judge jailed him for just four – and he was released after a little more than two. Not long afterwards, he snatched, raped and murdered Sarah Payne. He should still have been in jail for the original offence.

The judges and the magistrates who pass these sentences are not accountable. If I decided not to arrest a suspect and he went on to kill someone, I would, rightly, be in serious trouble. I'd be suspended, and our entire investigation looked at independently. If the court releases a serious offender and he kills someone, there is no comeback, no challenge. Not only that, but the magistrates and judges look with disdain upon those who call for firmer action.

A while ago, I posted a comment on my blog about the case of Craig Dodd, Ryan Palin and Raymond Atherton. I didn't say much – I just outlined the facts, and waited to see what the response would be.

The facts were as follows: Mr Atherton lived in Warrington, he was 40 years old and a vulnerable man with learning difficulties. Dodd and Palin were teenage scum who liked to torture him for fun.

Over a period of months, they and others regularly visited his flat uninvited and used it as a place to smoke their cannabis and drink his cider. While there, they would use him as a plaything to assuage their aimless boredom. Sometimes they burned or shaved his hair, and scrawled graffiti on his walls and face. Other times they beat him up, urinated in his drinks and poured bleach over him. On May 8 2006, Dodd and Palin viciously beat and kicked the defenceless man half to death. Then they urinated on him and threw him into the river Mersey where he died.

They were convicted – of manslaughter, which is, in itself, ridiculous. But their original sentences – life – were overturned on appeal by Lord Justice Rix.

The noble and learned lord decided instead that Dodd should serve a minimum of three and a half years and Palin a minimum of three.

Most of the comments that came into my blog were from outraged police officers or members of the public. 'Life is cheap, and becoming cheaper,' said one. 'Three years is nothing in a lifetime – the length of an average college course.' Another said: 'Of course, they can't help it. It was their upbringing / drugs / drink / mother / loss of teddy bear / teacher / abusive father / not watching enough TV / watching too much TV / poor living conditions / lack of self respect / prospects / poverty / girlfriend left them... Oh, the excuses are endless.'

One dissenting voice came in, from a magistrate. He wrote: 'The facts do not justify the above rant-fest... The appeal judgment hinged on a technical legal point.'

That's where we are with magistrates: yobs burn a man's hair, beat him within an inch of his life and throw him, soaked in their urine, into a river. And we're supposed to worry about 'technical legal points.'

IF I COULD CHANGE ONE THING...

...about the media reporting of cases like that of Dodd and Palin, above, it is that reporters should not use the phrase 'was jailed for' but should, instead, talk about the actual time the convict will serve.

People read the papers and they see that a given criminal has been sent down for ten years and they relax, safe in the knowledge that one of them is away for a long time. But he's not.

Over 50 people who were sentenced to 'life' after 2000 have *already been released* – in one case, the person spent 14 months inside.

Those who are jailed for 'four years' often serve just eight months.

They get time off for a guilty plea – irrespective of whether or not they were absolutely bang to rights and had no choice in the matter.

They get time off for good behaviour inside jail (effectively, if they don't murder a warder).

Any time spent on remand – in better conditions, wearing their own clothes, with privileges they haven't had to earn – comes off, too.

If they agree to wear a tag for a Home Detention Curfew, ostensibly restricting their movements to a set area and time (usually, the place of abode during the night), that's more time off. They can cut the tag off or vandalise it, as hundreds have, or ignore the restrictions – the chances of them being swooped on immediately and brought back to jail are zero. If we come across them in the town centre at midnight, and we know they're in breach, we have no power of arrest for that.

Then there's the end of custody licence (ECL) initiative, which gives up to 18 days off a sentence for no reason other than our

Government didn't think to build enough prison spaces. (We actually pay convicts to leave jail early, and lots of them still refuse because they quite like it inside.)

Ah well. At least they don't commit any more crimes after getting out early!

Except that they do – hundreds of them, including rape, burglary, assault, drug dealing, robbery, wounding and more. Amanda Murphy could confirm this, except that she was battered to death by her boyfriend a few days after he was released early from 20 weeks in jail for an earlier attack on her.

GET IN LINE

IN Ruraltown, the criminal underclass – when not breaking into your house, stealing your car or mugging your kids – mostly spend their time drunk, asleep, eating, watching telly or fighting.

When they're not doing any of that, they're in queues.

They queue for 'The Housing', they queue for 'The Sick' and they queue for their benefits.

They queue for their methadone and they all queue to get in to The Ugly Duck on a Friday night. 'Ladies Drink All Nite For Free' at The Ugly Duck.

After drinking all nite, they queue for some chips or a burger.

Then they queue for a taxi or an ambulance, and, if the latter, they queue to be seen in A&E.

Finally, they queue at the police station – as either victims or offenders, depending upon how things went the night before.

I can't speak for The Ugly Duck or the other services, but in the nick the genuine citizens with the real problems who are waiting in the same queue are usually drowned out by the noise and disturbance of our criminal friends and their 'family groups'. Often, the genuine folks leave before we can see them, to avoid the abuse and bad language (from the criminal underclass, not us).

Until recently, if we wanted to nick Joey Stubbs for his latest fail-to-appear, we had to trawl round his house and known addresses and all the places he might be queuing. We would ask the girl behind the counter at the Housing Office whether he was expected in there later on, but the response you got depended very much on which girl was in the chair. Jo was helpful and would tip you the wink; Stacey, Carole and Helene were very sniffy about helping us locate any of their 'clients'.

However, since the introduction of various bits and pieces of recent crime and disorder legislation, our 'Partner Agencies' have to share information with the police over certain issues.

These 'Partner Agencies' include the Housing, The Benefits Agency and any pharmacy involved in the supply of methadone. And guess what? 'Information' can include opening times, appointment schedules and planned events. So I no longer have to try (and fail) to schmooze Stacey, Carole and Helene with the Gadget charm – I just tell them I need to know when Stubbsy is in next. Then we swoop down and arrest him. Preferably before he has fraudulently gained whatever advantage he was after, thus allowing genuine claimants to do their business in peace.

Oh, how I laughed the first time I employed the legislation.

There are two great things about this tactic.

Firstly, it *always* works.

Secondly, liberals *hate it*. They throw their collective hands into the air and start mumbling about 'confidentiality' and 'Human Rights', as if behaving in a criminal and anti-social way isn't a lifestyle choice that Joey Stubbs and others like him have freely adopted.

The services he receives after waiting in all these lines are paid for by you, so I thought you should know that there is some value for money to be had out of the situation (and some decent, useful criminal justice legislation emanating from the Houses of Parliament).

CHRISTMAS

THE Inspector From Upstairs rings me as I'm head down in a load of paperwork.

'Gadget,' he says. 'The Boss wants to see you.'

'Which one?' I ask in amazement (the Senior Management Team having long ago abandoned any thoughts of involving me in anything political).

'The real one, the Chief Superintendent,' he says.

Well, I'm always pleased to meet someone I've only ever heard about in the newsletter, so I put down my pen, straighten my hair and set off immediately.

The Chief Super's office is on the top floor. He has a nice swivel chair, a stress ball and a great view of the town. I'll probably never have an office like that.

'Gadget, is it?' he says, with a warm smile. 'Nice to see you. I need you to organise a little something for me.'

He hands me a folder with a document inside. I leave.

Back downstairs, I look at the document. It's the template for something called 'Operation Inclusive Festival', and it explains that we need to 'embed' the festival formerly known as Christmas into the various different 'faith groups' in Ruraltown.

I phone the Inspector From Upstairs to ask what this means. He sighs the sigh of a man used to dealing with idiots such as myself. 'Come on Gadget, you have to involve the other religious groups in' – he lowers his voice, conspiratorially, as though he can hardly bear to say the word – '*Christmas*. It's part of the Citizen Engagement plan.'

I reach for the phone directory and telephone the nearest mosque. This is right on the edge of Metro City, some miles away.

'It's Inspector Gadget here from the police, sir,' I say to the man on the other end of the line. 'Can I involve you in Christmas?'

'Well, not really,' comes the reply. 'Sorry.'

'But I haven't even told you what it's about yet,' I say.

'Well, I know what it's about, it's about 'Operation Inclusive Festival' and it's part of your Citizen Engagement Plan.'

'So why aren't you interested?' I say.

'Oh, it's not that we're not interested, it's just that I'm now fully booked with every other police station in this part of Metro City. I might be able to fit you in next year if you book now?'

Not a bad idea, but it's too early to say who we'll be interested in 'engaging with' next year.

'Look, thanks for your time, sir,' I say . 'I won't bother you about next year now, but I might be back in touch later?'

Eventually, I come across a sympathetic elderly Sikh gentleman who is here to pick up some lost property belonging to his daughter.

He takes pity on me, winks knowingly and agrees to come down from Metro City to judge the Christmas 'teddy-bear' competition for the children at the recreation club.

The Inspector From Upstairs is reasonably happy.

'I suppose it will have to do,' he says, grudgingly, secretly hating me for my partial success. In the brutal business of fourth floor politics, a 'Diversity' result is worth ten 'Crime Detections'.

MYSTERY SHOPPER

I AM sitting down for the first time in four hours.

My leg hurts from where it was kicked, hard, an hour ago, and I am very tired.

The white, sweat-shop manufactured, threadbare, cheap-bleached shirt which, according to Ruralshire's Chief, is suitable for operational work, is a damp, sodden rag under my body armour and jacket.

I must be getting old: it hurts to walk to the microwave. But a man's got to eat, so I reheat some left-over lasagne in a plastic tub and get it down my neck. It doesn't taste the same without Debbie and the juniors around the table, laughing and joking.

I don't eat with the troops. They don't want me around when they're letting off steam, and I don't want to be there, either. Someone has to respect their privacy, even if it's only for a few minutes snatched between emergency calls.

I grab a tattered bit of paper from my back pocket. It's soggy, smells of alcohol and the ink has run. This is because I've had to shut the Silver Bar down again tonight and someone threw beer over me.

On the paper is my list of on-going tasks.

Tonight, I have attended two traumatic death scenes, been in a fight with two idiots in a car park, assisted the arrest of a complete animal outside the railway station and done the PACE reviews on a dozen prisoners. I have served ID papers, and signed numerous authorities for Section 18 Searches and other PACE-related matters.

And I closed the Silver Bar. Again.

The Sergeant is after me for my notebook and statements from the car park and station.

It's only 10pm.

I open some random email from la-la-land while I eat.

I see that in addition to all of this, I am to be subject to a 'mystery shopper' at some point before September.

This person, a civilian volunteer, will turn up at the police station, wind me up with some spurious story and then see how I deal with it before admitting that they are a plant sent there to test my customer service skills.

They will not be doing this to the civilian front office staff because UNISON have objected, saying that fake scenarios could stress out their members. While this is obviously rubbish, good for them. Where are the Police Federation in all this? Sadly lacking as usual.

I finish my lasagne. I'm off out again, limping and wet, but I'd rather be abused, spat at and attacked by the drunken mob outside our nightclubs than go on some magical mystery tour invented by the keyboard rattlers.

ONE OF OUR AIRHEADS IS MISSING

CHARLIE is 14 years old, he lives in a care home and he's vanished.

Again.

Charlie is a MISPER.

There are two types of missing persons.

The first type is persons who are *actually* missing.

They might be stressed husbands who left work four hours ago and haven't come home. They might be mums with post-natal depression, or old people with Alzheimer's, or kids who are playing in the park and have just forgotten the time. We don't get many calls like this, and we take them very seriously indeed.

In fact, we had one yesterday.

I was busy listening reviewing prisoners in custody and making up shortfalls in manning levels and, in the background, I could hear the troops on the air giving the despatcher the familiar coded reasons why they couldn't go to the outstanding nonsense jobs.

Offensive texts from an ex-girlfriend? Solution: turn your phone off.

Strangely enough, all the guys were either 'putting fuel in the vehicle' or had 'pressing paperwork from yesterday to complete' etc. Then, an urgent message suddenly came out for a missing five-year-old girl. She had vanished from the back garden at her parents' house and they were beside themselves with worry.

In a flash, every unit on the ground was available and responded. And I mean every unit. A co-ordinated search was carried out and the child was found safe and well an hour later. The parents switched from weeping to joy, and the neighbours and the police were buzzing. We were thanked again and again for the response. I was happy, the troops were happy, the community was happy. Taxpayers' money well spent. (When I returned to the nick, I struggled to find a single Home Office target or performance indicator that we had hit or achieved, and no detections had been filed. In statistical terms, the incident never happened – we had 'failed' to provide 'best value' during that hour. Does anyone in their right mind believe that the public would have preferred us to have attended the 'offensive texts' call instead? What total nonsense all this performance rubbish is. But I digress.)

The second type of MISPER are persons who aren't really missing at all – like Charlie.

In fact, in our area – as in any area – the vast majority of these cases fall into this category.

Most of them are wayward teenagers who have disappeared from one of the foster/children's homes on our patch. They're kids with no obvious future except crime, unemployment and poverty: disturbed, unwanted youngsters from broken homes, born to underclass parents who just drop them and never bother to pick them up again. Usually, mum or dad is in the middle of some drug or alcohol daze, or has a new partner who doesn't want to know. The result is young boys and girls left to fend for themselves, out in the big wide world at the age of 10 or so. They end up in care, and they abscond very regularly – some of them several times a week – after being told by the staff that they can't smoke cannabis, or can't drink, or simply because they want to go and hang around in town with their mates. The staff watch them stroll away (they are not allowed to detain them), and then they call us.

They're undoubtedly tragic, these kids, and they'd break your heart if you let them.

What they *aren't*, though, in 99.99999% of cases, is in the clutches of a predatory paedophile.

Despite this, we have to pretend that they could be.

This is because although their parents, social workers, foster carers, doctors, teachers and everyone else may have failed them horrendously, it is PC Snodgrass who will go to the wall if one of them goes missing and something bad *does* happen.

As we've seen before, the one thing Chief Constables fear above all else is media criticism, or an IPCC enquiry, so every time Charlie vanishes, we ramp up an entire system.

How this starts is with a risk assessment.

In theory, this is to decide which of three levels of response we adopt: high, medium or low.

In practice, it's really about getting some poor bastard's name on it – usually that of a Duty Inspector like me – so that if and when things get bent out of shape they have someone to stick it to. Call me cynical, but that's the way I see it.

Let's go back to the theory. It sounds sensible: if someone is at high risk, let's have a high level of response.

The problem is, what is 'high risk'? If it means any kid who goes missing, you can forget it. A high level response requires a helicopter. It needs search dogs, a Gold* command (Assistant Chief Constable or above) and incident command posts. It needs large teams of level two-trained officers – the specialists who you see on the TV news, dressed in white overalls carrying out painstaking, fingertip searches. Charlie's *always* disappearing and he's not alone in that: if we act like this for *every* kid who goes missing in our area *every* time they do it I'm going to need eight helicopters *a day*. I will need *hundreds* of people. It's impossible.

As for low risk… well, no-one is ever going to be low risk, are they? I mean, would you put that on a form if you were me?

So what happens is, we end up recording the vast majority of MISPERs as 'medium' risk (I *think* I'm supposed to make that judgment based on an e-learning package I did on the computer

---

*We operate a Gold, Silver and Bronze Command Structure in the UK national emergency network. Generally-speaking, Inspectors are Bronze with more senior ranks rated as Silver or Gold.

once). Hence, the entire, bureaucratic, time-consuming, box-ticking, arse-covering exercise that is the risk assessment is actually a big fat sham.

Thankfully, I also have common sense to fall back on, and I think I still know the difference between a MISPER who actually is a problem and a MISPER who isn't.

The five-year-old who went missing from his back garden, he's a problem, as is the battered wife whose sister says she hasn't seen her for several days and the 15-year-old girl with the mental age of a four-year-old.

Charlie, who has just legged it from his care home for the eighth time this month, is not.

In fact, like the vast majority of the MISPERs we judge as medium risk, he is low risk, or even 'no risk'. They're all just teenage kids who go missing regularly and know how to hide from us, usually with a network of similarly errant teenagers/adults who will put them up.

Medium risk doesn't mean we just shrug our shoulders and don't do much about it, though. There's still a whole list of things that have to be done – at least 50 of them, on forms which are about eight pages long.

For instance, you have to:

– Search Charlie's home and any outbuildings

– Check for any diaries, letters and calendars he might have, seize them and put them in evidence bags

– Question all people in the home.

– Carry out house-to-house enquiries locally and in areas of interest.

– Do an area search of the places that Charlie is known to frequent.

– Alert CCTV.

– Broadcast his disappearance to other officers.

– Get it on to the briefing.

– Put him on the Police National Computer as 'locate-and-trace'.

– Go to his school – even though it's long after dark, and he doesn't go to school most days anyway.

– Visit his last two known addresses.

– Contact his family and friends, and physically go round and check for him there.

The list goes on for quite a while yet – and everything, of course, has to be written down and recorded in triplicate, just in case something bad does happen, so you and your bosses can prove you did all that was humanly possible to prevent it.

So I take two officers off my shift and put them to work on finding Charlie. They trawl the canal towpaths and the children's playgrounds and the underpasses and all the hidden away places Charlie likes to meet up with his mates and they eventually find him, mildly pissed, lying in a rosebed next to the bandstand in the park.

By that stage, he's quite happy to get a lift back to the home. They drop him off, knowing they'll be out looking for him again within the next three or four days.

I could give you many, many examples. Jade is another 14-year-old who also lives in a care home in one of our towns. She has an 'Acceptable Behaviour Contract' with the home: if she generally does as she's told, once a week she's allowed out to go and buy cigarettes. Yes, I know this is illegal but they have to work with what they've got; if they just say *No* to her, what's going to happen? What sanctions do they have? (One day, undoubtedly, Jade will find a no-win-no-fee lawyer who will sue the local authority on her behalf for allowing her to smoke.)

She's supposed to go to the local shop, or to her mother, or to whoever it is that provides her with the fags, and then come straight back. She gets half an hour for this, and *every single time* she doesn't come back. Instead, she goes into town, nicks a load of make-up from Supadrug, swipes some vodka from the offie and spends the afternoon getting smashed with a load of older kids. All our medium risk responses grind into action and we get officers out looking for her. Sometimes we find her, other times she comes back of her own accord. Depending on how she's feeling, it might be that night, but more often it'll be a day or two later. The following week, we'll go through the same thing all over again. And the week after that, *ad nauseam*, until they're no longer juveniles.

As a normal person, unfamiliar with the way these things work, you are probably thinking that this all sounds a bit mad.

If she keeps going missing, why don't the care home staff just ban her from going out in the first place? (Because she'll ignore them and go anyway.)

Why don't they lock the doors? (They aren't allowed to.)

Why don't they grab hold of her? (They don't want to get done for assault.)

And Jade and Charlie are but two of many. At any one time, I will have half a dozen of these cases on the go.

Earlier, I explained how the 20 officers available to me on paper are actually more like ten or twelve actual cops. Part of that is because a couple of those absent officers will be off working on bogus MISPERs, spending the entire shift going to house after house after house, looking for people and following up leads, shuffling the paperwork, checking the CCTV, getting enquiries followed up. If it's been longer than a day or so, all ports have to be warned; after 48 hours, a Detective Sergeant looks at it, and the day after that a Detective Inspector gets involved and we set up an incident room. But thank goodness, most of them come back long before that stage. Then they go missing once more and we start all over again from square one.

Clearly, there are major knock-on effects on our ability to do actual, proper police work.

We've had discussions with social services about some of our regular absconders.

'Look,' we say. 'Kayleigh has gone missing 15 times now. We don't want to treat her as missing any more.'

'Oooh,' they say, with a shocked air. 'Just because she's gone missing before does not mean she cannot be murdered, raped or abused *this* time.'

It's very easy to quantify a dead child; it's much harder to measure the effect of the loss of thousands and thousands of police hours per year spent looking for them when they're in no danger whatsoever.

SOCIAL SERVICES

WE DEAL with Social Services a lot.

They're under-resourced, under-staffed, hard-pressed. Lots of chiefs, not enough indians; it's a familiar story.

I remember calling them one time – we had some assessment or other that needed doing. It's a centralised number, and the woman who answered the phone said she was in a town right on the other side of the county, miles and miles away.

'And you're coming all the way from there?' I said.

She said she was covering the whole county.

I said, 'We have a population of two and a half million people – don't tell me that there's one of you on duty?'

'That's right,' she said.

'How long is it going to take you to get here from where you are now?' I said.

I could hear her mentally totting up the hours.

'Hmmm. I've got to go to Bigtown, where I've got an attempted suicide of a lad who tried to kill himself in a cell. Then I've got to go to a hospital in Nearby, where a 13-year-old girl has just given birth to a baby and her parents have kicked off and taken it away. Then I've got to go via Roundhouses, where I've got a child who's been burned in a fire and I have to do a safety assessment on the house. I should get to you in about... um... nine hours?'

Every police officer who reads this will be nodding now – most social workers too, probably.

So I have some sympathy for them. They're not paid very well, they're pilloried and screamed at when things go wrong and the risk assessments that they have to make are huge. Unfortunately, some of them are lazy, incompetent, hard-eyed bastards with not an ounce of compassion left in their bodies.

I had a child who was missing. He was called Sean, he was 12 years old and he was not one of our regular MISPERs. He'd chosen a Friday night to vanish, but luckily it was during the World Cup – because of that, we had a lot of officers on duty.

I started the whole machinery working, sent some people out looking and they came back with him inside the hour; he'd been sitting down by the river, smoking and chatting to a fisherman in the gloaming. That was a result – we love it when we find them quickly.

However, it soon became clear than this was just the start of our problems. Sean told the officers he didn't want to go home. His dad was beating him up, he said, and his mum couldn't or wouldn't do anything about it. He pulled up his top and showed them: he was covered in bruises and burns.

The two officers reassured him that they would take him to the police station instead. They brought him to my nick and the Sergeant came to get me.

'I think we need to do a Police Protection Order here, guv,' he said.

A PPO means we take a child into emergency care. To do this, the matter has to pass a threshold test, which is that there is *immediate* risk of *significant* harm. 'My mum said that when her boyfriend is round next week he is going to give me a good kicking' is not good enough, because the risk isn't immediate (this doesn't mean we do nothing, we just can't draw up a PPO). On the other hand, I've taken kids into care if we find them in the back of a car without a seatbelt on, and the parents are saying, 'F**k you, we're not putting one on.'

In this case, a PPO was obviously justified, and we took the boy into police protection.

As an Inspector, and the 'reviewing officer', I have a list of tasks to perform. The first of these is to ensure that the child is safe. To do this, we must have two officers, from the on-paper strength, sit with him.

There have to be two of them – each watching that the other doesn't molest him; this is the surreal world in which we live. OK, I made sure Sean was set up with two non-sexually-predatory-paedophile officers.

Under the Children's Act, the child's view of what has happened to him is very important, so next I went to see him to ask what had been going on. He told me the same story, about his father beating him and his mother not caring, and showed me all his injuries. Nasty stuff. But after years of doing this job, you do develop an instinct: while clearly there were problems at home, there was something wrong with his story. I couldn't put my finger on it, so I left it at that and went on to the next tick-box on my list.

As the reviewing officer, I need to have our paperwork faxed to Social Services and then speak to them as soon as possible. This is supposed to trigger a non-negotiable, statutory response from them. That response is sending someone down to see the boy, looking for accommodation for him and taking him off our hands, for now.

I had the papers faxed over, and then got hold of the duty social worker.

'I need you to house this kid, Sean,' I said. 'He obviously can't stay at the police station.'

It's acknowledged, rightly, that a police station is not a suitable place to keep a child for any length of time.

'Hmmm,' she said. 'We've looked at what's been faxed over and we understand that the father, the one who has been beating the child, is no longer at the house.'

'Well, he's no longer at the house because he has run off,' I said. 'He's run off because he knows that we're looking for him and we want to arrest him.'

'So that means the house is now safe for the child,' she said.

'Well, there's a good chance he might go back,' I said.

'But if he goes back, surely he will be arrested?'

Like we can station two officers outside every house from which someone nasty has done a runner, hoping they show up again so we can nick them.

'Er, no,' I said. 'If he goes back they'll have to ring us, and we will have to go back out there, and by the time we arrive he will probably have run off again. In the meantime, Sean may well have had another beating.'

'Why don't you keep him at the police station until his father is arrested? Then he will be safe and he can go home.'

I thought about the drunks, druggie thugs and abusive scumbags who would soon be filling our cells and shook my head. 'No, we have a child here that needs care. And I am not sending him back to the house while the dad is outstanding.'

This went on for a while, them telling me that I needed to take him back to the house, me refusing. I asked to speak to the supervisor, who gave me the same line: we can't help you, we have no-one, we've got no places, it's Friday night, you've got to take him home.

In the end, I went back to speak to Sean again.

'Look, mate,' I said. 'I think we're going to have to take you back to your mum. Is that OK?'

It wasn't.

'Don't worry,' I said. 'We're going to arrest your dad. Once we have him in custody we'll keep him away from the house.'

He got very upset, on the verge of tears. It still didn't seem quite right to me, but he wouldn't elaborate beyond being adamant that he would not return home.

I went back to Social Services. This time I got someone else.

'There is no way this boy is going back to where he lives,' I said. 'I don't think we could take him there even if we wanted to.'

The person on the other end of the phone got very irate at this. 'I want your name and number,' she said. 'I'm going to raise this with your superiors.'

I looked at my watch. 'I'm happy to give you all my details, but I should point out that it is now three in the morning. I need your names, too. I am going to enter it onto our log that in six hours you haven't made any attempt to house him.'

Eventually, they changed their tune. The supervisor called back. 'Right,' she said. 'Can you get him to such-and-such an address in Overtown?'

'What is it?' I said.

'It's a half-way house, a hostel. There's a room waiting for him there.'

'OK, we can get him there and do that. Is it a registered Social Services place?'

'Yes.'

'Fine. Who do we ask for when we get there?'

'Oh, it's not manned,' she said. 'It houses new prison releases and people like that. You can tell him there will be a key under a flower pot around the back. He can let himself in. Tell him he's in the top room – it's the only empty one.'

I thought of my young lad, asleep in his bunk with his brothers and my wife at home.

'Wait a minute,' I said. 'No. That's not a place of safety. I am keeping him here under the Police Protection Order.'

I didn't back down. My force has faults, as they all have, but I knew that no-one would drop me in it for making the right decision here. Finally, at about 5am, Social Services homed him somewhere decent.

Just as I was going off duty, CID said that they wanted to go and get him for a statement. The poor lad hadn't slept for 22 hours: I told them to leave him be. And then I walked out of the nick and left the case behind. Often, that will be the last you hear of these things, but as it happened two weeks later I saw someone in Child Protection.

'Blimey, Gadget,' she said. 'It was a good job you didn't send that kid back home like they wanted.'

It turned out that it was his *mother* who was the offender, not his father. The lad just didn't want to admit to two burly coppers in stab vests that he was being beaten up by a woman.

I rang up Social Services. I wanted to vent my frustration on them – to point out that if I had followed their instructions I'd have been putting the victim right back with the person he was running away from. I asked to speak to the supervisor I'd dealt with.

'She no longer works here, I'm sorry,' they said.

'Well, can I speak to the other woman, the one who wanted the boy sent to the halfway hostel?'

'Sorry, she's left too – she now works in Othershire.'

'OK, I need to speak to the first person I called, then.'

'Ah... she was an agency worker. Her contract has finished.'

'Look, I need to speak to *someone* about this. Who is dealing with this case?'

'Sorry, we can't tell you that. It's confidential.'

Furious, I went to my force's Social Services liaison office. I spoke to a really nice woman there, who said, 'Tell me about it and I'll write it all down. I get loads of these.'

Nothing I told her surprised her.

There are good social workers, obviously. But of all the agencies we work with, they are the least likely to find ways to help you, the quickest to quote rules and regulations and put up barriers. I'm honestly not sure whether it's because they're so overwhelmed that they have just given up, or because they are of very poor calibre in the first place.

HOW LOW CAN YOU GO?

I HAVE puzzled long and hard over why it is that some law-abiding people are so vehemently against the police.

In the minds of many on the left, we are a bunch of racist misogynists who like to go around beating up, fitting up and otherwise hassling basically innocent people – downtrodden, put-upon but essentially sound folk who just need an understanding shoulder to lean on and a little guidance to help them find their way back to the right path. If we actually *do* manage to arrest someone who is guilty of something, it can only be by accident.

I think they believe this because they have no real knowledge of what we do and no real contact with our regular customers. They have a lot of theoretical arguments gleaned from books, but these don't survive contact with reality.

I'll often find myself wishing I had a few of them along for the ride on a given day, so that they could see with their own eyes how basically decent most police officers are and how appalling the enemy truly is.

I'd like them to meet, for instance, the Mahoneys. These are a family of southern Irish travellers who like to pimp out their teenaged kids to businessmen in cheap motels near our local airport.

We bumped into them a while ago after our local child protection officers saw the 14-year-old niece of the family being offered up on an internet escort service, and happened to recognise her as a MISPER from our briefing posters.

We followed the trail back to the caravan site where we thought she lived, but she was in hiding – or being held – somewhere else. The Mahoneys agreed to hand her over to Social Services but *only if* we returned a sizeable amount of cash which we had seized under the Proceeds of Crime Act because the girl had earned it for them.

This is their *niece* we're talking about, their own flesh and blood, for God's sake.

They were all arrested and she never was returned; later we heard she had been seen in Ireland, but the Gards were unable to locate her.

I'd like to introduce some of our detractors to people like Mrs Weaver. Mrs Weaver is an 82-year-old widow who lives in a council house on an estate in one of our towns. She keeps the place tidy with the help of her son, who pops round once a week to trim her privet hedge or clean her windows or mow the little front lawn.

A couple of my officers popped round themselves the other day, and sat with her while she cried her eyes out about the theft of her purse by two distraction burglars.

They're particularly unpleasant people, these: they always target the elderly, because they find them easier to trick and they know that, even if they are caught, old people make terrible witnesses. Their eyesight is usually poor, and their memory for faces is not as good as it once was, so they usually fail to pick out offenders at ID procedures. If it gets to court, they're easily confused by defence lawyers and they get flustered and emotional and find the whole thing a terrible ordeal.

How do they know where the old people live? They look for bungalows or neatly-kept houses like Mrs Weaver's, and cars with disabled badges. They will follow meals-on-wheels vehicles, and they look through wheelie bins on collection day to identify single occupancy houses where less rubbish is thrown away. One gang round our way opens letterboxes to smell for incontinence – not a problem Mrs Weaver suffers from, but one which does help identify some old folks.

When they've found their target, they will identify the property with various coded chalk marks to indicate the type of place it is… a repeat victim, for instance, or one who has no money, or one who keeps his money in a drawer, and so on.

One favourite *modus operandi* is to pretend to be from 'The Water Board': they knock on the door wearing hi-vis jackets, speak very quickly, and tell the old dear that they are carrying out works in the road and that they need to check the stopcock. In Mrs Weaver's case, she had let them in and they had sent her upstairs to turn on the taps in the bathroom to 'check if everything was OK'. When she came back downstairs she found the house ransacked and her purse gone. It had about a hundred quid in it, but she was most upset because it had also contained a precious photograph of her late husband on his wedding day.

Another is to have a child knock on the door and say their dog is loose in the garden, or that their ball has gone over the fence. The kind old lady goes into the garden with the kid, who has been told to keep her talking and searching for the non-existent ball as long as possible. Meanwhile, the father goes in and steals the life savings.

A day or two after Mrs Weaver's job, a more innovative couple of scumbags struck – they told an 85-year-old Second World War veteran that they were from Social Services and that they needed to take a sample of his blood. Coming from a time when you obeyed authority, he sat down and prepared himself; while he did that, they went through his house.

It's not small beer, this. Individually, they may only make 10 or 20 quid a time, but sometimes they get a lot more and, if they hit 20 houses a day, they can make two or three thousand pounds in a week.

They make me sick, these people. I hate them. The trail of misery and sadness they leave behind them has to be seen to be believed. They don't care about their victims – in fact, I've seen them laugh about them – and they are not dealt with harshly enough.

I know of one prolific offender who was sentenced to three years for these sorts of offences in 2007 and is *already* out (mid 2008). His brother was sentenced to six years, and will probably be out next year. Think about that: it might be *you* that his sons are robbing in 20 or 30 years' time, because dad's experiences aren't going to put them off.

The fact is, apart from one man who was secretly raping his teenage daughter and the odd kid caught with cannabis, I have not come across any generally law-abiding people who have just 'lost it' and done this kind of stuff. *All* the people I deal with are known to us, and well-known. *Every time* I've got them into custody and run them through the PNC, I've found they have previous for something. They are all known for domestic violence, child protection, robbery, drugs, burglary or something. All that's different is how low they are prepared to go.

CHILDREN AND DEATH

DEATH comes calling at strange times, in strange ways.

A skip lorry has left the road, gone up an embankment and flipped over on the slope. It has then rolled back down onto the road and crushed the rear of the car which was travelling behind it. The driver of the lorry is unhurt, as is the woman driving the car. Unfortunately, her young child is still in the back.

Standing at the side of the road, looking at this scene, on a sunny Wednesday morning, I watch as a firefighter crawls and squeezes his way into the wreckage to see if there is any hope. He comes back out, grim-faced, shaking his head, and we know.

We have closed the road and now everything goes into slow time. At serious accidents, the immediate priority is to save life, but if there are fatalities and there is nothing that can be done, the bodies are left *in situ* for the time being while everyone stops and takes stock. The safety of fire crews and everyone else there becomes more of an issue – is there petrol swilling around, for instance, or is the wreckage unstable? They start planning the body extraction, the police investigation begins.

They're going to have to bring in huge lifting gear to haul the lorry off; it takes a long time, hours, but eventually they lift it away and we all stand for a few moments, staring at the squashed car. Most of us have our own children. The firefighters gather around in a circle, helmets off, listening to their chaplain as he says a few words: this is something they always do before they extract bodies.

Then they get to work, stripping and sawing away the twisted metal and getting the poor little kid out. Suddenly, one of them breaks away and walks quickly to a nearby hedge, gesticulating angrily.

On the other side of it is a journalist, taking photographs. He has ignored our cordon, and tramped miles round, across the fields, through the woods and back down to get a shot of this.

He is arrested, to prevent a breach of the peace.

As the undertakers arrive, I wonder at the nature of life.

Months later. A young boy – he'd have been about nine or ten – has somehow drowned during a school swimming lesson. We are called, along with the paramedics. CID send a Detective Inspector to decide whether it is suspicious, a 'Sus Death' as we call it. He deploys his experience and knowledge through a three pint filter (well, it is after 4pm) and decides against any escalation.

The child's mother arrives and there is a scene of hysteria by the ambulance. The DI watches in silence. 'There's nothing for me here Gadget,' he says.

There's nothing here for anyone, I think.

I know the swimming teacher; she is from my part of the Ruralshire border. She's beside herself.

The other children are very quiet. One by one, their Balkan nannies rush them home in German cars.

Even the Paramedics, usually 100% reliable with a smile in the worst of situations, will not make eye contact.

A crowd of Emergency Service workers and other parents stand around the mother. Everybody cares and everybody understands.

Everyone involved will feel this, in some way and to some extent, for the rest of their lives.

HATE CRIME

THERE'S no doubt that there are some really nasty, evil racists in Britain. I'm white but I have close family who are not, and I'm more than aware of how poisonous some people's actions and beliefs can be. I'm also absolutely clear that we need to stamp on them, hard.

Am I convinced, though, that the Government, and the police, are approaching this undoubtedly serious issue in the right way?

No. As with domestic violence, I think our well-meaning approach may actually end up exacerbating matters.

Unless you've been living in a cave for the last five years or so, you'll be familiar with the phrase 'hate crime'.

In the police, we *love* hate crime. That is, we hate it – but we love to find it, because it provides the clearest possible proof, post-Macpherson*, of our anti-racist, pro-diversity credentials.

So what is 'hate crime'?

According to the Home Office, a hate crime is 'Any incident, which constitutes a criminal offence, which is perceived by the victim or any other person as being motivated by prejudice or hate.'

We also deal with things call 'hate incidents', which are exactly the same except that the 'incident' doesn't have to constitute a crime. I'll talk more about hate incidents shortly.

In both cases, the 'prejudice or hate' must be inspired by the victim's race, colour, ethnic origin, nationality or national origins, religion, gender or gender identity, sexual orientation or disability.

---

*Macpherson – the investigation by the judge Sir William Macpherson into the murder in London of the black teenager Stephen Lawrence by a gang of white thugs, and the subsequent botching of the investigation into the crime by the Met, which led to the police being described as 'institutionally racist'.

Where we identify hate crimes, such offences are likely to have more resources and attention spent on them than other similar but non-'hate' offences.

Additionally, if offenders are brought to justice they stand a very good chance of receiving a much stiffer sentence.

Two things to say first.

One: I don't think any particular area of discrimination is more or less important than any other, but since most cases we come across involve race that's the area we'll look at here.

Two: I am solely interested in arresting criminals and I believe justice should be entirely blind. I am not concerned with the skin colour of a victim or offender, his or her gender, what they do at night and with whom, or which god they pray to, or anything else except that they receive justice under the law. (That I am not a racist will be a grave disappointment to the PSD officers no doubt reading these words at this very moment, trawling for clues as to my identity and looking for some way to nail me to the wall. There is no more serious allegation to make against someone in the modern day police than that of racism.)

The key elements of the Home Office definition of hate crimes or incidents are these: they must be *'perceived'* by the victim *'or any other person'* as being motivated by prejudice or hate.

I cannot believe that the legislators intended those five words to have the impact they've had.

Most crime is judged objectively.

For instance, Adams is said to have assaulted Baker. This is not a matter of opinion: it either happened, or it didn't.

If Adams carries out the assault in such a way that other people might be left in fear, this is an affray. But it is not enough that the police say that other people were in fear; it's not even necessarily enough that we produce the people themselves and they say they were in fear. Instead, English law uses a 'reasonableness' test: would a person of reasonable firmness at the scene have been in fear? The court must use this test to try to decide the case.

When identifying a hate crime, this objectivity and 'reasonableness' test are not necessary; all that is required is that the victim, entirely subjectively, 'perceived' that the suspect's behaviour was motivated by hate or prejudice.

Additionally, if *'any other person'* perceives that the suspect's behaviour was motivated by hate or prejudice, the same applies. Amazingly, you might think, this can be so *even when the victim himself* believes the offence or incident did not involve hate, and actively requests that it's not logged as such.

This is something of a departure from the normal principles of law, but is that a problem?

Well, imagine Adams assaults two people in identical circumstances and causes them both the same injury, a broken jaw. One victim is from an ethnic minority group, and there is evidence that Adams attacked him because of that. The other is someone close to you – your daughter, perhaps – and there is evidence that Adams attacked her because he thought she was 'looking at him funny'. Assuming that your daughter is white or, if not, that there were no racial overtones to the attack on her, how will you and she feel when Adams gets three months less for her injury than for that inflicted on his other victim?

Perhaps you will see some bigger picture in this, as our lawmakers seem to, but will people in the wider community accept the idea that we have different classes of victim now? I'm not so sure. And where does that lead? I can only see it causing problems, not solving them.

Don't get me wrong: I'm not worried about violent scumbags getting longer in jail. I think they should *all* get longer. I'm just not sure that it matters what particular type of hatred motivates the blow that breaks a jaw. Is one jaw worth more than another?

The other point to bear in mind is what I said right at the top: the police *love* to find hate crime. Hate crime detections look fabulous on our figures, so the more offences we move to that pile, the happier we are. And 'any other person' can be a police officer or a civilian call taker, can't it?

There's a PC in my station whose job title is 'Community Liaison Officer'. His job is to look at every crime where the victim comes from an ethnic minority background (or is from one of the other hate crime target groups) and identify those which could be motivated by prejudice or hatred. All he needs to do is make the decision, and that moves a given offence from 'crime' to 'hate crime'.

He has a detective who works solely for him, personally investigating every possible hate crime.

It's not their fault – they're disciplined professionals doing their jobs – but sometimes this leads to absolutely nonsensical situations.

Here's a recent one. Two 15-year-old girls, Kelly (white) and Jasbinder (Asian), are having a row in a classroom. Kelly calls Jasbinder a 'slag'. There is no racial abuse used, but someone at the school believes, with no evidence that can be attested, that it may have been racially motivated. We are called and the offence is logged as a hate crime. The detective goes down to the school, arrests Kelly, takes her home and gives her a home caution. Result: one detected hate crime.

People are not stupid. They know that there is absolutely no chance of getting a detective to go to a school to effect an arrest like this if the alleged 'slag' and her accuser are both of the same race (remember, this is not an assault). It may play well with the journalists who write the *Guardian*'s editorials when my force's hate crime stats are 10% better, year-on-year, but how does it play with Kelly, her family and friends and everyone else on the estates they moan to about it?

WHEN TWO TRIBES GO TO WAR

SOMETIMES, the people from ethnic minority communities themselves don't want any part of hate crime, either.

I've known victims say, 'I don't want this recorded as a race crime because I don't think it was one,' and we do it anyway.

Our strategy as to how to overcome any objections the victim might have is to say they have 'Gone to WAR'. This is a handy acronym which means they have either Withdrawn, Acquiesced or Resisted. (Note: there is no other recognised response, such as knowing that there actually is no problem.)

There was a classic example of this in action in the 2006 World Cup.

Football world cups are the ACME of public disorder events, and, on Response, we were braced for trouble. With several large towns in my division, if and when England lost – especially if it happened during the later stages of the tournament, especially if it came down to penalties, and especially if we were playing a team like Germany or Argentina – we knew it would be followed by a tsunami of violence and criminal damage. Who knows why this happens? It just does.

A major concern among the senior management, though, was about the potential for racial attacks on premises attached to the countries we faced.

England reached the quarter finals and were drawn against Portugal.

This was a bit of a result. Germany and Argentina got each other, we avoided France and there is no traditional history of enmity between England and Portugal. Perhaps most importantly of all, we don't have much of a Portuguese community for our local morons to turn on.

We do have one Portuguese restaurant, though, in an outlying town.

They had been following the tournament enthusiastically – there was a Portuguese flag in the window, their waiters were all wearing replica shirts and there had been no problems at all. Come the quarter final, their regular customers were all going to turn up in England tops and the plan was that they would all watch the match together, have a few beers and generally enjoy themselves. It was fully booked. They were all friends: you couldn't have wished for a better example of how mature adults from different countries can sit and enjoy sport together.

Unfortunately, our top brass were not convinced.

The SMT had drawn up a grid of the town, and it told them that this restaurant was a hot spot, a flashpoint, and that there was likely to be trouble there.

As the match approached, we started having daily updates on the restaurant: officers were sent round every day to check whether there had actually been any threats and the hunt was on for intelligence as to any planned attacks.

The owner wasn't so sure. 'There are no problems,' he said. 'If Portugal lose, we have a drink and everyone is happy. If England lose, the same... we're just going to have a good night.'

In saying this, he has gone to WAR.

'Withdrawing' might have meant him shutting the restaurant for the night. But we can't have that – we need the restaurant to stay open, because we can't have people being threatened out of their homes or businesses. How would that look? (I know there was no threat, but that's not the point.)

'Acquiescing' is where the victim says, 'Look, this is all just a bit of fun... we don't mind the Portuguese jokes, honestly.' This is a bit like being 'in denial' – the racism is real, the victim just doesn't know it. Put another way, he doesn't know his own community – the one he has lived in for 30 years.

'Resisting' is actively fighting back in some way.

None of these applied: there was no racism and he wasn't a victim, he was just a bloke planning to have a good night in his restaurant. But in our minds he was at WAR, so we gave him the protection we said he needed.

This involved taking large numbers of officers out of the town centre and inserting a massive police presence around that restaurant. As the diners arrived, in their England and Portugal tops, they were greeted by a phalanx of a dozen cops, dressed virtually in riot gear. Another carrier-full of PCs was on display, constantly patrolling nearby.

Unsurprisingly, it rather ruined the atmosphere. Nothing happened, but nothing would have happened anyway.

Everyone nearby assumed that the manager had called us, of course, and he had to unpick that for the next six months. And the locals, they gave us loads of abuse. 'Where were you when we were burgled?' they said. 'When we called you loads of times because the kids' park was being trashed, where were you then? Now that we're playing Portugal in the World Cup *here* you all are?'

The problem is, there is no box you can tick in the SMT handbooks which says, 'This is a nice part of town where everyone gets on and there really isn't a problem.'

You cannot achieve any National Competency Framework Objectives out of that scenario.

You cannot evidence your portfolio with Diversity Community Objectives.

Writing, 'Everything was fine and no-one got upset' does not compute. That way, promotion does not lie.

The biggest tragedy in all of this is that what was, presumably, introduced with the best of intentions is beginning to produce the opposite effect of what was desired, and is driving people apart. My fear is that as this continues, *proper* racist crime – the vicious assaults, the attacks on homes and cemeteries, the threats and intimidation – will attract less sympathy from an increasingly cynical public and the job of the police in bringing these offenders to book will be made concomitantly harder.

MORE THOUGHTS ON DIVERSITY

IT'S NOT just hate crime. I mentioned 'hate incidents'. These are things that people do or say which are not crimes but which the police still get involved in.

A typical recent example involved a 14-year-old boy calling a 12-year-old Welsh girl a 'sheepshagger' because she wouldn't share her sweets with him in the local park.

This is an ongoing incident: the current position is that a local Neighbourhood Police officer will attend and speak to the boy in front of his parents about the consequences of using racist language, and warn him that if he does it again he will be arrested. When this happens, the PC will update the 'Non-Crime Incident Report' with what the boy said, and details of when he was seen.

The boy will then have a Local Information and Intelligence File made on him, including his name, age, address, the details of his parents and information about this incident. This will effectively label him as 'racist' for the next five years, at which point the file will be either 'weeded out' or continued, depending on what he has been up to in the intervening period. By 'label him as racist' I mean if these kids are stopped at any time in the next five years, and a police officer or PCSO asks the Control Room for a 'Person Check', their details will come back from the local system (not the Police National Computer) as 'known to police'. If the officer then asks for further details, the Controller will open the file on their screen and find details of this Race Hate incident. He or she won't read out the whole report – due to time constraints and multiple radio traffic, they are trained to summarise – but will say something like 'known for a non-crime race hate incident in 2008'. The officers will then develop their attitude to the kid based upon that information. It may be wrong to do this, but they'll be trying to deal with several kids at once and they're only human; if our boy gets just a bit stroppy he may well get arrested quicker than he otherwise might. I suspect, too, that that label would prevent employment in the emergency services; while we do want to weed out real racists, are 14-year-olds who insult Welsh kids using a well-worn stereotype the sort of people we're after?

By the way, a Non-Crime Incident Report *can* be upgraded later to a Crime Report if more detail comes to light – if, for instance, the boy blurts out to someone that he also shoved the girl (which would make it an assault). Additionally, the NCIR still has to be scrutinised by the Community Liaison Officer to make sure that he agrees with the course of action. He could still insist that the boy is arrested, perhaps on the basis that it was a racially motivated public order offence.

You can't challenge any of this, of course. There are people who will object to me just raising some of these questions. The best I can hope for is to be ignored. Here in Ruralshire Constabulary, as in all forces and most public sector organisations, we use four tactics to stifle any meaningful debate – especially when the subject matter may be uncomfortable, and even if the objections are sensible.

1. We link your views to 'change', and label anyone who does not agree with them as 'resistant to change'. Being resistant to change is almost as bad as being called a racist in today's police service. ('Openness to Change' is a competency we are all assessed on each year.)

2. Discredit the individual making the argument, rather than the argument itself. For this, you can use any of the 'isms'. Link the person's view to an 'ism'.

3. Disguise the language describing your view, so that nobody can actually understand what you mean. For instance, create a 'Neighbourhood Performance Management Tasking Group'.

4. If the debate is about a group or individual, give them 'victim status'; this places them beyond criticism, entrenches their views and absolves them of responsibility for their actions. (Note: this does not apply to *real* victims.)

There is a final tactic, for emergency use only. That is to agree with the common sense you are hearing, promise to adopt it, and then... don't. Later, say that you have, and use tactics 1 to 4 against anyone who complains. I call this 'doing a Hazel Blears'.

IT'S A SHAME ABOUT RAY

RAY was an idiot, and I didn't much like him.

Until his ASBO, he used to get pissed and hang about outside the railway station. After the ASBO he was still there, just sober.

When Ray was younger, he was a 'five hander'; when he got older he just used to shout at everyone. And he was an old man at 29, thanks to the alcohol addiction he inherited from his absent father.

His mother is a waster. She used to shack up with whoever Ray brought home from prison. These boys were always younger than Ray. She always misunderstood their intentions. The truth was always discovered in an empty handbag, contents scattered over the fake terracotta tiles in the kitchen of their house on the Fields Estate.

They always stole Ray's drugs too. As a constable, I spent hours taking pointless statements in the front room of that place.

Ray's criminal career was a kind of 'looking glass' affair. He started out bad and violent and graduated to sad and useless.

By the end, although always on the edge of any trouble in the town centre, he cut a rather pathetic figure, whose reputation as a bottomless pit for cheap drugs protected him from the worst excesses of the new generation.

I knew something was wrong when he suddenly started to self harm and inhale lighter fuel. By the time he died of a heroin overdose, Ray was doing 12 cans of butane a day. He blamed this latest addiction on the courts which had inflicted the 'alcohol in a public place' ban on him.

When I heard he was dead I pondered for a long while. I really thought hard about it. And about him. And about his mother. One of the Sergeants asked me what I thought, and I told him that I think it's a shame about Ray. And I meant it.

EAST MEETS WEST

THE Balkanisation of Ruraltown in recent years has been astonishing.

The Jenkinses are moving out of Empire Crescent today.

The PSU* team stand around dressed in black Kevlar and Gore-Tex. Over the years they have cultivated a 'bored' look, used to convince the locals that they are unconcerned about being outnumbered; they chew gum, lean on their shields and chat about football and the new girl on Response Team Five. The PSU are needed to keep order while the family load the contents of their home into an HGV. The removal companies in Ruraltown refused to do the job; a firm from Metro City has arrived, and they are working fast.

The house itself is boarded up; the Jenkinses were one of three or four families who owned their own houses in the road and, like all the others, they have decided to default on the mortgage and hand the keys back to the bank, rather than tough it out any longer.

I am present in my role as 'Public Order Bronze' – the sacrificial lamb, should anything go wrong. But things have already gone wrong in Empire Crescent. It's like a rough bit of Eastern Europe has been picked up and dropped in the middle of our town almost overnight. The Albanian/Kosovan/Romanian gangs struggle for control over the lucrative market in stolen prescription medication, peddled to England's eager, home-grown white trash. They have benefit money to spend, and these guys will flog them anything which can be smoked, injected or snorted.

Jenkins Snr worked for British Gas as an engineer. He parked his van outside his house and found it vandalised most mornings. He tried leaving it around the corner to fox the vandals, but then it was stolen. His mistake was to report the problems to us.

The family became a constant target from that point: violence, threats, paint daubed on the house, dog mess put through the

---

*Police Support Unit, comprising an Inspector, a Sergeant, six PCs and a Protected Police Cell-Van (Riot Van)

letterbox, rubbish tipped into the garden. The final straw came when their family pets were killed.

I remember deploying the PSU in support of a Community Officer who tried to investigate that crime. We helped with the 'house to house'. I asked a fat man dripping in gold and wearing a fur coat and grubby jeans if he had seen anything. He drew a swollen finger across his neck said to me, 'I cut your f**king head off, you come here again Englishman.'

I take it that's a 'No', then.

I called the Neighbourhood Policing Team and asked the skipper what the plan was to tackle these people. Five minutes into a lecture about the various ways in which a 'multi-agency engagement process with the minority ethnic population' could help, I replaced the handset quietly and let him carry on talking to himself. Why not? He is just about the only one left who believes any of it.

They don't like us talking about any of this, let alone writing about it. None of it fits the official story and, in these strange times, the story is what counts.

But how *can* I stay quiet? I have dealt with families where every single one of the children over seven is a professional thief.

If you chase these people on foot, they will throw their babies at you so you have to stop. If they're making off in vehicles, they'll place the babies next to the wheels of police cars to prevent you driving after them. Not long ago, we had a very interesting briefing – a formal warning from the Home Office to all police forces, though I didn't see it make the papers. Based on experience and also written material found during cell searches, it concerned the tactics employed by some eastern European females (I suggest you look away now if you're squeamish). As they're arrested, they put their hands down their knickers and rub them over their privates. When a male officer nicks them, they grab hold of his hands. Then, as soon as they're in custody, they claim that he has raped them. They know that a British policeman will immediately be tested for forensic evidence, and that that will sow confusion and slow us down. If they muddy the waters, put doubt in our minds, maybe they will make us think twice about arresting them and while we hesitate they can get away.

And when that's all failed, and we get them into custody, they don't bat an eyelid. They are totally unconcerned about being photographed, and having their DNA taken, and being fingerprinted and interviewed. Here, we give them a coffee and a choice of menus and get them a lawyer and an interpreter, and they face no sanctions to speak of: this is all as it should be, but I doubt it's how they do things in Romanian and Albanian and Kosovan police stations, so it's no surprise they're relaxed.

In court, sometimes they will strip all their clothes off, stand in the box and scream, and not stop screaming. If the ushers go near them, they will bite and kick and scratch and fight. The idea is to behave so unacceptably that a British court will not deal with them and will just bundle them away. If it doesn't work, who cares? What has it cost them?

As I watch the Jenkins' possessions get hefted into the red box van, I look at the tracksuited youths eyeballing us and remember a conversation I had with one Romanian interpreter, a man who was married to an English teacher here. He said to me, 'You haven't got a *clue* what's coming your way.'

STOP AND SEARCH

THE most effective tool for dealing with low-level street crime is stop and search.

Burglars go equipped with screwdrivers and crowbars or have stolen gear on them; drug dealers have little wraps of hash and coke in their pockets or mouths; muggers carry knives. If you want to catch these people, the best way is to stop them and search them. Of course, officers act on suspicion and intelligence reports and neither can always be right. The inevitable corollary to this is that a lot of innocent people will unfortunately get stopped and searched (as well as some guilty ones who manage to get rid of their drugs and weapons when they see us coming).

The only sensible response to this, surely, is to accept that this is a minor inconvenience compared with what would happen if we allowed burglars, drug dealers and violent thugs to proceed unmolested.

I have a lot of experience of being stopped and searched by the police myself. When I was in the Army, serving in Germany, I was regularly pulled over by the French cops on the roads between Calais and Holland – it was the 1980s, PIRA terrorists had started operating on the continent and they often travelled on British number plates. Equally, if you went out for a beer on a Saturday night in somewhere like Paderborn or Osnabruck, you could easily be pulled to one side and frisked three or four times by the Bundespolizei. They had problems with squaddies getting tanked up and fighting, and they needed to disrupt that behaviour. It never occurred to me to protest: I'd nothing to fear because I wasn't committing any crime and, anyway, it was in my best interests. If PIRA bombers got through, I was a target. If drunken soldiers kicked off, I might be in the way.

Unfortunately, not everyone sees it like this. A few newspaper commentators, experts and criminologists and some – but by no means all – members of the black and Asian communities believe that the police deliberately stop more black and Asian people because we are all racists. I don't believe this to be the case – no bobby I know gives two hoots what race a suspect is – but the suspicion, helpfully, is probably fuelled by the Government's own figures.

This summer, the Home Office revealed that there were 1.87 million stop-searches and stop-and-accounts (where we stop you and ask you where you're going or have been) last year.

Each of these required the filling-in of a lengthy form, containing lots of information about the person stopped and the officer, such as the date, time and place of the stop, the reason for it and its outcome, what the officers were looking for and anything they found, the person's self-defined ethnicity* and his name, or a description if he refuses to give one. The Home Office says these forms should take seven minutes to complete. I'll come back to this aspect of it shortly, because it's highly relevant.

---

*There are 16 'SDEs' and 'other'; we often get white teenagers describing themselves as Asian (or 'alien', come to that) and, if arrested, demanding cells which face east and halal meals – they don't know the first thing about Islam, but they do find it very amusing watching us scurry around meeting their non-existent faith requirements.

The figures showed, further, that black people were seven times more likely to be stopped and searched than white people, and Asian people were 2.2 times more likely.

On the bald face of it, this looks like clear racism on the part of the police. But the raw data seldom tells the full story.

For instance, in large parts of the country, in the rural villages and small towns, I'm sure very few people are *ever* stopped. A major reason for this is that – as the residents are always complaining – there is very little in the way of a daily police presence there to carry out stops in the first place. Who lives in these rural areas? Mostly, white people. In contrast, in the high crime areas in the cities where the proportion of ethnic minority residents is historically higher, the police are more active. So far this year in London, there have been around 20 stabbings of youths by other teenagers. In my village there have been none. Where *should* the police be stopping and searching kids?

However, I think there are other factors in play, too.

First, let's look at the supposed seven minutes it takes to fill out the forms. I bet it *does* take seven minutes, in the nice, controlled environment where they designed them. But on the street? Let's say you need to stop and search a gang of four youths who resemble descriptions of a group of shoplifters just reported legging it from PC World. You have to get them to stand still and listen to you, and perhaps grab one or two of them who keep trying to walk off. There's nowhere to lean your pad. It's raining and blowing a gale. Your pen keeps stopping. The first lot of information they give you is all bulls**t, and you have to start all over again. Other kids are hanging around – perhaps just shouting stuff, possibly getting quite threatening – and you have to back them off a couple of times. You have to break off to listen to the radio now and then. You have to call for back-up. The people you've stopped don't speak English, or claim not to. They won't stand still for the actual searches. It all adds up to a nightmare which can take *far* longer than seven minutes per individual. Back in Germany, the Bundespolizei asked if they could pat you down, you said they could and it took them 15 seconds before you were on your way. In Britain, after our little PC World job, even if things go swimmingly, the fourth person in line will have waited *28 minutes* for the copper to finish dealing with him. If he's entirely innocent, why wouldn't he be hacked off?

Now, complaints. All complaints against the police are taken seriously but complaints from members of ethnic minority communities are taken particularly seriously. In the post-'Macpherson Report' world of institutionalised racism, any hint of an allegation of racism is absolute poison to your career. Thus, any officer stopping any black or Asian person and not doing it to the absolute letter is very foolish, because if the person stopped later complains about the search he or she will be in major trouble. This means that stops of black or Asian people are likely to be most assiduously recorded (along with stops of folk like MPs' children, heads of pressure groups, anyone who says he's a lawyer and anyone stopped in view of CCTV cameras). What are the odds that some searches of white people are likely to be informal? I'm not saying this would be right, or that I approve of it or even know of it – it just sounds likely to me.

All of which leaves us in the ironic position that those people most likely to be offended by and complain about having their time wasted by a stop-search are precisely those people we don't want to offend or have complain about us – entirely innocent members of the black and Asian communities. The other irony, of course, is that because black and Asian people tend to live in poorer areas, for historical reasons, they are disproportionately the victims of crime. We are stopping and searching people for their benefit.

What are the solutions?

I suppose we could do more to ensure beyond doubt that every single search is performed to the letter of the law and recorded as such. But this would cost a huge amount and would tie officers up in even more paperwork than they're already swamped with. When the Government released this number of 1.87 million stops, the papers multiplied it by seven minutes and said it all added up to 25 years of police time spent filling in forms. The real figure, I think, is much higher than this, and doesn't take account of all stops. There's talk of scrapping stop-and-account forms, which is a move in the right direction. Stop-search forms certainly need modifying, too. It may be that there *are* people out there who will say that they really don't mind if the police take even longer to come to their burglary/assault/robbery just so long as they know that every time Darren and his eight mates are stopped in the park with their bottles of White Lightning, nine long forms are painstakingly filled in. But I suspect most would prefer we just took away the cider, quickly recorded the fact that we'd done it and then got on with policing.

POSTCODE POLICING

THERE'S a lot of talk about the lottery of 'postcode prescribing', where NHS patients in one city are denied drugs that those in another receive.

We don't hear half so much about postcode *policing*, but it's every bit as prevalent.

Some forces arrest for things that other forces would just give 'words of advice' for. The significance of this is that Mr X of Ruralshire stands to get a criminal record, whereas Mr Y gets no such stigma for committing exactly the same offence in Othershire.

Here's an example. We nicked two 19-year-olds outside KFC one Friday night. CCTV had called a fight in: it was relatively minor stuff, and the classic six of one and half a dozen of the other – a bit of handbags over a girl which had left Shane with a slight fat lip and Dwayne with the beginnings of a black eye. It also left them both with criminal records, each for assaulting the other.

By the time we got there it was actually all over. In the absence of aggravating factors or serious injuries, or one of the two being an obvious victim of an assault by the other, there was a time when we would have dealt with a matter like this informally, using a method called 'IP Declined'. How it worked was, officers would get in between the two idiots and push them apart. Then we'd talk to them separately.

'Look, Shane,' we'd say, 'what happened here?'

'He was looking at my bird,' Shane would say. 'We had words and then we smacked each other.'

'How about you, Dwayne? What's your story?'

'He thought I was looking at his bird, which I wasn't. We had words and we smacked each other.'

'OK,' we'd say, 'if you want to get nicked, fine. But if you prefer, you can shake hands and sign this pocket notebook here to say you decline to get involved.'

Nine times out of ten, they'd sign and we'd send them on their way: 'You're a pair of fools and you should be ashamed of yourselves. Get yourselves home to bed. You go that way, you go the other, and if we see you doing this again then you *will* be coming in.'

Result: two young lads who will grow out of their stupidity one day *don't* have criminal records, and a group of officers who would otherwise have to spend the next four or five hours with them at the police station can instead stay on the streets to deal with any serious incidents that might occur.

In some forces, officers still regularly operate this system.

Not in mine.

Nowadays, we look at that incident as two crimes which might be detected to meet our targets.

We dress it up in the language of ethics and safety, of course. One of those two men *could* be a victim, couldn't he, even though he says he was as much to blame as the other. (Maybe he just doesn't want to admit it – he might be frightened, or embarrassed, or have a cultural agenda which prevents him from doing so.) Then there are the legal and safety issues: for instance, what if one of them collapses later and it turns out that the police were there but didn't do anything? These 'what ifs' can be, almost literally, endless, and if we try to cover each one it ends up paralysing us. But never mind: for all of these reasons and more, we must separate them and bring them in.

Overhanging the whole thing in this instance is the spectre of our process.

Remember, I was directed to Shane and Dwayne's scuffle by CCTV. If CCTV calls in a fight, and an operator at Headquarters types onto his or her log that there is an assault in progress, that's it. That log is a legal document and, once it's opened, someone pretty much *has* to be arrested and crime reports *have* to be taken. You're not supposed to use your discretion, talk to the lads and send them on their way: you're supposed to cuff them and stick them in a van.

I know that many readers will think that, for a variety of reasons, this is fair enough. People fighting in the street *should* be arrested. But it's often even worse than that. I'm not exaggerating when I say I have come across incidents where ordinary people end up being arrested and taken to the police station for, literally, a bit of pushing and shoving.

After I wrote this part of the book, my publisher queried this. He said, 'What if two men are out in town having a pint together one night, and on their way home they end up throwing each other around in horseplay?'

The answer is, it depends.

If we saw it happen, and we were satisfied it was just two blokes messing around, they'd probably be OK.

If it was called in on CCTV, though, that would be different. We would be directed to the scene by the operators, and would stop the two men and ask what was going on.

They would say, 'Nothing.'

One of the PCs would say, 'Can you just stand there with my colleague, please?' Then he would phone the CCTV. 'I'm in Centre Street with those two males... what have you got?'

The operator says: 'The one in the white t-shirt clearly pushed the one in the dark t-shirt, causing him to stagger backwards. Dark t-shirt then barged white t-shirt and *he* staggered back, and then it looked like they were squaring up.'

'Roger, thanks for that,' says the PC. He then calls the force comms centre and asks the team leader what's on the log.

'Let's see,' says the team leader. 'Erm... right, it says *assault in progress*.'

And that is that: the two men are coming in. 'Right,' the two cops say. 'Allegations have been made by the CCTV operators that there was an incident between you. I am arresting you on suspicion of assault.'

To overturn it, once it's on the log, is a massive and very risky job, no matter how minor the 'offence'. The officer who does that – who accepts that they were just horsing around – will be scrutinised and questioned and examined and, overtly or not, criticised by his superiors. Someone from Headquarters will email over a list from the last ten years showing cases where people were just 'horsing around' and then hit their heads and ended up in comas, or went on later and stabbed each other. *This is how the wife beaters get away with it*, they will say. *The police believed them when they said it was nothing serious*. No-one is trusted, certainly no front line bobby. In the end, many cops just say, *It's not right, but let's just get them in*.

That means DNA, fingerprints, photographs, a night in the cells and an interview in the morning. If the two men are daft enough, they might accept a caution or a PND ticket for disorderly conduct, rather than wait around to be interviewed. If they don't, once it gets to interview they will be refused-charged – ie released without charge, when it becomes apparent that the whole thing is nonsense. But they will still have been through a fairly unpleasant, and certainly inconvenient, ordeal over absolutely nothing, and what really upsets me – more than the fact that this is (in my eyes) a massive abuse of state power, more than the waste of police time and more than the petty, bureaucratic nature of the people who have decided that this is how we should now police – is that the scumbags who really do kick the living s**t out of people are in the cells next to our two guys and they get treated in *exactly* the same way.

Two other things to say about postcode policing.

Firstly, it changes *within* forces. I was chatting to some cops from our own G Division the other day. We were swapping anecdotes about public disorder, and I made what I thought was an innocent comment: 'And then we arrested him for drunk and disorderly.'

The G Division skipper looked in amazement at me. 'Good grief, boss,' he said. 'Your team arrested someone for d&d? We're forbidden from arresting for that. We have to use Section 5 Public Order Act because it's a notifiable crime, and we can get the detection out of it.'

This is the notifiable/non-notifiable dichotomy I mentioned earlier: G Div wants detections, F Div wants to keep the figures down. But never mind the figures, what about the arrested individual? Applicants for some government jobs will find that 'public order' offences bar them unless there are 'exceptionally compelling circumstances'. This does not apply to those convicted of being drunk and disorderly.

Secondly, it even changes within *divisions*. Areas are designated as crime 'hot spots', based on analysts looking at crime across the area. Officers are 'tasked' to hot spots and given strict direction (usually in writing) as to how to deal with particular offences there. So an incident which might result in words of advice in Acacia Avenue (not a hot spot) could end in arrest if it happened in Jones Street.

KIDS

LAST week we were cautioning too many juveniles; this week, apparently, we are locking too many of them up.

How do we know this? Because Frances Done CBE says so.

Who is Frances Done CBE? She is the head of the Youth Justice Board (YJB) for England and Wales (but don't hold that against her – she once had a proper job, as a chartered accountant).

About 2,900 young offenders aged between 10 and 17 are currently locked up in secure children's homes, training centres and Young Offender Institutions, and I can guarantee you that every single one of them needs to be there for your safety.

In June this year, Ms Done said magistrates and judges needed to impose fewer custodial terms on such offenders. In what was described as 'her first major interview since being appointed in February', she told BBC news she was determined to 'drive the numbers down'. Instead of incarceration, Ms Done suggests greater use should be made of community penalties.

She was worried, she added, that 'new Government plans to tackle knife crime' meant there was 'a risk more teenagers could be locked up'.

This all came against the background of the YJB missing its three-year target of cutting youth custody numbers by 10% – despite the fact that they fell as a proportion of sentences imposed.

I'm sure Frances Done is a very intelligent and charming woman, but I'm not sure I set much store by her views on youth crime.

I'm not even sure why the YJB *has* a target for cutting youth custody numbers in the first place. Surely they should leave the question of youth custody to the parents of the youths, the police officers who arrest them and the courts they put them before? Not to mention, the youths themselves. If more youths involve themselves in offences for which custody is the answer, then, *ipso facto*, more of them will find themselves in custody. If fewer do so, youth custody numbers will take care of themselves.

Look, I know there are a huge number of great teenagers out there. The vast majority of Britain's youth would no more think of sticking a knife into your ribs than of flying to the moon.

The trouble is, there *are* those – a tiny, tiny percentage of the whole – who *would* do that sort of thing without a second's reflection, would laugh as they did it and would further delight in sticking the mobile phone footage up on YouTube. As someone who actually spends time dealing with the latter sort of kids, let me assure you that it is actually *extremely* difficult to get custodial sentences for them. I work in Ruralshire, not Moss Side, I accept that – but still, I have put young people through our youth courts on dozens of occasions for the most heinous stuff, and I haven't seen a single one sent away.

A couple of examples. Ronnie Carling was a persistent MISPER from the age of 12 until he turned 16. We were always being called out to spend all night looking for him (he always turned out to be safe somewhere with friends or relatives) and then returning him to Social Services homes and foster carers 30 or 40 miles away. Once there, he would sleep, eat and then immediately run away again after arguments over whether or not he could smoke indoors and so on.

One day, we found him in a house on one of our estates; while we were sorting out some social workers to come down, he threatened me with a knife. Luckily, I was able to rush him and take the blade away, but it could have been very serious. He was 13 years old at the time. Last year, now aged 17, he stabbed a boy in the head with a pair of scissors because he wouldn't hand over his mobile phone during a street robbery. He did not receive a custodial sentence for either of these incidents, both of which could have ended in death, and he has more than 20 offences on his record.

Troy Wallis is another such youth. I hate to stereotype, but Troy is a teenage scumbag, the latest of three generations of scumbags from the same family. His folks will turn their hands to anything, from armed robbery to rape and beyond, and he's showing all the signs of following them down that road. There is absolutely no chance that Troy will listen to me, or his teachers, or Frances Done CBE from the Youth Justice Board, and turn out alright in the end. I wish it was different, and it doesn't mean we shouldn't try, but I'm sorry, that's the way it is.

A couple of years ago, I was on the street on public order duty on a Saturday night. We were in the High Street and there was a disturbance outside McDonald's, which there always is. A fight had broken out between a group of youngsters – proper punches were being traded, and there was broken glass everywhere. As far as we could tell, there were about six of them involved, all aged around 14 or 15. Two or three girls were also among the combatants. (The involvement of girls makes it quite difficult for us; the way they binge-drink and fight and generally behave means, occasionally, that they really do need to be got a grip of, put on the floor and cuffed, but there are still cultural issues about male officers laying hands on them. Partly it's old-fashioned, residual chauvinism, partly it's the fear of complaints when you inevitably end up accidentally touching them in intimate areas as they're rolling around and struggling like all-in wrestlers. Some officers have got over this, some haven't.) Anyway, it was all going off, one thing led to another and one of the PCs, a youngster called Jimmy, grabbed hold of a 14-year-old boy.

It was Troy.

Jimmy told him he was nicked for assault and by way of reply Troy swung round with his fist and smashed Jimmy in the side of his head. I saw this happen, and grabbed Troy's other arm; he started kicking and screaming and swearing and threatening us. Meanwhile – I only saw this later on CCTV – one of his mates ran over and tried to boot me in the back of the head with a flying kick. Luckily, one of my other PCs saw him coming and managed to grab his leg while he was in mid-air.

We were still struggling with Troy. He may be a 'young person' but he's violent and he was utterly out of control. As usually happens, Jimmy got one handcuff on him and then he broke free and started using the loose cuff as a weapon. He flailed at me with it and as I moved back he ran towards me and tried to head butt me. I could sense other people crowding in: they could have weapons, this could get very nasty. We needed to get Troy under control, *now*. Enough was enough. I gave him a hard right hook, flush on the jaw, which dropped him instantly. When he hit the floor, he chipped a tooth and split his lip. There was blood everywhere, but he was subdued and everyone else backed off.

I *hated* doing that. Bizarrely, it hit me far worse than seeing multiple deaths in car accidents. I have a 13-year-old son, and punching a lad of a similar age seemed wrong. It *wasn't* wrong – it was legally well within my rights under the circumstances – but I felt very guilty. As soon as we'd got him and the rest of them squared away, I went to see my boss. 'Look, sir,' I said. 'I've smacked this boy in the face. It was lawful, minimum force and all that, but I don't feel great about it.'

A couple of weeks later, the same senior officer came down to see me.

'You know Troy Wallis?' he said. 'That lad you punched a while back?'

'Yes,' I said. Thinking, *He must have made a complaint.*

'He's just bottled a man in a pub and the guy has lost his eye. He's down in custody now, laughing about it. If you were still feeling guilty about him, don't. He's a little s**t and he couldn't care less.'

Now, do nice, well-meaning people like Frances Done see Troy when he is spitting and punching and kicking people, and giggling about having just blinded a man?

No. They see him when he's on his best behaviour, talking about his hard childhood and his deprived circumstances, and how none of this is his fault, and if only people would listen, and there's nothing to do round here, and it's all down to society...

So they write long reports about how teenagers shouldn't go into custody and insist that 'community penalties' should be used instead.

In a way, this shouldn't surprise us: most people involved in the Youth Justice Board and the media and in the higher echelons of the police and the Home Office not only have zero experience of Troy but would, themselves, feel thoroughly chastised and punished by community service.

Does Troy? Er... not so much. People like Troy are among those who – according to a 2008 National Audit Office report – are routinely skipping community service by claiming they overslept or forgot they had to show up.

The *real* problem, though, is that even when Troy *is* turning up to paint out the graffiti he and his mates sprayed all over the skate park on Friday, he's only doing this for a few hours a week. The rest of the time he's free to indulge his tendency to beat you up, steal your car or stick a broken Rolling Rock bottle in your eye.

The big lie – or the big mistake, take your pick – is that people like Troy and the rest of the tiny minority of truly violent and unpleasant young offenders on our streets are basically just like the rest of us, only they've copped a raw deal or behaved out of character – so there but for the grace of God, go I. The courts are encouraged to reflect this mindset in sentencing, and the YJB is clearly fully signed up, too.

We need to grow up and accept the truth that some kids are so poisoned that they are pretty much lost to us. Every now and again I am privileged to get a wake-up call – a young lad sitting in a custody area laughing at having blinded someone – which shows this.

Our Young Offenders' Teams act as their surrogate parents. One of my PCs, Gary, is a virtual dad to a large number of children on the estate where he's based. I was chatting to him just the other day. He told me how a 15-year-old girl had come to him, at one of his community surgeries, to talk about her GCSE results.

'She wanted me to sit down with her and work out what she should do next in terms of college,' he said. 'Me... some copper she hardly knows. How sad and depressing is that?'

'Why don't the school careers people do that, Gary?' I said.

'Oh, she's got behavioural issues,' he said. 'There have to be three teachers present whenever she sees one of them, and they have to be restraint-trained. Chances of getting that combination together are zero, so basically the careers people can't or won't see her.'

People like Gary, they find these children when they're lost, they take them home and will even make a meal for them if there is no-one there. They spend their lives explaining right and wrong to them, and drawing up behavioural contracts. They arrange for parenting orders, to force their mums and dads take them to school. And we are the *only* ones who ever say *No*.

Some of the Neighbourhood cops find it rewarding work, in its own way. That's all fine. But this is why no-one comes to your burglary – we're too busy bringing up other people's kids for them.

HEAVY METAL THUNDER

ARE people being robbed blind of copper pipes, electric cable and lead from the local church roof round your way?

I thought this was a national trend, caused by the high price of metal on the world market, leading to high prices for scrap metal in local areas and, therefore, an increased incentive for feckless thieves to switch, temporarily, from conning old ladies out of their pension money.

Apparently not. According to the *Ruralshire Chronicle*, it is the fault of the police. More specifically, it's my fault. It's my fault because I was the only Inspector available (or stupid enough) on Friday afternoon to provide a statement about the problem.

The Detective Inspectors had been in the pub since 2pm and my uniformed colleagues are too interested in promotion to go near reporters.

Faced with the possibility of a 'police declined to comment' situation, I was asked to talk to the local paper by our media officer.

In a moment of madness, I informed the journalist that metal theft is a national trend, caused by the high price of metal on the world market, leading to high prices for scrap metal in local areas and, therefore, an increased incentive for feckless thieves to switch, temporarily, from conning old ladies out of their pension money.

She smiled, nodded her head in apparent agreement and wrote it all down.

She then asked me what the police were doing about it and I dutifully spun her all the items on a hurried list dictated to me by the DCI from his mobile next to the bunker by the 9th at the Royal Ruralshire.

I saw the results this morning in the shop as I bought some bacon. The *Chronicle* blames Inspector Gadget for not doing enough.

I wanted to ring her up and point out that, with the few Response officers I actually have on the ground, they're lucky we can answer the emergency calls, let alone personally guard every church and manhole cover in F Division.

But I thought better of it, and went home to make a bacon sarnie instead.

EVEN THE KIDS THINK WE'RE A JOKE

I'M sitting in a marked police vehicle, a big Volvo jam sandwich, in the left hand lane of a road cutting past a retail park.

I'm in a line of cars, with the traffic lights on red up ahead and a KEEP CLEAR box directly in front of me.

Down the right hand lane comes a shiny Mercedes convertible. It's moving at a rate of knots – at the last second, all I see is a silver blur in my wing mirror, and then it's braking hard and pulling a sharp, tyre-squealing left right past my bonnet and cutting across the waiting traffic to zip through into an access road leading to a line of shops.

My first response is almost to crap myself. My second is to think, 'I'm in a bloody marked car – I'm not having that.'

I stick the blue lights on and go after it. She – it's driven by an attractive blonde woman in her early 40s – stops in the NEXT car park, puts the roof down and gets out. Her young daughter – 13-years-old or so – gets out of the other side. They're just about to go into the shop to buy a pair of kitten heels or some skinny jeans or whatever it is that NEXT sells when I catch up with them.

'Excuse me, madam,' I say. 'Can you just stop there a second, please? I need to have a quick word with you about your driving.'

I want to explain that she has just committed what amounts to Careless Driving at the very least, and could have been a lot worse – she could easily have hit a motorcyclist or push bike rider obscured from her view on my nearside. I ask for her licence, and while she is fishing around for it in her Prada bag and I'm talking about the danger of cutting through traffic at speed, her daughter pipes up.

'Shouldn't you be out catching murderers and rapists?' she says.

I am, momentarily, speechless. She's 13, from a good family, and this is how she speaks to a police officer in front of her mum.

What has gone wrong?

People are like this now, even at a young age, because the Government has turned us into clowns. We go out looking for detections for cream cake throwing, and even the kids think we're a joke.

DEATH KNOCKS

IF YOU ask any Response team officer, he or she will tell you that they'd rather be at the scene of a fatal accident – terrible as those scenes can often be – than be sent to see the family.

When someone dies unexpectedly, there are (usually) relatives to be informed, undertakers to be arranged, often a police doctor or a GP to come out. That's all down to us: we visit the house and knock on the door and their lives change forever.

Delivering these sorts of messages is horrible, people are crying, sobbing, distraught, but it has to be done and it has to be done in person; in training, they tell you about officers who have written something on a slip of paper and stuck it through the letterbox because they couldn't find anyone at home. It's hard to imagine how anyone could be so stupid or insensitive as to do that.

You have to be incredibly careful. Any normal law-abiding person who has the police call on them automatically assumes the worst. They'll open the door and – particularly if they have kids who aren't at home – they'll almost faint. Of course, quite often it's nothing serious at all – it might be some house-to-house enquiries after a burglary, or perhaps a car has been stolen and they were the previous keeper. So you get into the habit of saying, 'Don't worry, there's nothing to worry about.'

The problem is that you get so used to saying that that when you do have bad news to deliver it's still often the first thing you say.

My first 'death knock' will stay with me forever. I was a PC, quite new in the job. Back then, death knocks were often left to bobbies; unfortunately, as I've risen through the ranks this horrible task has followed me. Now it's usually down to a Sergeant or an Inspector.

A woman was driving home in her Ford Fiesta from work one afternoon. Her route took her on a long, straight stretch of road, notorious in our patch for nasty accidents. She was hit, head-on, by a drunk. It was hideous: she wasn't killed outright, but she had life-threatening injuries. Clearly, her family needed to be informed, and fast.

It took the people at the scene about an hour to work out who she was, because everything was smashed to pieces and she was unconscious, but eventually they found something that identified her and I was sent to her house with a colleague, Paul. It was a nice, neat little place on the edge of one of our towns. I knocked on the door in uniform and two young children came to the door.

'Can we come in?' I said, trying to work out what the set-up was. It's difficult when all you have is an address. It turned out that she had a husband, these two youngsters and an older son, a lad of 16 who was at the cinema. The two younger ones – they were around 14 and 12 – were waiting for her to come home to make their tea. Dad was at work, none the wiser.

Paul called big brother on his mobile at the cinema, but he thought it was a hoax call from one of his schoolmates and put the phone down. So Paul drove off to find him: we didn't want him coming back past the scene of the accident and happening across his mum.

I couldn't tell the other children too much about what was going on. 'Your mum's been in a car accident,' I said. 'Has she got an address book we can look at?'

One of them fetched it from the kitchen. I flicked it open and found she had written down, in the front of the book, a whole screed about what to do in an emergency, who to contact, the works: mum and dad's work numbers, grandparents, uncles, aunts, everything.

The door went. It was the next-door neighbour; she'd seen the police car arrive and then leave, and she wanted to know if she could help. She was a Godsend; she'd been the children's babysitter when they were little, and she sat with them while I started making calls. Obviously, I wanted the husband, but he'd left work – it was 6pm or so by now – and his mobile was going straight to voicemail. You can't leave a message about this kind of thing. The only person I could reach was his brother, who didn't know where dad was but agreed to come down from where he lived, miles away. So aunt and uncle are en route, with me hoping they get there soon so that I can extract.

Then my phone rang. It was one of the lads, calling from the hospital.

He said, 'Don't say anything, just listen. She's dead.'

I looked at the children, sitting there looking at me. The neighbour, who was making the children something to eat, glanced over. She knew.

'I've just got to nip outside,' I said. 'Can I leave the children with you for a sec?'

I had to get hold of Paul, preferably before he picked her eldest up at the cinema. I didn't want him telling the boy everything was OK, or deciding to take him to the hospital to see his mum. But I couldn't get a mobile phone signal. I was wondering what to do, and shuddering at mental images of Paul driving the boy to A&E and bouncing in, asking where Mrs So-and-so was, when he turned into the road. Thank goodness.

I let the lad past and stopped Paul on the pathway: he looked at me and, like the neighbour, he knew straight away.

Shortly afterwards, the aunt and uncle turned up. We took them aside and I spoke to the uncle, and then we left.

That night, my wife and I filled out an emergency page in our own address book.

ASSAULTS ON POLICE

I DON'T care whether you're a 16-stone rugby player or a skinny 18-year-old woman, when you first join the police the thing that worries you most is the violence.

Whether you like it or not, you're going to get involved in fights, and lots of them.

We don't deal with normal people. We deal with aggressive drunks, drugged-up sociopaths and angry thugs, who attack you from behind, kick you while you're on the floor, bite you, scratch you and cover you in their spit and blood and vomit and worse. If they get a chance, they'll stab you, or smash you with a lump hammer, or run you over in a car. They'll fight you in broad daylight, or in the foyer of Asda, or in their house, or in a pub, or down an alleyway or anywhere you have the temerity to question their behaviour or lay hands on them. They are not people like you or me, or the people who get arrested in *The Bill*. They are semi-feral, wild things full of hatred and anger at everyone, and they have no morals, no empathy and no compunction about hurting you.

I've been relatively lucky so far in my career – I've had nothing *really* serious happen to me. That's a relative term, of course: it's more serious than most people expect to face during their working day. In the northern part of the division, where I was a patrol Sergeant, I was assaulted pretty much every day. Punched, kicked, spat at, head-butted, pushed around, knocked over. As a Sergeant, you go to pretty much every incident, and anything after 9pm usually has pissed and aggressive people on the end of it, so the odds are you're going to take a battering now and then.

I've had officers knifed, and one was repeatedly stabbed so hard with a shattered chair leg that it actually started to penetrate the vest.

I've had a PC deliberately run over.

Women officers get trashed, too – there's not a lot of chivalry knocking around Ruraltown I'm afraid. You hear a lot of talk about female officers not being any good in a fight, and they can struggle with big, determined males. But then, we all can; in my experience, most of our girls are pretty tough, mentally, and you don't mind having them alongside you. One of them, a friend of mine, was really badly bitten a while back, and went down with a very nasty infection. She was off work for some time as a result.

Another woman I worked Response with had her nose broken by a 16-year-old youth, much bigger than her. There were reports of a massive fight going on at one of our big, edge-of-town leisure multiplexes – the kind of place where there's a cinema, a McDonalds, a bowling alley, a bar or two and a nightclub. (Incidentally, when they build these places, they attract yobs in from all over, alongside the decent folks, but we get no extra police to deal with it, it's just an addition to policing the town centre. There's often no CCTV – they are private places and they won't pay for cameras to cover the carparks and outlying areas – and I've been there numerous times for assaults and even stabbings.)

Sure enough, as we pulled up, there was a wild west-type brawl going on between five or six people out in front of the bowling alley, with a big crowd around, laughing and cheering them on. They carried on going at it right in front of us – the days of people scattering and running for cover when the cops arrive are long gone.

Why bother? They can take us on, and if they lose they won't get any real punishment for it. Assault-police often just doesn't get charged.

We jumped out and the woman PC ran for this 16-year-old as he rained blows and stamps down on another youth who was curled up on the floor. As she grabbed his arms from behind, he turned round and decked her. Blood everywhere. She got up, sprayed him and started handcuffing him, at which point his girlfriend started attacking her, too. Fair play, she got them both under control, but she was off work for three weeks and she looked like an England prop forward till the facial swelling went down.

Different night, same place. There was another report of a fight and we turned up in a van. There were only three of us in it, but they didn't know that. Out front, a crowd of about 20 people had spilled out of one of the bars and there were two small groups of men, each lot shouting abuse and throwing beer at the others. As we watched, one of them tore his shirt off – they always do this, for some reason – and started walking towards the rival gang. He was well-known to us: called Wally, he is a multi-tattooed moron of a football hooligan who had just got out of prison. I could see the veins on his neck standing out and his eyes bulging – there was something almost comical about his rage, but nothing funny at all about his intentions. Wally is the sort of bloke who would slash your throat and do 10 years for you without thinking about it. He doesn't give a toss and he was completely off his face. A few of his mates, being slightly less moronic, managed to get him under control and they bundled him into a car and drove him off, to general jeering and beer throwing from the ones left behind. Things started to calm down then, but he'd obviously got the better of his friends in the car because a few minutes later they came back.

Then they started slugging it out. I have to be honest, I was reluctant to leave the vehicle.

We put on the sirens and the flashing lights, but they took no notice, so we screwed up our courage, called for urgent assistance and got out into the middle of the melee.

It was all over one bloke, one of our local idiots, who had started something on the dance floor. Whatever he'd done, there were men there who were trying to kill him; I'd have been quite pleased to see the back of him, to be honest, but unfortunately we can't have that. Taking blows all the way, we managed to drag him back into our armoured van and lock the doors, and then they started to try and turn it over.

By now, at least, some assistance had started to arrive – but it was pitiful, under the circumstances. I had one Community officer from a town 20 miles away, a traffic unit with one female officer and, eventually, a dog handler. We had a dozen people here who needed to be arrested, and a PSU would have struggled.

We got out of there before they managed to overturn the vehicle, thank goodness.

'Cheers, mate,' said this idiot.

I just looked at him. *I've just risked my life for you,* I thought, *and you won't be thanking me next week when I'm nicking you because you're the one kicking someone while he's down.*

That was very shocking. The two other officers I was with, one of them went on a long career break afterwards; the other one is still around, and we still talk about how potentially dangerous that night was whenever we meet up.

Nightclubs are usually nasty and dangerous, not least because we're hugely outnumbered and because there are always a lot of very drunk people – many of them women in very short skirts lying in the road with their legs everywhere, which always starts blokes fighting. And the women fight, too. They're vicious and aggressive and they don't come quietly, and if you try to cuff them you can end up like the late PC Tony Mulhall.

PC Mulhall was filmed trying to restrain a woman called Toni Comer after she was ejected from a Sheffield nightclub and needed arresting for criminal damage. CCTV footage of him striking Comer on her upper arm was soon all over the internet, and this was followed by a huge chorus of disgust at his actions. It was presented, almost, as though the officer had hit her for the fun of it, but the fact was that he was attempting to get his handcuffs on her as she tried to kick, punch and twist his testicles. His actions were later found to be an entirely lawful use of force, though not too many of those commentators who had criticised his actions found the space or time to publicise this (or to suggest ways in which violent and unwilling drunks can be arrested without using force). PC Mulhall later died in Snowdonia; at the time of writing, I don't know if the incident, the subsequent stressful investigation and his death are related.

I remember being outside a club one night. It was an under-18s event, and it was massively over-subscribed. The managers had to shut the doors, leaving 300 teenagers queuing, forlornly, to get in. Nowhere else for them to go, mums and dads have dropped them off, and they're all drunk, having necked bottles of alcopops before they came out to get in the mood. They're restless and angry and upset, but the real problem is the local scumbags who have started to show up, like sharks smelling blood.

They want to get in amongst these kids and do them over, nick their money and phones and jewellery, grope the girls and punch the lads. The only thing stopping them is me and one colleague. We are the 'police presence'.

One well-known local thug came over to me as his mates, 20 or more of them, watched from the sidelines. 'Are you scared?' he said.

'Of what?'

'You're on your own.'

I looked over at the club. There were a couple of bouncers at the door. Sometimes you can rely on them for help, but sometimes they're in the country illegally, or they have criminal records, and they don't want to know. The two guys on duty that night, we had arrested them both previously for burglary and car theft, so they were going to be looking the other way if it all came on top.

On the radio, I could hear the other Response officers dealing with assaults and robberies, but they were away in other parts of the town. There was literally no-one else. There wasn't going to be any help for quite some time if things developed.

I turned back to the youth. 'Why would I be scared?' I said. 'Of *you*? I don't think so.' Then I read him his fortune and told him, forcefully, to go away: if you don't become robust and difficult, and potentially worse than they are, you are going to go under. He did go away, sucking his teeth and rolling like a gangsta from the hood instead of a teenaged English muppet, but I have no doubt that if something had happened, and either my colleague or I had gone down, they would have been straight in on us. That's when you're in real trouble, and a serious kicking is the *best* you can hope for. I don't want to sound melodramatic, but with youths jumping on your head, and kicking you in the face, death is a possibility.

You get people puking on your boots, and you can't bend down to wipe it off because you know that as soon as your head drops they're going to attack you. I have been rolling around on the floor fighting with people, trying to restrain them, spraying them, trying to get cuffs on them, with 60 others around me, baying for blood and some of them trying to drag me off or kick me. One night, we broke up a mass brawl between a group of soldiers and a load of drunk civvies. One of the squaddies was on the floor getting his head thoroughly kicked in. I stepped in between him and the attacker to protect him, and my colleague chased after the bloke who'd been doing the kicking. As I stood there over this injured soldier, someone tried to rip my radio off me. He turned out to be quite a senior banker in London, in town for a stag weekend. We wanted to do him for affray, but he had some high-powered barrister who managed to twist the whole thing in knots and the CPS dropped it. But you have to ask, what was this bloke doing trying to take my *radio* away?

Another night, we went to a park to reports of a disturbance. We found 40 people fighting with baseball bats and bottles and hammers and sticks. There were six of us; you look at each other, with your heart pumping and your throat dry and your hands shaking a little, and then you get out and run into the middle of it all. We arrested two people and that took all of us, fighting, literally, for our lives.

I don't know how we got to the position we're in. Obviously, it doesn't help if all your officers are working 9-5 on Neighbourhood Policing, or in various teams, and the 12 people you started the night with are all back at the nick filling in forms. It doesn't help, either, if the people you arrest get released with a PND they never pay. I think it goes deeper than any of that, though, to a cultural change in British society. Some time in the last 10 or 20 years, it became acceptable to attack the police. Violence became endemic. I'd like to fill a police carrier with a couple of MPs, an Assistant Chief Constable, a sociology lecturer or two and four judges and pitch them into the middle of a mass brawl one night.

Other countries still have a handle on this. Attack a police officer in the USA, or Saudi Arabia, or most other countries, and you soon know about it. We had a Captain from the Gendarmes come over on a fact-finding exchange visit one week. Nice bloke. He came out on a Saturday night with us.

After the third or fourth violent incident we'd been to, he said to me, 'These nightclub fights, where you're putting a couple of officers into a group of twelve men throwing fists… why? How?'

'It's just the way it is,' I said.

'What about back-up?'

'Well, in theory we have PSU, but I can't actually get one of those down here – it would take 25 minutes.'

I told him about the girl with the broken nose. He raised his eyebrows at me. 'You know what, in France, if someone hit a Gendarme on the nose, breaking his nose, there would be major repercussions for that individual, for his family, for his employment, everything. The court wouldn't even listen to a defence. They would throw the key away. What would happen here?'

I looked at him. 'Nothing would happen here.'

THE RICH GIRLS ARE WEEPING

I HAVE that nervous feeling you get while trying to drive, read a map, listen to urgent updates coming over the radio and talk to Control on the hands-free. As usual I'm on my way to a serious drama. As a PC a small percentage of the calls I attended were real dramas. Now, all the calls I attend are real dramas.

This is because there is only one uniformed Duty Inspector at a time in F Division, and we are expected to attend the serious incidents personally. The patch is so huge that there is more or less always a serious drama for me to rush to.

Dealing with the incidents does not present me with a problem. I have spent my career to date in Response or specialist uniformed front line policing of one kind or another, and one of my blog correspondents summed it up nicely by saying it is like going to watch the same play each night, only with different actors.

This one is a double fatal road crash on some fast road in the north of the division. Four more are seriously injured.

I'm using the map to see how to avoid the road closures the response teams have already put in. The Controller, who can only stand by in horror, is phoning me every ten seconds with information I already know. It helps him to transfer the tension.

This is the worst kind of drama for us. It's the kind where we have arrived before the other emergency services – specifically, before the paramedics. The officers from the Response team are trying to save lives and calm the shattered relatives who were in the car behind and saw it all.

This has taken place outside a private school for girls. The daughters of the privileged have just returned from the ski slopes of Europe. The snow is not as good this year in Villars-Gryon, and now life will never be as good again because you shouldn't see what they have just seen, and are still seeing, at 15 years of age. Or at any age.

Our people work fast without speaking. They eye their Sergeant as he sweats under his armour. He nods at a car, points at a victim, puts a finger to his lips indicating a distressed witness; all the time, he's on the radio, closing roads, eyes tightly shut as he accesses his mental map of the area.

I arrive. It's my old team. I was their Sergeant once. I'm there to keep a broader perspective and to think strategically about what the division needs to do next. This lasts for as long as it takes me to see the first body.

Everyone is here now. Like some bizarre, colourful ritual; fire and rescue personnel, paramedics, an air-ambulance. The huge rumbling dual carriageway is a silent, deep red-stained strip of concrete. I stand and catch my breath, and behind me, the rich girls are weeping.

PAPERWORK

IN CASE you've missed it, there has recently been much discussion of the amount of paperwork British police officers now have to wrestle with.

Chief Inspector of Constabulary Sir Ronnie Flanagan produced a report on policing which said the amount of form-filling was 'truly staggering'.

Gordon Brown said he was 'looking at how we reduce the amount of paperwork officers have to undertake'.

Even Mr McNulty joined in, revealing that he would be 'investing in new technology to make crime fighting more effective and to save officers' time'. This new technology appears to be, er, Palm Pilots (handheld computers to you and me). So instead of filling in forms that don't actually need filling in, bobbies are now to be bent over in the street trying to type the stuff in using tiny keyboards as the world goes on around them. In McNultyworld, there will never be a gang of yobs jostling and spitting at you, it won't be raining, or snowing, or so sunny that you can't read the screen, the machines will never crash, or get lost, or stolen, or snatched and stamped on, and the batteries will never die just as you reach the end of the longest of the unnecessary forms that are the same as they ever were, only now created in binary code.

So given all this hot air, how have things changed, paperwork-wise?

Well, sadly, it's not good news. Her Majesty's Inspectorate of Constabulary produced a 190 page report (*of course* it was 190 pages) in July this year in which they revealed, shock horror, that front line Sergeants were spending 45% of their time writing. So, tell me something I don't know.

Things have actually got worse, as I'll show you in a minute. But first, let's look at a simple crime from earlier this year – since all these highfalutin promises were made.

It's late one midweek evening in sleepy Ruraltown. For once, nothing much is going on.

Suddenly, Mikey O'Brien shatters the peace and quiet by throwing a brick through the window of Beachtastic Breaks, the travel agents in the High Street.

Mikey is 17 years old and he is off his face on cheap cider. He has numerous previous convictions, and is always being arrested for similar offences (last week it was a bus stop window, and the week before that he ran a screwdriver along the doors of 40 cars in Old Road).

On this occasion, the whole event has been witnessed by a taxi driver, a waiter at the Indian restaurant opposite and two people walking home after a normal night out.

It has also been recorded on the town's excellent CCTV system.

In fact, the CCTV operator is still watching, and he radios through to a police patrol as he sees Mikey lob the brick and then sit down on the pavement outside the shop.

Mikey doesn't run away – why bother? He knows from long experience that nothing will come of this when it finally gets to court.

When the patrol arrives, the first thing he does is admit the whole thing, with a sneer.

'Yep, I done it,' he says. 'Nicci works there, innit, and she's a bitch.'

Nicci is his 'partner' and they have had a row. Somewhere in Mikey's mind, a proper response to this is to smash the window of her place of work.

After a brief but violent scuffle, the patrol arrest him on suspicion of criminal damage and he is taken to Ruraltown police station, booked in to the custody area and interviewed about the offence the next morning, when sober. (We won't go into how long it takes to book him in and conduct the interviews – yet.)

The crime – the actual lobbing of the brick – took far less time to commit than it has taken you to read about it.

A relatively simple job, you might think. Not in the crazy world of British policing.

Here's a list of the paperwork required from the patrol who were unlucky enough to arrive at the scene and arrest Mikey:

– A full, handwritten, pocket notebook entry detailing the incident, the grounds for his arrest and anything he said about the incident.

– A typed arrest statement containing exactly the same information, only in more detail.

– A typed form requesting the release of CCTV tapes. We don't need the CCTV, but we still have to view it. If we don't, Mikey's lawyer will claim it contains evidence exonerating his client of the offence that four people and the CCTV operator saw him commit and to which he has confessed.

– A handwritten custody 'search and booking-in' form.

– A property sheet, listing the contents of his pockets.

– A typed Persistent Offender form, containing the same information as the arrest statement but in a format which prevents 'cut-and-paste' (meaning everything has to be re-entered).

– A typed Young Offender form, containing the same information as above, but in yet another format.

– A typed or verbal 'update' for the computer log held by the Control Room, containing – guess what? – the same information as all of the above.

– A typed Crime Report, with the same information as in the notebook, arrest statement and Young Offender form, but with the details in different fields which, again, cannot be cut-and-pasted.

– At least two MG (Manual of Guidance) forms for the case file, summarising all of the above.

– Witness statements from at least two of the people who saw the whole thing occur.

– A PNC check of all his previous convictions.

– A witness statement from Beachtastic Breaks saying that Mikey didn't have permission to smash their window.

– A print out with a map showing their address.

– An 'intelligence report' about the incident.

– A typed Domestic Violence form (because Nicci was mentioned by Mikey as a reason for his committing of the offence) with all of the same information again, and a complete risk assessment for her, even though she wasn't there at the time. (This risk assessment will take hours and is likely to involve several appointments made with Nicci which will be broken by her when officers arrive at her home to find she's gone out to the pub.)

– The paperwork for Mikey's fingerprinting and DNA record. This will run into at least four pages.

– The Custody Record. This will be at least ten pages long (though admittedly this is completed by the custody team and not by the patrol).

– The brick will have been seized as evidence: there will be the forms and statements to be filled out for that.

– A typed 'update' on the 'Night-time Economy Incident' diary sheets.

– A three-page Community Impact Assessment briefing form for the Inspector (because Mikey is a 'traveller' and therefore his arrest has an 'impact' on the 'community'). As the Inspector, this enables me then to fill out a longer version of the same thing, totalling six pages.

– A handwritten two-page form for the Licensing Officer

discussing where Mikey might have purchased the alcohol he had drunk, again containing all the details of the offence.

There will also be a 'control sample' of the glass from the window for CSI, and associated paperwork, so that the defence can't claim later that he did smash a window, just not *that* window

They then take it to the Sergeant, who looks at it and then fills out *his* paperwork, another huge tranche of forms and writing.

You may think that this is insane for such a simple job. You would be correct.

We collect all of this because we live in fear of Mikey getting to court and saying, 'I didn't do any of this. I just said I did because the police bullied me. Now prove it.'

It's about worst-case scenario policing: every job we go to, we have to assume that it is going to go really bent at trial.

This isn't a triple murder, it's a smashed window. A smashed window, moreover, which Mikey has already admitted breaking.

Imagine what happens if it's slightly more complicated than the incident described.

What if Mikey *doesn't* admit the offence?

Or if there are two offenders, and each blames the other?

What if drugs or a weapon are found in his pockets when he's searched – as they usually are? Mikey will be arrested for those offences, too.

We haven't even talked about nicking him for resisting arrest, or assaulting the police, or about the lengthy booking-in process (we'll get there in a minute).

If any or all of these factors come in to play, the whole process doubles or trebles in size and complexity.

If any of these forms contains a single mistake – even a genuinely unimportant error, like a digit wrong in a postcode, which could easily be corrected by the admin clerk who discovers it – it will be sent back to the arresting officers for correction.

We *need* paperwork. We need to know that the police are not fitting people up, or maltreating them in custody. We need to keep a close eye on domestic violence offenders. I don't know a single police officer who believes otherwise. But do we really need *all* of this? Of these forms, half are duplicating information for the Crown Prosecution Service and the remainder are 'data mining' exercises to satisfy various national or local initiatives and ensure we're hitting centrally-imposed targets.

Meanwhile, as Mikey puts the brick through the window, ratty-looking Kevin Jones is carefully squeezing his skinny frame through an open window in old Mrs Carter's kitchen. He's going to steal her pension book and any cash he can find. It will take the police six hours to get there after Mrs Carter calls the burglary in, sobbing.

BOOKING IN

IF ONLY it were *just* about paperwork.

When Mikey gets nicked, he admits he chucked the brick through the window.

That doesn't mean he 'goes quietly', though.

People like Mikey have an exaggerated sense of their own personal space, much as they like to invade other people's.

You look at him, he swears at you. You touch him, he pushes you away. You tell him he's under arrest, he really kicks off.

He's still kicking off when he gets to the nick.

What happens now?

Well, he has to be booked in.

It's a quiet night, remember: amazingly, there isn't a queue of other offenders ahead of him.

It takes about 10 minutes to calm him down to the point where his handcuffs can be removed. As soon as they're off, he takes a haymaker of a swing at one of the officers who arrested him – we are *always* being attacked in custody* – so he has to be subdued again.

After another 10 minutes, with a couple more officers standing by in case, the cuffs come off again.

Now it's time to take his fingerprints and photograph him. But hang on – didn't we say he was arrested last week for smashing a bus

---

*If you visit http://coppersblog.blogspot.com/2007/08/call-that-knife.html you'll see some dramatic footage of a man attacking a PC with a knife in custody. This is the sort of utterly chilling and quite deadly violence that officers now face every day.

stop window, and the week before that for screwdrivering 40 cars? Yes, we did. But every time anyone is arrested, we have to fingerprint and photograph them (we only have to DNA them once, thankfully).

This might seem mad, but there have been cases where people have appeared in court and their defence has been, 'It wasn't me who was arrested.'

Police constable: 'Yes it was, I recognise you from the other 50 times we've arrested you.'

Defendant: 'No, it wasn't. It was some other geezer claiming to be me.'

PC: 'It was definitely you.'

Defendant: 'Prove it.'

Naturally, the courts won't take the word of two arresting officers and a Custody Sergeant over that of a heroin addict career burglar and car thief.

I suppose we could have him apply one thumbprint on the custody record by way of proof that he was actually arrested. But then... who witnessed the thumbprint being applied? And so on, forever.

So we fingerprint fully and photograph, every time. And some of these people are being arrested three or four times a week.

Sir Ronnie Flanagan and Tony McNulty and anyone who's never been in a custody block and has no common sense will tell you that you can fingerprint and photograph a person in five minutes. Especially with today's high-tech, easy-to-use kit.

Well, you can.

If the kit works, which it very often doesn't.

If the suspect will stand still and stop shouting and swearing and threatening people, which he invariably won't.

If they're not refusing to do it without their solicitor there – and if the solicitor isn't 45 minutes away.

If there's not a queue of six other people ahead of you, all waiting to be booked in, all kicking off, demanding their lawyers, shouting, spitting and threatening the officers.

I'm not a Luddite – I'm not complaining about the technology, or the fact that Ronnie and the chiefs recognise the problems and are trying to solve them. But I'm talking about *reality*. We don't deal with reasonable people, who do as we ask when we say, 'Here you go mate, stick your fingers on there and I'll just press this button.' We deal with people who go, 'F**k off copper... *make* me do it!'

Mikey does this and generally messes around for a bit, but we finally get him done. The process takes an hour.

We go through a few things like which of the 12 dishes (seriously) on our custody menu he would like for tea, would he like satin sheets or just cotton, would he prefer an X Box or a Playstation etc etc?

Then we also have to risk assess him.

The very last thing any police force wants is a death in custody. Partly, this is down to natural human empathy and the fact that we are not intrinsically evil, but mostly it's because it will bring the mother of all headaches crashing down on top of the Chief Constable. The IPCC, the newspapers, the family on the telly demanding enquiries... as I've said before, you don't want any of that. So we ask our detainees a huge number of time-consuming and often quite pointless questions and dutifully tick off the boxes as they reply.

We ask them things like, 'Have you ever self-harmed in the past?'

Or, 'Are you going to harm yourself while you are with us?'

'Do you suffer from mental health problems?'

'Do you have any illnesses or injuries?'

'Do you suffer from any heart condition?'

'Are you on any medication?'

'Have you seen a doctor in the last 24 hours?'

There are 12 pages of these questions. Some of them don't sound all that pointless, and indeed they would not be if we were dealing with rational, normal people who had temporarily veered from the straight and narrow, and now realised the error of their ways and wanted to co-operate. But – and I'm sorry to repeat myself again – we're not dealing with those kinds of people, we're dealing with people like Mikey.

So what happens is this.

We say, 'Are you going to harm yourself while you are with us?'

If they *are* they say, 'No', and when they do we have to explain how we let it happen.

If they *aren't* they say, 'Why?'

So we say, 'Well, you'll get an officer to sit with you and your cell door will stay open while you're with us.'

So they go, 'Oh, yes, in that case I am going to self-harm.'

That's an officer tied up, watching the prisoner, for the rest of the shift.

We say, 'Do you suffer from any heart condition?'

They say, 'Why?'

We say, 'Because if you do we're going to have to bail you straight away.'

So what do you think any regular crook with half a brain says as soon as he comes in? 'Oh, mate... I've got chest pains.'

Unless he's murdered someone, or committed some other really serious offence, that's him out of the nick.

Later, we might ask him to sign a medical consent form so we can check with his doctor that he was telling the truth. No problem: he just refuses to sign the form, and that's us stuffed – there's no way we'll get a warrant to carry out the check, because it doesn't affect the case. We'll end up having to make an appointment for the offender to come down to the police station, and only interview him in half-hour stages. Then he'll develop chest pains in the middle of an interview, and the tapes will have to come out and be sealed in the presence of a Sergeant, and the grit of more delay and hassle and cost is thrown into the machinery.

Remember, there *are no* chest pains and there *is no* heart condition: I've had more than one prisoner with 'chest pains' ask me if he can go outside to have a cigarette while we're waiting for a decision from higher up as to what to do with him. 'Oooh,' I'll say. 'You don't want to be smoking if you're having a heart attack, mate.' It's a small victory, but it cheers me up.

It's very rare that anyone says, 'It's a fair cop, guv,' comes into custody and co-operates, and yet the whole system is predicated on the idea that that's how people *will* behave. In fact, they all know the system, and they all play it.

The first thing the female shoplifter says is, 'I've got two kids under the age of five who are at home alone.'

Yes, she is at risk of getting prosecuted for neglect, but she knows she won't be. We send patrols round to the house and no-one answers the door.

So she says, 'They must have gone to their aunty's, then.'

We say, 'OK, where's that?'

She says, 'Oh, I don't know the address.'

If it was a murder case, clearly we'd launch a major initiative and go and find these kids. But for a shoplifting... we just have to let her go, because if the children *do* exist (and often they don't), and anything does happen to them, we're going to be in a world of trouble. The IPCC are going to drop a ton of bricks on us: She *clearly* told you there were unsupervised children, and yet you kept her in for four hours. *What were you playing at?*

Along with all of this, there is the waiting for other people to arrive: lawyers, appropriate adults (in the case of juveniles or those with mental health problems), interpreters, Mental Health Assessment Teams, social workers, doctors... if they're drunk, or on drugs, or injured, it all takes longer still.

By the time we get through all of this rigmarole, Mikey is finally ready to be interviewed. Then he fires his lawyer and demands another one. When she arrives, he fires her and demands *another*. Eventually, we have to press on without a solicitor – so the interview and our evidence and everything else gets challenged when it finally goes to court.

The British Criminal Justice System is no longer about whether or not Mikey broke the window in Beachtastic Breaks, it's about delay, and how much he can muddy the waters, and what can be done with the procedure.

In the old days, if Dixon nicked Mikey in Dock Green, he would take him down to the station, put him in front of the Custody Sergeant and read out the reasons why he'd been brought in. The Custody Sergeant would make sure he was fit and well, lock him up and Dixon would be back out on the street. The following morning, Mikey would be up before the beak (where he'd get a proper punishment for his behaviour).

I'm not suggesting a return to 'the old days', though there are certainly elements – speedy justice, a penalty to fit the crime – that I like. I can see the need for some of this modern stuff: who wants prisoners hanging themselves in their cells, or dying of heart attacks, however unlikely they may be?

But I would like law-abiding, honest taxpayers, many of whom are fed up with the service they get from us, to understand that – whatever Tony McNulty or Sir Ronnie Flanagan or anyone else says – when we arrest people like Mikey for breaking a window, we are off the streets for a minimum of four hours, and very often we're finished for the entire shift.

THINGS CAN ONLY GET WORSE

I'VE said a few times now that, not only are things not getting better, they're getting worse, despite all the headlines and Green papers and Ronnie Flanagan and Palm Pilots.

If you're a credulous soul, you might believe the Home Office press releases.

OK, here's a list of bureaucracy which has been increased or introduced in the last six months alone:

New Inspector Handover Form

Form used by Duty Inspector to hand over to the colleague who follows him or her. Now more complicated and patronising, and not really designed for the oncoming Inspector – more for the Chief Inspector to monitor the latest mad schemes, and check whether they are being followed. Now contains boxes to tick for each action taken during a shift, despite the fact that there are already 'team reports', a computerised Command and Control system and various Custody logs in existence, which clearly describe everything which happened during a shift anyway. Time to complete? Depends on how busy the shift is, but it could easily take 20 minutes to duplicate the other records.

New, more complicated electronic PDR

Designed to be less complicated, but it fails spectacularly in this due to the annoying fact that once an entry is made it can't be changed without returning the form to the originator (who is probably on Rest Days or Nights). He then has to 'unlock' the form and send it back to you. You make the change and return it to the originator, who agrees the change and forwards it back to you again. You then send it to a Reviewing Officer, who has to go through the whole system just described if he wants to make any changes etc etc. Clearly designed by and for people who just work days, who only have to walk across the corridor to contact each other and who know they'll never have to rush out to an immediate-graded call or be required to work shifts. Time to complete? *Ad infinitum*.

New more complicated and longer MISPER form

This is a new electronic MISPER form which is gigantic in size, and will not let the author progress until they have completed the sections in order. Like the PDR, this cannot be printed and filled out by hand, so the officer has to return to a police station and log on to the server to start the form. If circumstances change or move on, you cannot indicate that fact without returning to every single section of the form one by one. The form contains absolutely no more information than the old one, but it is couched in more politically correct language and repeats itself more often. Time to complete? Depends when/if the person is ever found.

New MG14 for Conditional Cautions

This is a form which needs to be completed by the officer, the offender, the CPS and any appropriate adult who may be involved. It also needs the victim to agree. The form is a duplication of information already contained on the MG5, the arrest statement, the Custody Record and the Prisoner Handover Form. This new national form has to be completed electronically, printed and faxed to CPS, completed by them and faxed back. Then the offender is involved, followed by the victim (at a separate location), then the Custody Sergeant and finally it is finished and placed in the file. Copies go to all the persons mentioned, plus the court. Time to complete? Depends upon how quickly all those parties do their bit and send it back.

New more complicated National Accident Form

There is now a more complicated and longer form for accidents. You have to attach it to numerous extra forms designed to gather statistics for the Government about the causes of crashes and the conditions of the roads and vehicles involved. This is largely a duplication of information already available on the Command and Control system, or in officers' note books, but due to the incompatibility of Government IT systems it all has to be written down by hand and submitted again. Time to complete? Not sure… but more than used to be the case.

New, longer and hideously more complicated TIC Form

The bureaucratic system for taking offences into consideration (Jimmy gets caught smashing one car mirror and 'coughs' to all the others he has done in the street in an attempt to show willing in front of the magistrates for a more lenient penalty) now consists of a hideous form with signature boxes for three different officers to sign as each checks on the other to make sure that the offences are legitimate and correctly written up. Remember, they are not checking the investigation, this is just a bureaucratic system for treble-checking the paperwork involved. Time to complete? If each officer really does check before signing, this can take half a day.

New Quality Assurance Forms

These forms are filled in by Sergeants and Inspectors every week as a kind of Customer Service system. You have to come in from patrol, switch your radio down, and start telephoning a certain number of people who have called the police in the last few weeks to check the service they have had. You then have to fix all the problems, even if they are not within your gift, which means sending loads of emails to people who are probably on Rest Days or Nights etc. At the moment we do ten per month each, but this may rise soon. Time to complete? Depends upon what the public have to say.

New Victim Care Forms

These forms are filled in by Investigating Officers and their Sergeants every day as another kind of Customer Service system. You have to stop investigating crime, switch your radio down, and start telephoning a certain number of people who have been victims in the last few weeks to check the service they have had. You then have to fix all the problems, even if they are not within your gift, which means sending loads of emails to people who are probably on Rest Days or Nights etc. At the moment, we do every single victim. Time to complete? Depends upon what the victim has to say.

New Witness Care Forms (Pre Charge)

These forms are filled in by Investigating Officers and their Sergeants every day as *another* kind of Customer Service system. You have to stop investigating crime, switch your radio down, and start telephoning a certain number of people who have been witnesses in the last few weeks to check the service they are receiving. You then have to fix all the problems, even if they are not within your gift, which means sending loads of emails to people who are probably on Rest Days or Nights etc. At the moment, we do every single witness. Time to complete? Depends upon what *they* have to say.

New Witness Care Forms (Post Charge)

These forms are filled in by civilians working in the Criminal Justice Unit and their Supervisors every day as yet another kind of Customer Service system. More calls, emails, problems to fix and responses required. Time to complete? As above.

Needless to say, there is no evidence whatsoever that a single criminal has been caught despite all of this new paperwork.

In fact, in many cases, officers will have had to abandon pressing work to meet the time-limit targets for completion of all of the above.

MOTORBIKE LIES

YOU know how, in the piece about domestic violence, the court gave more weight to the word of career scumbag and semi-pro wife-beater Tony than mine, and let him off even though I *saw* him beating up Mary outside the supermarket?

Did that surprise you? It surprised me, the first time I gave evidence in a trial.

I know me, and I know I'm honest. I also knew the guy I was giving evidence against was a thoroughgoing liar who was as guilty as sin. Sadly, that doesn't count for much, and it no longer surprises me when criminals with 50 or more convictions for dishonesty are believed and I'm not.

A while back, I was out and about. As Duty Inspector, my job is to control my area and command stuff on the ground as it develops, but I do get more downtime than the bobbies. I very much believe in leading from the front, so when I do get a moment free I'll take myself off to the crime hot spots in our area and see what's happening. Sure enough, on this particular night, as I was trawling through one of the outlying estates, I heard an immediate-graded emergency call come out to an incident a quarter of a mile away. It was confused, but it seemed as though there were three people, two men and a woman, fighting in a country lane just outside town. Some criminal damage had happened to something or other; one of the men had called us about that and, while he was on the line, it had all 'gone off'. The operator could hear a major disturbance going on in the background. As I was right on top of it, I called in and said I'd take it. I stuck the lights and sirens on and was there within a couple of minutes.

As I drove into the lane, with other units responding as well, I was confronted with a scene of mayhem.

In front of me are the three of them, the woman with a bottle in her hand, all trading massive blows. Lying down by the side of the road is a motorbike, and in a ditch, half on its side, there's a people carrier. Lots of shouting, screaming and swearing.

I get out of my car and jump straight into the middle of it, hoping they'll see sense when a copper joins in. They don't. In fact, they're so spittingly angry that they don't even acknowledge that I'm there, I've just become part of the fight, and I'm not strong enough to separate the three of them. Now I'm being hit and jostled, too. I press the red button on my radio – if you're in danger and you need back-up but haven't got time to talk, this puts you on 'ambient listening' for 15 seconds and your colleagues can hear what's going on. 'Put the bottle down,' I'm yelling. 'Stop fighting.' All the sort of things I need the other officers to hear so they get the picture.

Other units arrive, and the woman breaks off, goes over to the motorbike and starts kicking it, hitting it with the vodka bottle and scratching it with her car keys.

The two men are still trying to fight each other. Out comes the spray. One of them is trying to head butt me, but I spray him straight in the face and luckily he goes down. My colleagues all weigh in and everyone gets nicked. The woman is still screaming and shouting, and is absolutely pissed out of her mind.

I grab her and, finally, she starts to quieten down. 'Where did those keys come from?' I ask.

'Over there.' She points to the people carrier.

'Is that your vehicle? How did it get in that ditch?'

'I f**king put it there, what do you think?'

'Right. You're nicked for drink drive, affray and criminal damage.'

The two men were also charged with violent disorder or affray.

What had happened was, she'd been meeting her lover in this lane so they could have sex in the people carrier – I mean, who said romance was dead? Her husband had got wind of this and turned up on his motorbike. Upon finding them together he had lost his rag and the trouble had started.

It went to court. I stood up in the box, swore the oath, looked the magistrates in the eye and said these people were kicking lumps out of each other when I arrived. I told them to stop, they wouldn't, and I had to spray one of them, blah, blah, blah.

And they were found not guilty of everything.

How the hell did that happen?

Well, having patched things up behind the scenes and realising they're now in this together, they all lied through their teeth.

There wasn't a fight, we were just messing about.

Yes, this is my motorbike but there's no damage to it – and even if there is, she's allowed to damage it because she's my wife and I told her she could if she wanted to.

No, I didn't drive the people carrier there while drunk, and put it in the ditch, I drove it there and then I had a drink. In fact, it wasn't 'in the ditch', it was just a bit badly parked. I'm not a great parker – is that illegal?

The drink drive, fair enough, that was a bit of a wing and a prayer: I didn't see her drive, she said she hadn't admitted to it, and if she had she was drunk while she was doing so.

But the affray – I had arrived and *seen* everyone fighting with my own eyes. I'd been in the middle of it.

I am a police officer with a lot of years' experience and a totally unblemished record. No complaints against me ever have been found.

What does a not guilty verdict mean?

The CPS prosecutor – a great guy, actually – told me afterwards that he had really pushed it but that the magistrates had felt it was my word against theirs and so... well, you understand how it is, Gadget.

'So I'm lying?'

'No, there just isn't enough evidence.'

'No, there's my evidence. They are saying that I am lying and that it didn't happen. I've stood in court and said that these three people were fighting, and the magistrates have said, "We don't believe you."'

Maybe they think I have some strange agenda against this trio that I have never met before?

I said, 'What about the tapes of the 999 call, where there is a massive disturbance clearly going on in the background?'

He said they were ruled inadmissible because of some technicality over the way that they were copied back at Headquarters: the statement was signed by the same person who did the copying, or something like that.

I said, 'What? Are they saying that we made those tapes up, too? That we got some digital engineers, recorded these people's voices and mixed them all up and pretended that there was a disturbance going on when really there wasn't? Are they saying that the police are going to do all this to fit up some drunken lovers meeting to have sex in a people carrier? Have I missed something? Is this Watergate?'

'It's not like that,' he said.

This is a real departure. I know about the Birmingham Six, but that was bloody years ago, and I wasn't involved. There is no police corruption in cases like this. Police officers don't wrap themselves up in lies and conspiracies about low-life beating each other up, because why would we? Risk our jobs and pensions and two years inside with all the nonces in the special wing to fit up some woman caught shagging her boyfriend?

It's very hard to take. There is a sudden realisation that the court is looking at some thug in exactly the same way they're looking at you, despite the fact that he has a five-year history of nasty, violent scummery and you're blemishless.

Some cops are now being fitted with cameras, so that magistrates and juries can see stuff with their own eyes. But where does that end? It will end, I can tell you, in a total devaluation of oral evidence: if the camera doesn't get the images, or the battery fails, or the video is incorrectly uploaded, annotated or signed for, that will just provide utterly guilty defendants with another get-out.

DEFENCE LAWYERS

THE thing you grow to understand about the Criminal Justice System is that it is entirely misnamed. As the story above shows, it has very little to do with delivering justice to criminals or their victims. It's not about finding out the truth, it's *not* about deciding guilt and it's *absolutely* not about punishing the guilty.

It's far more like a combination of Charades and Monopoly – lots of people pretending to be what they're not, a huge element of chance and, occasionally, someone is unlucky enough to go to jail.

Among the key players in this game are defence lawyers: they know the rules inside out, they control the dice and they never really lose.

Some of them are quite upfront about all of this, and their honesty is refreshing, if nothing else.

A month or so back, I had two people in custody for a very serious armed robbery. Because it was such a heavy case, with other outstanding offenders and threats to life to deal with, we had authority to hold them incommunicado. This means that we don't have to allow our suspects their phone call, tell anyone we have them in custody or give them immediate access to a solicitor, and it requires a Superintendent's authority. (On my authority, we can 'delay intimation', which means they don't get to tell anyone they are in custody but they can have a solicitor.)

In the middle of the night, the custody phone went. It was a lawyer.

'I am phoning because I want to represent people who I believe you have in custody,' he said.

'I'm sorry,' I said. 'I'm not going to discuss who I have in custody with you or anyone else.'

'It's alright,' he said. 'The family have told me. They were there when they were nicked.'

'Really?' I said. 'As I say, I am not going to discuss with you or anyone else who I have in custody. All I can say is that if there is anyone in custody who requires your services we will get in touch as and when you're required.'

He laughed and said, 'Well, it was worth a try.'

'How does this work then,' I said. 'Are you one of those ambulance chasers?'

'No,' he said. 'The family called me.'

He was a reasonable chap and I decided to have a chat with him. I said, 'How can you represent really serious criminals?'

He said, 'I'm not going to try and justify it to you. Pretty much all the people who I represent are absolute s**ts. They are lying, cheating, evil, violent, nasty scum who would turn on me as quickly as they would turn on you. To be honest, mostly, I despise them. Any normal person would. But they still have the right to a hearing. We have a system and it needs people like me to make the wheels turn.'

'But if you get them off, how do you sleep at night?'

'Look. If you're going home tonight and you call in at the pub and you have a few pints, and you get nicked leaving and you're over the limit, and suddenly you're going to lose your job and your pension, and everyone is going to know you're an ex-copper who's a drink driver, who are you going to ring? And if you ring me, and I tell you that they haven't filled in the forms properly, and you can walk away from this, and you might even get some money out of them... think about it. Are you seriously telling me that you wouldn't ring me and you would not be glad to hear that?'

'I don't drink and drive,' I said. 'But if I did I suppose I'd ring you... anyone would.'

'Anyone would,' he said. 'You're right. I'd want legal representation, you would, your Chief Constable would, and hardcore criminals are no different. That's how I operate.'

Of course, just because one might use errors in the system to evade a drink-drive charge does not mean the system is working properly – it means the reverse.

Imagine a man wanders down your street tomorrow, smashes the passenger window in your car and steals the briefcase you have carelessly left lying in the passenger footwell.

Luckily, a police patrol are nearby and they see it all happen. They arrest him, but he's drunk and bolshy and he attacks the two officers first, giving them each a black eye.

Now, what do you imagine the law has in store for him once he gets to court?

The first thing that will happen is that his lawyer and the CPS will put their heads together and do a deal.

'OK,' says the defence brief. 'We'll plead guilty to the theft as long as you drop the criminal damage and reduce the assault-police to a public order offence – an obstruction, or a drunk and disorderly. If you don't agree to this, we're going to contest all of it, and we'll take you all the way.'

The CPS guy has a think. What he has in front of him is someone who is prepared to cough to theft and a public order offence, which is two ticks in two boxes; if it goes to trial, it will take more time and money and the guy could get off. Plus, back in the office he has an in-tray groaning under the weight of another 150 similar ongoing cases. It would be nice to clear this one.

'Alright,' he says. 'We'll do it.'

Straight away, this sends an interesting message out to criminals. If you're going out stealing from cars, don't bother quietly feeling a few door handles until you find one that's unlocked – just smash your way in to the first one you fancy, because you ain't going to pay separately for that. And if the cops catch you, why not have a swing at them, too? You won't pay for that, either.

So the two sides appear in the Magistrates Court. Standing in front of the magistrates is a thoroughly contrite and respectful man in a shirt and tie admitting he nicked a briefcase from a car and talking about his heroin addiction and the fact that his girlfriend has just had a new baby.

'Did the person get the briefcase back in one piece?' they say.

'Yes, Your Worship, the police arrived in time.'

'So nothing is actually missing?'

'No.'

'Right, we will deal with this by way of a conditional discharge. If you are found guilty of stealing anything within six months, we reserve the right (which they never seem to use) to take this offence into consideration when we are sentencing you for that one.'

Result: one violent, drunken scumbag walks out of court, grinning. As he passes the arresting officers in the corridor, he grins at them, gives them the finger and says he hopes their kids die of cancer. Then he goes out and does it again and again and again.

As I said, it's not about the truth, it's not about justice and it's definitely not about punishment.

I know I complain about magistrates a lot, but to be fair to them they don't know the full facts – that he blacked the coppers' eyes, and smashed the car window. So, for once, we can give them a pass.

The defence solicitor, though, she knows the full details, doesn't she? She's seen the police officers' statements and she knows the car was smashed up and she knows the guy was drunk and she knows he did it, because he's admitting the rest. I might not be able to *prove* she knows it, and she'll never admit it, but she does.

Now she's watching him walk out of court, and she feels good about that.

I feel a lot of contempt for that kind of defence lawyer.

I speak to a lot of them in the course of my working life. 'It is a game, you're right,' said one I came across recently. 'I don't care whether he's guilty or not, that's not my issue. My job is to represent him to the best of my ability. If I have someone who's bang to rights, I tell him to keep quiet, say nothing, not to me, not to the police. *Let's find out what evidence they've got*, I'll say. *That's what it's about. It's not about whether you've done it, it's about whether they can prove it.*'

I often say to lawyers like that, 'Can I – without wishing to be rude or judgmental – make a suggestion, that you seriously need to reset your moral compass?'

They tend to bridle at that, and start talking about miscarriages of justice, and the process and the system and PACE, but that's not the truth, that's smoke and mirrors. There is no way that hundreds of thousands of low-level scumbags, who make other people's lives hell for decades on end, should survive and thrive on the back of the actions of a few bent or stupid coppers in the 1970s. It isn't good enough.

REVIEWING

MOST of the contact I have with solicitors nowadays comes when I'm 'reviewing' a suspect in custody. Reviewing him means checking that he is being fed and watered, is reasonably comfortable, has legal representation if he wants it, and so on. We carry out several reviews according to a schedule laid down by PACE and, after 24 hours, we have either to release him, or charge him, or go to court for an extension, which requires a Superintendent's authority.

The idea is that the Inspector is independent – he's not involved in the investigation and his arse is on the line if there's any jiggery pokery. The reviews normally take place in an interview room with a solicitor present.

Not long after my promotion to Inspector, I went in to carry out a six-hour review. I sat down with matey boy and his lawyer and started running through the usual questions about how he had been treated, and then we came to the part where we discuss, briefly, the progress of the case. If the suspect is in for vandalising a bus stop or nicking a loaf of bread, this usually takes about 10 seconds. However, it's very different when you have someone who's in real trouble.

This particular guy had stabbed another man and nearly killed him. To make matters worse (for the defence) we had pretty much everything we needed – forensics, eye witnesses, the weapon covered in prints, that sort of thing.

Faced with that scenario, his solicitor wasted no time in playing the only card he had.

'My client has not been interviewed,' he said. 'He has been here for six hours now and I want you to write that down.'

Sometimes at this point I say, sarcastically, 'Ah! So you've got no case, then?' But this guy smelled like trouble, so I said, 'I've been up to CID. I have spoken to the investigating officer and I am satisfied that the investigation is going as quickly as possible. They need to gather more evidence, there is some CCTV to look at and...'

The solicitor cut me off. 'That is not true,' he said. 'I know that there are detectives out having dinner at this very moment.'

'Well,' I said. 'As a reviewing officer, I am happy that they are moving as quickly as they can. But I'll write down that you are not happy.'

At this, he got up, left the room and started shouting at the rest of custody. 'This Inspector has called me a liar in here,' he said. 'This Inspector has accused me of lying, and I want witnesses.'

The Custody Sergeant came down the corridor. 'Is there a problem, guv?'

'I don't think so,' I said.

'You,' said the solicitor, pointing at him. 'Who are you?'

'I'm the Custody Sergeant.'

'Well, sit down and start writing.'

'No thanks,' said the Sergeant. 'I don't think I will.'

'He is calling me a liar,' he said, pointing at me. 'I told him that there are CID officers at dinner and he says that there aren't. He is accusing me of lying, and I have never been called a liar in 30 years' practice.'

'Hold on just a moment,' I said. 'I didn't call you a liar. I didn't even say that they were not at dinner. I said I was happy with the way the case was going. That may include the fact that officers who have been working for 14 hours solid have gone for a meal break.'

His tone tightened a notch, and he started demanding to see the Superintendent.

'Can I just have a quick word with you outside, guv?' said the Custody Sergeant. This is a man with a lot more service than I have, and it turned out he knew our histrionic friend well. 'This guy always does this,' he said. 'His client has got a big prison sentence hanging over him, so what he's trying to do now is to create a massive disturbance in here that rattles us and flusters us. Then we might not fill out a few forms correctly, we might not carry out our procedures properly, that sort of thing. He's going to make complaints about treatment in custody, which will have to be reviewed. He wants to make sure that you are now the subject of an investigation so that the next time you do a review you do it softer.'

I said, 'How do you know all that?'

He said, 'He used to come to Longtown a lot when I was Custody Sergeant there. We've had him thrown out of the nick by the Superintendent (which we can do under PACE) more times than I can remember.'

'Thanks,' I said, and went back into the interview room. 'Do you recognise that Sergeant?' I said. 'You might know him from Longtown?'

The solicitor looked at me and hesitated. 'I don't think that's relevant.'

'You are trying now to influence the investigation by being difficult, and you know what I am going to do if this carries on.'

He started huffing and puffing. 'This is ridiculous. I am writing all this down.'

'One more comment like that,' I said, 'and I will fetch the Superintendent, just like you've asked me to. And then you are leaving, and your client will not be represented by you any more.'

Instantly, his attitude changed. 'Fine,' he said. 'Whatever you say.' Just like that.

Spin back a moment. On the *other* side of all of this, a few miles away in an intensive care bed, is a man with a wife and two kids who has been stabbed and is currently fighting for his life. And the lawyer *knows* all this, *and* he knows his client did it, too. He's not interested in the truth, though. He's just thinking, *There are too many witnesses, there's too much blood, there's too much forensic evidence... f**k the case, we'll go for the procedure.*

He just wants to win the game and make his money. Where is the moral basis for that?

I understand the right of everyone to have a fair trial and a defence, but that shouldn't be based on lies, it should be about what actually happened. Justice should not be about tactics and no comment and finding out which side has the cleverest lawyer and digging around for technical procedural mistakes.

EBAY GUM

APOLOGIES for the truly awful pun, but eBay really would gum up policing in this country if we allowed it to.

I spent time as a Neighbourhood Sergeant in one of our towns, and the four worst estates in the county came under my purview. My team and I knew everyone on them.

One day, I was reading a report which combined some statistics from the National Audit Office, the Inland Revenue, the Work and Pensions Department and various housing and benefit agencies. They had come together and done some national research on income, and they had discovered that one in five households in Britain were living way beyond their apparent means. That is, their savings, credit, benefits and earned money were not enough to support their lifestyles. So how were they supporting them?

Next time I was out and about on one of those awful estates, this came back to me. I started looking at the houses. It would go, rough house (washing machine in the garden), rough house (sofa in the garden, door boarded up), immaculate house – two four-wheel drives, nice red Tarmac drive, white fence posts, gnomes around a windmill, criss-cross leaded windows going all the way up, you could eat off the front door, satellite dish. And when you go into these sorts of places, there's a huge plasma TV with about 40 speakers giving you cinema-quality surround sound, the wife is dripping in jewellery and designer gear, the kids are wearing the latest Nike trainers and Man U or Chelsea kits at £80 a pop, and you think: *He's on the dole and she's on incapacity benefit. I can't afford to live like this.*

They're not even quiet about it. On these estates, it's three or four out of five who are at it – it only looks like one in five when you go nationally and include people like you and me.

There are an enormous number of people living very good lives on the basis of crime, and they're not all what you might describe as obvious scumbags. Before we had kids, my wife was a physiotherapist. She used to come home and say, 'My colleague Katie says her boyfriend has got a car stereo going... are you interested?'

Or you'd be stopped in the street outside your house and offered a new video camera which was 'an unwanted birthday present, mate'.

That was then. Now, you don't even have to risk walking up to a stranger with your hooky gear – just stick it on the internet.

Or, better yet, stick stuff on the internet that you don't even have.

If someone sells you a £1,000 TV for £199 and it never arrives, because he never really had the TV in the first place, that is a fraud.

But if he lives 500 miles away, what can we do? We can – and will – send the details on to the local force but that's about it. If they're based in another country, forget it.

Ebay fraud is not desirable. It's not good. But I take the view that people need to be more careful. If you think you've got a fantastic bargain, maybe there's a reason why. If you buy stuff at a car boot, you don't expect the police to sort it out for you if it goes wrong. What's the difference?

NO COMMENT

POLICING is still one of the great jobs (I've had a few, so I've got perspective), but as any police officer will confirm it can be terribly frustrating.

Not all that long ago, before I rose to the dizzy heights of Inspector, I went to the scene of an accident.

Someone had driven a stolen VW Golf across a roundabout and into a set of railings, trashing both the railings and the car and taking out a bed of busy lizzies and (almost) a pedestrian on the way.

Driver and passenger promptly got out and legged it, as any right-thinking person would surely do nowadays, leaving behind a small amount of cannabis resin, a packet of Rizlas and a half-drunk bottle of rum.

We arrived a matter of minutes later. After doing our best to tidy things up and get the car out of the way, I wandered over to a group of kids who had gathered nearby and were now hovering around and watching, slightly shiftily.

'Excuse me, guys,' I said. 'Did any of you see this accident happen?'

They all said they'd seen nothing, so I took their names, thanked them and moved on.

The following day, we started doing a bit of house-to-house in the area.

Amazingly, one guy had seen the whole thing happen from his front window.

'I don't suppose you could identify the driver?' I said.

He looked at me in surprise. 'Well, you spoke to him,' he said.
'When?'

'When you walked over to talk to those kids... he was there then.
The gothic-looking one, in the long black coat.'

Better *still*, he knew the youth's name – Darren Johnson – and
address. So we went round to the house, knocked on the door and
there he was.

I said, 'Hello Darren, remember me?'

'No.'

'I think you do. I spoke to you at the scene of that car accident
yesterday.'

'No.'

I arrested him, and we took him back to the police station and
locked him up. Then we set about getting all of our ducks in the
prescribed row. We'd already got pretty much everything: his prints
from the car, some CCTV showing him hurrying down High Street,
the witness. Then we got his girlfriend – the passenger – down to the
nick and she gave him up straight away.

'Darren was driving,' she said. 'When he crashed the car he told
me to run away.'

'Was he drunk?'

'Yes, he was.'

So far, so good. Then it started getting a little more complicated.
As we prepared to make disclosure to Darren's solicitor prior to
starting our interview, mum arrived at the police station.

'It's about my Darren,' she said. 'He's got serious mental health
issues so you can't possibly interview him about that crash. He
wouldn't have known what he was doing.'

'Who says he's got mental health issues?' I said.

'His doctor.'

'OK. Can you just give me the name of his doctor, then?'

I wanted to find out whether this was the 'Oh-no-I've-done-
something-wrong-so-I'd-better-be-mad'-type madness, of which we
see a lot, or the 'I'm-actually-really-mad'-type madness.

We bailed Darren until I could speak to the doctor.

I finally got hold of him a week or two later. I brought Darren
back down to the nick, stuck him in a waiting room and spoke to the
doc on the phone.

'This lad Darren,' I said. 'We've got him in at the moment over an incident. Can you tell me his state of mind?'

'Oh yes, he's quite mad.' (I'm paraphrasing slightly.)

'Right. Can you tell us a bit more about that?'

'No.'

'No?'

'No.'

'Why not?'

'That would break his medical confidence.'

'Well, I don't want to know the ins and outs of it, I just want to know how long he's been mad.'

'I can't tell you that.'

'Is it the type of madness that might make him… say… crash a car?'

'I can't tell you that.'

'You see, we think he's just using madness as an excuse since he crashed the car.'

'I can't comment on that.'

More on helpful doctors in a minute.

I rebailed Darren and arranged to have him looked at by a Mental Health Assessment Team. That takes several weeks to whistle up; when I eventually got them sorted out, it all followed a depressingly familiar pattern.

Their first question: 'Has he committed a criminal offence?'

'Yes.'

'Oh, we don't do that. Was he drunk at the time?'

'Yes, we think so.'

'Oh, we don't do that, either.'

Some time later – after more bailings and prevarication – we decided we would press ahead so long as we could satisfy ourselves that he was fit to be interviewed. To that end, I got him back into the police station and asked our own custody nurse to give him the once-over.

The nurse came down and sat in a room with Darren for an hour or so, asking him questions and so on. Then she came back out.

'I don't know whether he is mad or not,' she said.

'Why not?'

'He won't talk to me or answer any of my questions.'

'Is he fit to be interviewed?'

'Yes.'

'Can I have that in writing?'

'No.'

'Why not?'

'Because he never spoke to me. I can't fill the form out unless he spoke to me.'

Aaarrrgggh.

By now, about nine months had gone by. (Nowadays, because there are time limits in respect of bail, the CPS would probably have binned this job if I couldn't nail it within seven days.) Remember, we're talking about someone who was drunk and totalled a car; it's serious, but he's not the bloke who planned the Brinks Mat job.

I decided to take the view that, whether or not he was mad, we were going to interview him and see what we got.

We arranged for his mum and dad to sit in as appropriate adults (we didn't have to do this, he wasn't a juvenile, but there were these potential mental health issues to think about), together with someone with mental health expertise, and we all waited while Darren had a conflab with his lawyer.

Then, *finally*, we were ready to go.

The interview started.

'Darren, were you driving this vehicle on this day in Ruraltown?'

'No comment.'

I looked at everyone. 'Wait a minute,' I said. '*Please* don't tell me that after virtually a year, and after I've spoken to your doctor and I've run the case past every expert in the county I can get hold of, you're just going to go *No comment*.'

The lawyer looked at me. 'I don't know whether we're going to go No comment,' she said, sharply. 'That depends on what you ask.'

'I am going to ask him whether he crashed the car when he was drunk.'

That's the only question and it's a simple question, too. Yes or no. 'No comment' isn't 'No', it's 'No comment'.

The solicitor asked, 'What else do you want to interview my client about?'

I said, 'Failure to stop after a collision where there is damage to the roadside furniture. In other words, he smashed into some railings and knocked a lamp post over and it has cost £15,000 to fix it all.'

She said, 'That damage was there already.'

'No, it wasn't.'

'How do you know that the damage wasn't there already? Have you got a survey of the roadside furniture in the town prior to my client's accident?'

'It's on CCTV looking fine, just before the car arrives. You've seen the CCTV.'

She wasn't happy with that. I moved on. 'Darren,' I said. 'I spoke you at the scene and asked you if you had anything to do with it. You said No. What do you say to that?'

'I'm mad.'

'OK. Why did you give the police false details?'

'Well, I'm mad.'

It continued in this frustrating fashion for some time, the lawyer manoeuvring him around different procedural areas to try and get him off, with a No comment here and a No comment there. She succeeded, too, to an extent: we pinned the vehicle theft and driving without a licence on him, but the rest of it – drink-driving, aggravated vehicle taking, perverting the course of justice – he got away with. The drugs in the car? Not his – planted there by someone immediately after the accident. The alleged madness? Never raised in court (I can't prove this, but I suspect that was because they knew that the bench would bail him and get reports, and that might raise problems for the defence). So he pleaded to all the minor stuff and walked out of court, smirking.

If that's what we want from the justice system, fine. If we want kids to be able to steal cars and almost kill people with them while drunk and not be punished for it, OK. If it's *really* the job of a defence lawyer to string things out as long as possible, play the 'No comment' card at tactical points and try to bargain down the reality of crime to the point where offenders receive joke punishments that bear no relation to their crimes, good. Just so long as we know that's what we're all signed up to.

HELPFUL DOCTORS
(AND A&E RECEPTIONISTS)

SOMETIMES you wonder whether we're all on the same side, we few, we happy few, we band of public sector emergency workers.

Ambulance crews, on the whole, are great. The fire crews are pretty good, too (and we like the overtime when they go on strike and we have to pick up the pieces alongside the Army).

The nurses and doctors in A&E are mostly brilliant.

But hospital admin people and managers can be a different kettle of fish.

The other afternoon, one of my PCs – Sarah Carlisle – was overcome by noxious fumes during a building search. She went to our custody nurse, who did what custody nurses always do and sent her straight to the local A&E at Ruralshire General Hospital. I could have made that decision myself, but let's not lose the chance to spend a load of taxpayers' money on yet another layer of bureaucracy. At least someone was probably promoted off the back of deciding that policy.

When PC Carlisle arrived at A&E (with another officer, because it's not safe to leave us alone when we're injured) she was triaged and told to wait. 'It will be about two hours,' said the lady behind the counter.

That's par for the course for most people, I guess, and I'd have no complaints if Sarah had injured herself at home, off duty, but there's supposed to be a protocol in place which says that front line Response officers will be treated as soon as possible. It's probably annoying for members of the public sitting waiting with broken thumbs or split lips to see us jump the queue, but there's a certain logic to it: the quicker they get us stitched up, the quicker we can be back outside the nightclubs waiting to be bottled over the head again. If Sarah and her colleague spend two or three hours off the streets, that, in itself, increases public danger.

Reasoning that there was little chance of seeing a doctor this side of the Early Turn, PC Carlisle discharged herself rather than wait.

I sent her back to the custody nurse, who refused to see her because the original assessment had been for a hospital appointment and she didn't want to take the risk of treating her. In the end, we treated her ourselves by getting her home and ringing the on-call doctor service.

Later, I phoned up and spoke to the A&E manager about the situation. I was politeness itself and in return I received a large dose of bad attitude. Several members of the shift watched this incident with interest.

Luckily, we don't adopt the same stance when the staff at A&E press their panic button on a Saturday night, which they often do.

A month or so back, I went up there on an immediate graded call. Some simple-minded hooligan had gone in, off his face on Bargain Booze lager, and started attacking people. We pulled up outside; through the window, I could see a security guard curled up on the floor, getting a good shoeing. We raced inside, but chummy had seen us coming and had legged it out of the other exit and into a lurid green hatchback. We hurled ourselves after him but he disappeared in a cloud of gravel, exhaust fumes and drum 'n' bass.

We raced back inside and I ran up to the receptionist.

'That bloke who just beat up your security guard and ran off,' I said. 'Do you know him?'

'Yes,' she said.

'Great,' I said. 'Can you just give us his name and address?'

'Oh, I can't do that,' she said. 'I need to respect his medical confidentiality. He came into A&E as a patient.'

'*What?*' I said. ' You must be *joking*? Your security guard's got a broken nose. This idiot has terrified the staff and patients in here. We need to get to him now, before he gets all the forensics off him or kills someone or leaves the country.'

'I'm sorry,' she said, rather primly. 'I have to respect the patients' privacy.'

At times like this, I wonder if I'm mad, or she is, or the whole world is. I understand the point of medical confidentiality, but who are we protecting here, and why? Surely, there comes a time when you behave in such a way that you forego your medical confidentiality for the greater good? We're going to get a warrant anyway – all the delay does is increase the likelihood of a not guilty verdict in six months' time. And this woman *knows* the guy is guilty because she *just saw him beat up her mate with her own eyes* – her mate, by the way, who is only there in the first place to protect her, and who took the shoeing she would otherwise have got.

169

This kind of jobsworthiness is not confined to A&E receptionists.

The other day, I booked on duty and heard that four officers had gone to arrest a shoplifter who had been caught stealing whisky from an off-licence. As they arrived, he'd smashed a bottle and held it to the face of the bloke behind the counter. The four officers went in, rescued the terrified assistant and had a massive fight with the shoplifter. During the fight, he bit them and kicked and punched and head butted them, and bit them some more… it was a nightmare, but, eventually, they managed to nick him.

They arrived in custody with this maniac, all covered in blood, his and theirs.

In custody, as we have seen, we go through a laborious risk assessment as part of the process of booking-in our customers.

As part of the risk assessment, the suspect was asked whether he had any illnesses or injuries.

'Yes,' he said. 'I've got hepatitis.'

'A, B or C?'

'C.'

That's a particularly nasty form of a very unpleasant and possibly fatal illness. The officers had all been bitten by him, and his blood had mingled freely with their own; the potential for them also now being infected was not insignificant.

They were all taken straight to hospital for initial tests and seen by a doctor. He explained that they wouldn't know for some time whether they had acquired the condition. Some drugs were prescribed, and they all went off sick and home to bed.

It fell to me as Duty Inspector to see if there was anything I could do about this.

The first thing that crossed my mind was that the prisoner could be lying – either to cause maximum distress to us, or to ensure that, as someone with a serious illness, he was treated with kid gloves. So I rang the suspect's doctor.

'Hello, sir,' I said. 'Four of our officers have been bitten by your patient… can I just ask, does he have hepatitis?'

'I can't tell you that.'

'Why?'

'Medical confidentiality.'

'Yes, but this is a public protection issue. We need to know whether our people are at serious risk.'

'Get a warrant.'

Get a warrant?

I'm talking here about a group of young male and female officers – could be you, or your sons and daughters – who went to work that morning to do their job and keep the public peace and who now face a hellish wait to see if they're going to develop a potentially deadly disease. Their professional and personal lives are suspended for the next however long, and this doctor – who is supposed to have sworn an oath to protect people and save lives – won't even give me a steer as to the truth of the matter. My officers are sitting at home thinking, *Am I going to die? Will I see my kids grow up?* Again, we all need to know that our medical confidentiality will generally be respected, but if someone voluntarily decides to go to the next level and attack people using an illness as a weapon, in my opinion we ought to be able to say, Screw your confidentiality.

I put the phone down in some disgust and went down to the shoplifter's cell.

'Right,' I said. 'You've bitten my officers and they now think they're going to get hepatitis. That's not very nice, is it? Do you want to be helpful at this point and tell me whether you've really got it?'

'I have,' he said.

'Well, look,' I said. 'How about you have a test today for us?'

He agreed, reluctantly, and signed a medical consent form. We drove him down to the hospital, and blood was taken and tested for everything – the various hepatitises, HIV and all the other nasty little STDs and other viruses these people are often carrying.

Result: negative for everything, and I was able to ring the four officers and tell them they were in the clear.

I don't know what job you do. It probably has its share of risk and unpleasantness, because these things are not confined to the police. But it's not likely to be a job where maniacs routinely bite you and threaten you with broken bottles; I don't think we (the police, generally) get across how commonplace this kind of thing is for us, and I think doing so might counterbalance some of the flak we get for speed cameras, occasional officiousness and stupidity and the odd bent bobby.

SCALES OF JUSTICE

HUNTING detections to improve our crime figures is, slowly but surely, turning our natural supporters against us.

The ordinary people who make up the bulk of the British population are being criminalised in ways I never thought possible, all in the mad pursuit of ticked boxes and targets met.

The other day I was down in custody doing a review when an incredible disturbance suddenly erupted down the corridor in one of the interview rooms.

I listened for a minute or so and then thought I'd better pop down there and see what was going on.

I found the Custody Sergeant being screamed at and slapped around the head by a perfectly normal-looking woman in her early 40s. By 'normal-looking' I meant that she wasn't drunk, tattooed, dressed like a street prostitute, multiply pierced or clearly insane. She looked like a teacher, or an off-duty hospital matron: these have not been, hitherto, the sort of people who go loopy and assault police Sergeants inside the station.

After a swift double-take, I approached her and held her wrists.

'What on earth do you think you're doing?' I said. 'Sit down and stop assaulting that officer.'

At that, she spat in my face and shouted at me to f**k off.

We can't have that, so two PCs grabbed her and arrested her for assault. Then she *really* kicked off. We dragged her bodily through custody, thrashing and screaming past a row of open-mouthed solicitors, other prisoners, the custody nurse and people who were taking fingerprints, into a cell, where she started shouting and kicking the door.

When the dust had settled, I turned to the Custody Sergeant. 'What on *earth* was that all about?' I said.

'Well,' he said. 'I've just had to go and give her some bad news about her 15-year-old son.'

Let's rewind to the beginning of the story.

What had happened is this.

This lady, Josie, was one of those ordinary people I mentioned. She was estranged from her husband, but was struggling hard to bring their boy up. That is never easy for a single mum, especially for one with a teenaged lad, but she was doing her level best. Hardworking, steady job, not the slightest sniff of a criminal record. No record for her boy or husband, either.

The only blot on her horizon is her son Jason's low-level use of cannabis.

She's tried using her own powers of persuasion on him, and she's tried enlisting the help of teachers at his school, but boys will be boys and she is getting nowhere.

So she makes the *huge* mistake of calling us. 'My son's using cannabis,' she says. 'The school can't stop it, I can't stop it. Can you send a local bobby round to give him a telling off and tell him what's going to happen if he doesn't pack it in?'

A Neighbourhood Sergeant says, 'Oh, yes madam, no problem, thank you very much.'

He knows he could be looking at a nice easy detection here, for drug use. But he's not really *that* sad; he's also thinking *Maybe, maybe not... let's do the attitude test on the boy.*

The 'attitude test' is *highly* frowned upon by the training school gurus and everyone else who's never worked in the real world. On the streets, it's invaluable – we use it to stay alive. It's the most basic weapon in our armoury.

The test is this:

I stop you and say, 'Excuse me, sir/madam, can I just have a quick word?'

If you say, 'Yes, of course, what's the problem?' then we're already on the way to getting this sorted out.

But if you say, 'No, f**k off you pig b*****d!' then you've failed and you're about to get nicked.

So a couple of uniformed Neighbourhood officers go to see the boy.

They get in, sit on the sofa next to mum, teas with two sugars, and one of them addresses him. 'Right, Jason,' he says. 'Your mum has told us that you're using cannabis and I'm here to talk to you about it because it has got out of hand.'

Then he sits back and waits. If Jason says, 'P*** off, you're not my dad, I don't give a f**k what you say!' then the discussion will continue down the nick.

If he says, 'Yes, I'm really sorry,' then we can talk.

Jason goes for the 'I'm really sorry' option, and the officers think *Great... we're not going to have to bother nicking him.*

They'll take any dope he has, flush it down the toilet, give him a right bollocking, explain what might go wrong, and then leave. Everyone's a winner.

He has a small amount of resin in his pocket, which he hands over.

They're just about to go through the spiel about how bad drugs are for you, when mum says, 'Actually, whilst you're here, I'd like to have a look in his room but I don't know what I'm looking for. Will you come with me?'

The officers agree, and they troop upstairs. Unfortunately, Jason's a little more active in the market than he's been telling mum: on his desk, there's a set of scales, some little tools to chop cannabis up and a load of little bags – though no drugs.

'Is this stuff yours, Jason?' asks one of the officers.

'Yes,' he says.

'What do you use it for?'

'Well, I give my mates a bit of weed now and then – not for money, just because they're my mates.'

This moves matters on considerably, from possession to possession with intent to supply, on the basis of the evidence laid out in the room for all to see.

At this point, Jason is nicked.

'Er... wait a minute,' says Josie. 'I thought you were just going to have a chat with him? I didn't want him arrested... what's going on?'

She gets taken aside. 'Look,' says the second policeman. 'You didn't tell us he was supplying other kids. That's a lot more serious and we need to interview him about it at the police station. If he tells us the truth and we can get to the bottom of all this then the most likely outcome is that we'll just give him a Caution for Cannabis because it's his first offence.'

A Caution for Cannabis, also called a Final Warning for Cannabis, is normally handed out on the street as a way of getting detections for possession of cannabis without involving the court. Like a standard 'Caution', although it's on the Police National Computer for a long time it's not the same as a criminal record.

Josie's happy enough with that. It's still a bit of a win-win: we get our detection, and Jason gets off with a rap on the knuckles.

'OK,' she says. 'I'll get my coat.'

After the usual time spent booking-in, a lawyer is provided. She asks Jason what the police found, he tells her, and for once she says that it's best that he co-operates and tells the truth. We've said he's most likely simply to be cautioned, so admit to it; start to lie and we'll have problems.

So with mum and the lawyer present, Jason says, 'The drugs from my pocket are mine, those scales are mine, the plastic bags are mine and that little chopping knife is mine. I have got the scales and bags because I supply weed to my friends. But I only give them little bits and I don't make any money out of it.'

Well, that's fair enough. 'Go in there while we prepare the caution,' says the interviewing officer, 'and you'll be out of here in half an hour.'

Jason, looking suitably chastised, makes his way to a waiting room. Everyone's happy. Then, suddenly, things get really, really bent out of shape. When one of the PCs tries to create the caution, a message flashes up on the custody computer screen: *'There is a drugs operation going on in the area,'* it says. *'This is a hot spot for cannabis offences. Officers are directed that cautions are not to be issued – all offenders must be charged and dealt with.'*

This edict has come down from the Home Office, via HQ, because they have decided that we need to increase the number of people put before the courts for cannabis, and have given the force a target to hit. This sort of thing happens all the time: it tends to be localised and it also tends to change a lot. Next month they'll probably want more Street Cautions for Cannabis. It really is just bad luck for Jason: if he'd been arrested a few weeks earlier or later, things might be completely different.

The PC stares hard at this message for a few moments, thinking through its implications. Then he points it out to the Custody Sergeant. The Sergeant raises his eyebrows. 'Hmmm,' he says. 'Well, there's not much I can do about it. We've got to charge him, haven't we? So go and do it.'

The PC digs his heels in. 'Hang on a minute, sarge,' he says. 'I've just told the lad's mum and their lawyer I'm going to caution him. I'm not going back in there and telling them this.'

The Custody Sergeant sees where he's coming from. 'Right,' he says, with a sigh. 'I'll go and tell him. It'll be alright.'

He goes to see Jason and his mum. 'About that caution?' he says. 'No can do, I'm afraid. We're going to have to charge him.'

'What?'

'We are going to have to charge him.'

'Which means what?'

'I'm afraid he's going to have to go to court for possession with intent to supply cannabis.'

'But that will ruin his whole life,' says Josie.

'I can't lie to you,' says the Custody Sergeant. 'It probably will.'

'Let me just get this straight,' she says. 'I called the police to get some help with my 15-year-old son taking cannabis. We co-operate all the way along the line. I'm expecting a ticking off. Now, a few hours later, here I am sitting with you and you're telling me he's getting charged with being a drug pusher and going to court?'

The Sergeant then made the huge mistake of saying, 'Yes, but unfortunately we have our figures to think about.'

This is when I start hearing the yelling and shouting.

'I don't give a s**t about your figures, this is my baby. I have brought him up *on my own* and he has got a real *chance* in life. I've got him into the best school in the area. I work my *arse* off. I do *night* shifts. He's made a mistake, I know that, he knows that, we're trying to get it sorted, and now you're going to give him a drugs conviction before he is even 16!'

'Hang on a minute,' says the Sergeant. 'It's not me who put the cannabis in there, or had the scales and the baggies. It is a detection and we have to get the detection.'

Cue more screaming and slapping and the arrival of Gadget.

She kicked off so badly that she ended up getting charged as well. On the bright side, two detections instead of one.

I don't condone Josie's behaviour, but I do understand it. By abandoning common sense and ignoring the specific circumstances of the case in favour of catch-all directives generated on computers by unseeing, uncaring bureaucrats miles and miles away, we have wrecked her son's life. Employment opportunities are closed off immediately. He will find it hard to travel to America. He'll carry the stigma – and there is still a stigma – until the day he dies. The whole thing is screwed up. We've poisoned the relationships between the mum and her son and between both of them and us.

But there's nothing I can do about it. If I raise it with the Sergeant, his response will be: 'You want me to do nothing about a kid who is supplying drugs? OK, so put it in writing.'

As the Duty Inspector, I am responsible personally for the targets for sanctioned detections for drugs. If I step in, it's on the computer log. Once it's down on the computer, or has been called in to Headquarters, once someone mentions 'supply' or 'juvenile' (and definitely 'supply' *and* 'juvenile')... once all those things happen, our audit teams are all over it like a bad suit. I can't fudge these things with a bit of discretion any more. None of this, 'It's just a bit for personal use, so let's get rid of it.' I can't use common sense. I'd *like* to have stopped the clock, walked away from this, sat down with Jason and said, 'Right we're snatching all your equipment, I'm cautioning you for possession and intent to supply... now you're going to cough all the names of all the other kids you give dope to. You're a good lad at heart, you come from a good family, you've shown remorse, here's a rap on the knuckles, now on your way.' Then we would have gone round to all his mates' homes and talked to them, too. But now there are no deals, it's all set in stone by the system. The wheels have started turning, and Jason is going through the mincer, whether we like it or not.

And why? Because the Government has told the tabloids that it is cracking down on drugs offences. Nothing wrong with that, I'm all in favour – except, what kinds of drugs offences? Does anyone think that the Jamaican Yardies and the Turkish Mafia and Essex gangsters who bring in kilos and kilos of coke and cannabis and heroin are at all affected? The proper pushers on the estates, with knives and guns and really nasty attitude problems, even they aren't really touched. It's just kids like Jason who get tipped from 'caution' into 'conviction'. Still, our figures look great.

GOOD WEATHER FOR AN AIRSTRIKE

I recently had a childish conversation with an Inspector from another force. We were on a training course, and fell to discussing why we had joined the police in the first place.

He said he had joined to get into fights and drive fast, legally.

I told him that I joined to drink coffee and eat lots of doughnuts.

Here are four reasons neither of us joined.

1. To sit behind a desk, doing admin.
2. To bring up other people's children.
3. To react instantly to tabloid headlines.
4. To learn to be ashamed of everything our grandfathers fought for in two world wars.

As for the course, it was pretty much irrelevant. Needless to say, we spent the whole time learning (yet again) about diversity, being careful what we said at every turn and generally sticking our heads up our own backsides. Catching and dealing with criminals, not so much.

The training staff inhabit richly-carpeted offices and produce lazy, cynical and damaging claptrap.

They can deliver this unhindered by reality, and have an arsenal of 'isms' and 'phobias' with which to label anyone who has a different opinion.

As I stood in the carefully-landscaped grounds of the training centre, I looked up at the sky and remembered my time in the Army. *Good weather for airstrikes*, I thought.

DAFT PUNK

The Chief Superintendent asked me the other day if I was interested in forming a new squad to tackle street gangs in Ruraltown.

I was initially very happy about this, for two reasons.

First, there are no street gangs in Ruraltown. This means that I can run this new proactive team in the town while pretty much choosing my own terms of reference.

The second reason is that a new 'youth crime reduction' initiative (stopping street gangs) means a *budget*. A budget means new kit, kit which can be passed over to the Response Teams (who have no budget) when the initiative is over.

Why does the Divisional Commander think that there are street gangs in Ruraltown, when there aren't?

He thinks this for three reasons.

The first is that the local newspaper has told him so, mainly via its 'Letters to the Editor' section.

The second is that the District Commander has confirmed this, because he doesn't know the truth himself and does not want to disagree with his boss.

The third confirmation came from an analyst at Headquarters who provided statistics linking all the volume and street crime to the same young offenders. Further analysis showed that all these persons were known to each other. *Ergo*, they are in 'gangs'.

My view, and the view of most front line and Neighbourhood cops, is more prosaic. These offenders all come from the same estates and play (or played) truant from the same schools. They are unpleasant, mouthy and violent, but they are not members of *bona fide* street gangs. They may ape the mannerisms of gangstas, and they wear their trousers very low-slung, but the thought of the Ruraltown Bloods versus the Ruraltown Crips triggers either fits of laughter or open-mouthed disbelief in my colleagues.

Sadly, the whole shooting match was never to be anyway. I discovered in the nick of time that this was not going to be a proactive team and there was, therefore, no budget for kit. The Boss had an altogether different kind of 'team' in mind. Gone were my visions of helmeted mobs of Ruralshire's finest, lead by yours truly, leaping from the back of riot vans and wading into the homies, sticks in hand. Instead, the Boss wanted a 'crime management' team of armchair warriors to 'validate' and 'reduce' the different types of crime associated with this problem. This will all be done between 9am and 4pm, in the relative safety of a heated office, using the latest IT systems.

Not really my cup of tea. While they're forming *their* team, I'll pop round to a few of the newspaper letter writers and ask for some names. Then we'll get to work on Lates and see if we at Response can solve the problem the old-fashioned way.

SUICIDE IS PAINLESS

SUICIDE is *not* painless.

I was called out to the scene of a hanging today.

A factory worker on the Ruraltown Industrial Park had taken his own life by looping his belt around a beam in one of the light industrial units, placing his neck in a noose made with the buckle and jumping from a stool.

The police presence was Response officer Mickey 'The Head' Thompson, Sergeant Dan, me, Michelle from the Coroner's office and some CSIs. Paramedics were, as always, present. The Detective Inspector was waiting outside. He had a nice suit on. I must remember to ask where he bought it.

As we all worked together to cut the victim down and try and preserve some of his dignity, a tide of human waste poured out of his trouser leg and splashed over my arms.

I'd like to 'soft soap' this for you, but it's best told as it happened.

I went outside and the DI in the nice suit helped me wash under an outside tap by the new car park.

I went back in as Michelle was closing the dead man's eyes and making him decent for the DI and the next-of-kin.

Mickey The Head and I were about to set off in search of his brother but, as so often happens, he arrived under his own steam; after a few tears and a ciggie from The Head, he made his way in to identify the body.

They had grown up together in Ruraltown, and had shared a room in one of the small council houses on the edge of the town for their whole childhood.

Back at the nick, I binned my shirt in the yellow Clinical Waste bag.

On my desk was a letter from the Federation about industrial rights. The Government isn't giving us the pay deal that we agreed to at arbitration. The Fed wants to know if we want the right to strike.

Industrial Rights. A pay cut. Targets. A hanging body, me *literally* covered in s**t, a bereaved brother and nine hours still to go.

I got home eventually. Everyone was in bed, apart from Kibble Chops. He's devoted to Debbie and the kids, but despite the fact that I rescued him from the nick his relationship with me is slightly more edgy – he needs me to exercise him in the forest every day, but has slight suspicions about my intentions with his mistress. He looked up from the kitchen floor and watched me as I tiptoed about, making myself a sandwich. Then I sat at the table, thinking.

The guy in the factory, not pleasant. But we've had worse. I've been to a few deaths over the last year or two where the deceased has been undiscovered for so long that his dog, driven mad with hunger, has started to eat the body. I looked into Kibble Chops' eyes. He licked his lips; I swear he was sizing me up.

NEIGHBOURHOOD POLICING

NEIGHBOURHOOD Policing is a great idea, thought up to deal with a real problem but then implemented with the usual lack of foresight, rank-and-file consultation and resources which seems to characterise almost everything the public sector does.

This means that it doesn't work – in fact, it causes more trouble than it solves – but this naturally doesn't stop the Government and ACPO trumpeting its success loudly and regularly, and threatening to roll it out to every square inch of the country as soon as they can.

In around 10 years' time, they will realise their mistake and change things again. Meanwhile, we're all stuck with it.

Where did it come from?

First, you need to understand what we in the police call 'the reassurance gap'.

It's debatable what's actually happening with crime. I wouldn't personally rely on the official stats – all we really know is that some types of crime are definitely down and some are definitely up – but insofar as it *has* fallen (and insofar as it's down to anything the police have done, as opposed to, say, economic factors or employment levels), it's generally accepted to be because of 'intelligence-led policing'. This was the national model which preceded Neighbourhood Policing, and it was invented by Sir David

Phillips, the former Chief Constable of Kent, using tactics like those used by the British Army in Northern Ireland to attack PIRA's cell structure.

Phillips deployed his officers based on analysis of who was committing what types of crime, where and when. Under this system, which is still in use, we focus on known criminals and carry out prolonged campaigns of disruption against them. We stop them when they're driving about – these people are often banned or not insured, or they don't have car tax or MOTs, or the vehicle they're in is stolen. We get warrants to spin their houses. We find out who's handling their stolen goods and make it hard for them to fence stuff. It's a bit more complicated than that, but the point is that it works. It's called the National Intelligence Model and all of our own 'business models' have to be 'NIM-compliant'.

The origin of Neighbourhood Policing came after it dawned on people that NIM was leading to arrests, and that once a bobby arrests someone he or she is off the street for hours and hours. During this period, he or she is not providing a visible presence on the street and that lack of a visible presence created this 'reassurance gap'.

I'll talk more about that later, but what it basically means is that *even if crime is falling* people feel less safe because they don't see any cops about.

The response to this is to create teams of officers dedicated to different areas, tasked with sorting out everything from low-level crime like vandalism and graffiti to dog fouling. The teams are a mixture of police constables and PCSOs, with some local authority support; they know their patch, and people know them, so they garner goodwill and gather intelligence and generally walk around reassuring the public.

Gordon Brown even said recently that soon everyone will know the mobile telephone number of their local neighbourhood policeman. Like so many of these things, this sounds great but is actually quite mad; some people will never call the number, but others will ring 15 times a day about things which aren't even crimes and expect an instant response every time.

Despite that, it is, basically, a good idea and I love it. Seriously.

My big problem is that the role has been created with no extra staff to perform it.

Everyone who *now* works as a Neighbourhood policeman was *previously* just a policeman – taken away from Response and Investigation, without those units' workload decreasing at all.

In fact, the workload is *in*creasing, because if you create what appears to the public to be a new cadre of officers, and make all sorts of promises about how you are going to crack down on minor crime and anti-social behaviour (and give everyone their local bobby's phone number) you have to back that up with action.

This wouldn't be too much of a problem if Neighbourhood backed it all up with their own action, but they don't.

This is because most Neighbourhood officers only really work weekdays, during the day. (In some areas of this country now, you cannot police effectively after dark without what I call a battlegroup – dogs, vehicles, Level 2-trained officers, firearms – available to you. Neighbourhood have none of this, so if they do go out late they end up getting surrounded and attacked and then we have to go to help them out anyway.)

We have a resources display board that goes up every day in our morning meeting. I happened to look at it last Wednesday. It was an average day, and there were *90* neighbourhood officers on duty (60 of whom were PCSOs). When they showed the early and late shift splits, not a single Sergeant was on lates – they were all on the day shift, 9-5. The vast majority of the PCs were on 9-5, too.

When does the low-level crime and anti-social behaviour actually happen, with all the kids hanging around outside the local Spar shop and giving people grief? It happens in the evenings, when Neighbourhood are all at home watching *Coronation Street*. So who goes? Response teams. That's the *same* Response teams stretched thinner than ever by the abstraction of our numbers to form the Neighbourhood teams. And it's not just Response, CID are in the same hole. On one of our divisions, the Neighbourhood team's detection rates are so low that they've had to build a number of specialist detective teams around what they're doing, just to catch up.

It's a circular form of madness that would drive you nuts if you thought about it for too long.

Again, I suppose even this wouldn't be *too* bad if the jobs we were covering for Neighbourhood were proper crimes that needed a police response. Sometimes they are, but quite often they aren't.

We (ie Response) recently had a call, after Neighbourhood had all gone home, to 'children playing cricket on the village green'. Being as we're a mainly rural county, and this is England, and there's an obesity epidemic and all, I thought that was to be encouraged. But apparently not. We had to go because the 'input code' on the system was that for an anti-social behaviour offence, and once it's on the system manoeuvring around it takes longer than just accepting it. Further, we had to send a Sergeant as a minimum because the area concerned had been designated a 'hot spot' for ASB. By the way, these hot spots can be identified based on the number of calls received, so if you call 100 times with the same complaint the Intelligence Analysts' system will throw it up as a hot spot. Local councillors who know how the system works (because they sit on policing panels) encourage their friends and neighbours and electors to call the police multiple times about stuff because they know this increases their chances of a speedy response. I don't blame them, I'd do the same, but it does tend to skew our reactions a bit, and is another one of the many ideas we work with that are not bad in theory. I often think it's a shame we don't live in a theoretical world.

Later, I printed details of the cricket call out and took it to the area commander.

'Look how low we've sunk,' I said.

He effed and blinded for half an hour, and said the job was f**ked (a common refrain among the police, I'm afraid).

But that is what Neighbourhood do: dog fouling and children ignoring 'No ball games' signs or 'throwing cream cakes in the street' (I'm not joking), and when they book off at 4pm or 5pm, this is what we cover on their behalf because the public have been told they should now expect that service.

That's all fine, if they understand the inevitable pay-off.

Often, on rest days, I listen to the radio phone-ins on BBC *Five Live*. There was one on a while ago about Neighbourhood Policing, and I heard a number of callers ring in to say that officers complaining about this nonsense were just the usual public sector whingers who needed to shut up and get on with it.

And I thought to myself, *Yes, you be cynical. Because it's* you *we're not coming to when you dial 999.*

If that sounds melodramatic, it's not just my opinion. In a recent edition of our trade magazine *Police Review*, one major force warned that having to put officers into the new roll-out of Neighbourhood Policing was stretching its emergency response to the point where its officers were doing things that were dangerous for them and the public, as a matter of course, every day. It's like stripping the ambulance service of paramedics: on the 999 side of our business, we are close to death point.

Neighbourhood has the reputation of being a dumping ground for the sick, lame and lazy. That's not entirely true: there are a lot of dedicated, excellent Neighbourhood officers out there doing really good community policing. But they do have their fair share of dead wood, and those people lack the resilience of front line officers.

Neighbourhood Policing sounds great in meetings, and press releases, but in the real world, where human beings can only be in one place at one time, and there are limits to the number of people the police force employs, if you introduce a new speciality like this *something* has to give. It's not – to use the cliché – rocket science. How can those at the top not see it?

When I took my boy to scouts the other night, there was a CCTV van in the village hall car park.

'That's interesting,' I said.

He told me that it was there every Friday now. Local youths had been hanging around the area smoking dope, somebody had raised this with the local Neighbourhood Police Forum and the Neighbourhood units had arranged for the van to come down. Now, that wouldn't have happened three years ago: back then, they'd have said, *Thanks, we'll put you on the list.* So that's excellent and, as a dad, I'm really happy. But as a Response Inspector with a more strategic view, I know that we don't have endless numbers of camera vans. If this one is here, it's not in a town centre where two or three officers are trying to keep a lid on the nightclubs.

Whenever I see PCs dealing with dog fouling, I know that one of us will be getting a kicking somewhere else.

OP CLEARSPEAK

WITH the combined political might and formidable intellectual weight of Gordon Brown and Jacqui Smith behind it, the Great Neighbourhood Policing Experiment is here for some time, as I say.

To help Neighbourhood and Response officers do a better job, my force has just launched 'Operation ClearSPEAK'.

Part of Op ClearSPEAK involves over 1,000 BlackBerry-type devices being issued to bobbies, and mobile telephones being withdrawn.

The idea is that duly-equipped officers will now be able to access their email and some of the constabulary IT Systems from outside the police station.

Sounds good.

But the coverage is very patchy, which means everyone ends up parking their cars in the same places around the force area. So members of the public walk past and all they can see is cops sat in cars, heads bowed, desperately fiddling with these tiny keyboards, trying to download their latest email or carry out a check etc. Meanwhile, *anything* could be happening outside the cars and even the best multi-taskers are so preoccupied with their screens that they have no chance of seeing it.

The other element of ClearSPEAK revolves around customer satisfaction.

Here are the steps we have to fulfil:

1. Member of the public phones the police and asks for assistance.
2. Control Room questions the caller to establish the level of response; if it is not an emergency, they re-route the call to the Divisional Incident Control Manager.
3. Divisional Incident Control Manager phones the caller and goes through it all again and then despatches a patrol, if required.
4. The patrol then gets emailed or phoned with the details, and has to phone the caller to go through it all *again* and then give them an estimated time of arrival, the officers' names and what action they think they will be able to take when they arrive, based upon what they know so far.

5. Any sane caller has now had enough and rings to cancel (or takes it out on the patrol when they arrive, and the patrol ends up dealing with the anger of the caller as well as the incident.)

But how many of our callers are sane? I don't know, but we get quite a few who aren't. A lot of the callers who ring in are not normal, sober people with real problems with whom you can have a sensible, adult chat about your ETA and a plan of action – they are utterly drunk or totally stupid members of the underclass who want you to come out and resolve some kind of bizarre, violent and totally unbelievable piece of tit-for-tat.

So when you ring them, they insist on talking you through the whole thing again, usually a new or different version with subtle tweaks they've thought up since they last rang, and you can't get them off the phone to actually get in the car and start driving out to them. Or they are not available. Or they gave the wrong number. Or the offender answers the phone. Or you call and they've changed their mind in the intervening minutes since the first call and don't want anything done now. Or they want you to forget the first row and concentrate on a new one they've just had with someone else. Or they can't even remember ringing in in the first place. None of these basic, everyday, entirely foreseeable operational scenarios – I can come up with another 20 in about 60 seconds if you want – have been imagined by the clowns who come up with this stuff.

It makes our lives a complete misery, but far more importantly it wastes time and money and causes unnecessary grief to all our decent callers with genuine problems.

Look, I'm sorry if I sound like a stuck record here, but you should try working with this stuff instead of just reading about it. At least you can put this book down for a bit if it all gets too much.

SAVE US FROM LORD ADONIS

LORD Adonis, the Schools Minister for England, wants a police officer in every school.

It's to help teachers to cut violent crime, apparently.

He told a union conference: 'Nothing is more imperative than that we keep weapons out of school. This is why we gave schools the power to search without consent pupils whom they suspect to be carrying weapons, and are proposing to extend this power.'

Trained officers could carry out searches for weapons where that was appropriate, he said.

Another bright idea by someone who has never told a bolshy 16-year-old to turn out his pockets in front of his mates and three girls he fancies.

Where are all the school cops coming from? What will happen to the work they were doing before? And will one per school be enough?

Three hundred kids are pushing through the metal detector and it goes off as Steven walks through.

Who makes the others wait while PC Smith searches Steven? What happens is Steven doesn't want to be searched, and struggles? What happens if Steven's five mates all get involved? What happens if Steven pulls out his knife, and it's actually a machete? You might need four cops with shields and Tasers to deal with that.

It upsets me when politicans dream up these tactical announcements for us. It's knee-jerk stuff, made up on the hoof for a day's good headlines.

The fact is, kids bringing knives into school can't be solved with metal detectors and bobbies. It's a much bigger problem than that, and it involves parents, our culture, attitudes to punishment, right and wrong and weak sentencing. All the police can really do is put people before the courts.

We don't admit this of course, we say things like: 'We are excited about this new initiative which allows the Ruralshire Education Authority to demonstrate their commitment to new statutory responsibilities under Crime and Disorder Act legislation. This new system will allow us to work with parents, children and school authorities to provide an enhanced level of protection for young people in our neighbourhoods.'

PCSOs

DID anyone ever march on Downing Street demanding PCSOs?

No, I didn't think so. So where did they come from?

They're yet another attempt to hide the truth while trying to solve an impossible puzzle – how to give the public what they want, when what they want is impossible to deliver with the resources available (or, perhaps, how to make the public *think* you're giving them what they want).

If you ask 90% of people what they want out of the police, they'll say lots of bobbies on the beat *and* a quick response to emergency calls.

I long for the day when senior officers and maybe even Government ministers stop trying to claim this is feasible and instead explain why it isn't, at least with our current staffing levels, working methods and the other demands on our time.

The idea of the bobby on the beat, walking around his local area, deterring crime, clipping ears and arresting villains, is cherished deep in the souls of many Britons, but life was never really like this, outside the pages of Enid Blyton. Even if it had been, you couldn't police that way now. But you can tell people this until you're blue in the face and they won't believe it.

If you have an officer on foot, all the thieves and crooks have to do is be on bikes or in cars, with mobile phones, and as soon as you plod into view, the calls go out and everyone moves to the next block and burgles everything there. By the time you run over that way, they have moved on again. We hear this on the radio all the time when we put officers on foot in the town centres – they spend their whole day chasing shoplifters around the town and getting nowhere.

And what about the other public demand – for a fast response to 999 calls? We are supposed to get to an emergency within seven minutes, and it can be 15 miles away – how do you manage that on foot?

We created Neighbourhood Policing in an attempt to provide some visibility, but it hasn't entirely worked for obvious reasons explored elsewhere in this book – mostly, the fact that even when you do put officers out on foot, as soon as they come across anything they are locked away for the rest of the day, booking in suspects and filling in forms.

This is the fertile ground of general discontent in which the PCSO was cultivated.

It started with a seed of true genius: why not put people out on the streets who *cannot actually do anything?*

They can walk around all day, be very nice and effective in their own way, friendly and useful, but they don't actually arrest any criminals so they're not going to have to come back to the nick and spend three hours booking them in.

Chances are, if you put them on the beat for eight hours they will *be on the beat for eight hours*.

It would not have been talked about in such cynical terms, but that is how Police Community Support Officers came to be.

As with almost all of these schemes, it wasn't properly thought through. I'm sure the Government spent more time working out clever answers to the potential criticisms of this new system than they did about launching it.

The first problem, as we have been telling our disbelieving bosses and the Government for years, is that the people we stop and talk to on the streets are not generally nice, reasonable types who don't mind standing still and answering a few questions. They're violent thugs and, half the time, they're tooled up and itching to kick off. So the PCSOs all need to be kitted out with stab vests. Of course, if it's really getting on top, they then need to call us for help. For this, they all have to have very expensive digital radio systems.

The result of this is that trained and newly-sworn officers will spend time office-bound because the stores are kitting out another big cohort of PCSOs and there are not enough stab vests to go round. There aren't enough Airwave radios, either, and they can't afford to buy any more, so they'll have to take radios back from prisoner handling teams and CID, which means that those officers – who we previously could have roped in for jobs if we needed them – can now no longer be used like this.

Vehicles are another issue: there aren't enough dedicated vehicles to get the PCSOs from one place to another, so we spend a lot of our time ferrying them around – time when we aren't doing our own jobs, and often when we actually need the vehicles ourselves.

There are other problems with PCSOs, of course.

What do you think happens when you stick another 300 people on the streets with no serious powers (they can issue Penalty Notices and that's about it)? Their only real role in life is to call us when something goes wrong.

Quite obviously – and I don't think you need special powers of hindsight to have seen this one coming – the result is a huge additional call-load for us to go to. Were we given a concomitant number of additional responders to meet this new workload? What do you think? OK, fine, some of calls are things we should go to. But they're not all, believe me. And where, previously, Mrs Local Householder was hanging on the line for 10 minutes waiting for a police response, now she's hanging on for 45 minutes, because we're all out and about, rushing around trying to follow up calls from the PCSOs.

I mentioned the Government dreaming up answers to criticisms. Here's the kind of thing I mean.

One of the few powers PCSOs *do* have – in theory – is to detain a person for up to 30 minutes while they wait for the police to arrive.

I've already explained how violent and nasty a lot of our customers are – but how many PCSOs have handcuffs, batons and CS gas to help them subdue their suspects as we're *en route*? That's even supposing they actually *want* to subdue people – PCSOs are not trained for confrontation, they don't routinely do this sort of thing and they're often easily intimidated. Add to all that, once they start grappling with a reluctant punter who wants to get away, we're looking at Use Of Force forms and all sorts of other stuff to cover our arses against the risk of litigation. The result: many forces *don't use* the power to detain for 30 minutes.

'Oh well,' say Government ministers. 'We have provided a whole range of powers to PCSOs – it's up to Chief Constables to decide which ones they use.'

It's not reality, but if you don't look much deeper into it it's a nice way of passing the buck.

The other questions running round my mind about PCSOs are these: what do they do for respect for the law, generally, and, over time, what do they do for the public confidence they are designed to shore up? Let me give you an example.

Earlier this year, I was off-duty in a town miles away from where I live, standing outside a shop, while my wife and kids were inside buying stuff. A kerfuffle erupted down the street and I saw a PCSO tagging along behind a group of teenagers. He was following them down the street, trying to call for assistance on his radio at the same time as scribbling in his notebook. The kids were screaming abuse at him and, as I watched, they stopped and rounded on this guy, got right in his face and started spitting and swearing and threatening him. People had stopped in the street, bags of shopping in their hands, and were watching all this unfold.

I got my badge out and walked over. 'I'm a police officer,' I said. 'You lot had better clear off right now or you're all getting nicked.'

They did as I told them, straight away.

I started chatting to the PCSO. He turned out to be a former naval petty officer who loved his new job. 'It's great a lot of the time,' he said. 'But then you get toerags like that. The main guy there has got bail conditions not to enter the town centre, so I was trying to get CCTV to record his presence, plus note down the details and explain to him that he is not allowed to be here and that I was going to inform the police. You saw what happened. They just turned on me, and there's nothing I can do about it. I was in the Navy, like I said, and what I would *like* to do to him for talking to me like that is take him into the alleyway there to read him his fortune. Clearly, I'm not in a position to do that, so I just have to put up with it.'

'Is this the sort of thing that happens every day?' I asked.

He said, 'With a certain section of society, yes.'

We all know the section he was talking about, of course.

He *did* look good walking up and down the High Street. It was a visible presence of a member of 'the police family'. The problem came when he was called upon actually to *do* something. The youths know he's powerless and now all the shoppers I saw standing round watching are thinking, *Maybe I don't feel quite so reassured as I thought I did, after all?* We're in the early days of this. Lots of people still think PCSOs are policemen, and some of the ne'er-do-wells are still doing as they're told. But it won't last forever.

I'm not absolutely against PCSOs. I have had lots of them work for me and I have always liked them. In many forces, sensibly, their ranks are filled with people who want to join the police. It can't be a bad idea to have them spend two years on the street on foot beforehand. They know their patch, they gather intelligence, they go to youth clubs and try to keep the kids off drugs, they do deal with some minor nuisance behaviour.

But as a long term answer to what really worries people, the worsening problems of drunken violence, street crime and general loutishness... no good whatsoever.

I predict that the end result of their introduction will be the exact opposite of what was intended: instead of reassuring the public and cracking down on yobs, we will embolden the yobs and spread despair among the public.

The *Daily Mail* recently put in a Freedom of Information request, asking for figures on the effectiveness of PCSOs. They found that, on average, they solve one crime every six years and hand out PNDs for anti-social behaviour, public disorder or motoring offences at a rate of one every four months.

A Home Office spokesman rather gave the game away in a statement issued to the paper. 'To attempt to measure their success solely by looking at the number of penalty notices and crimes they detect is to miss the point,' he said. 'Their primary role is to provide high-visibility reassurance, build confidence in communities and support police officers.'

The thing is, you can only 'provide reassurance' and 'build confidence' if you have the muscle to back it up. When youths can spit in your face and walk off laughing, I'm not sure how that works.

YES, BUT HOW DO YOU *FEEL*?

I HOPE I've established that the police cannot give all of the people what they want all of the time.

Whether we have officers on foot in Neighbourhood teams, or in cars on Response, or divided up into various squads targeting different issues, or sat on their arses in offices ticking boxes and sending emails, we can't prevent every crime happening and we *certainly* can't solve all those that are committed. To even get close to this would take cameras in every home and a police force three times the size of the Stasi – and we don't want that. Unfortunately, crime is a fact of life in a free country (and even in unfree ones).

However, I've argued, I hope consistently, that there are things we *could* and should do to make it a lot harder for the criminals and a lot better for their long-suffering victims.

We could cut paperwork and booking-in time to free up officers.

We could convert PCSOs and most Neighbourhood cops into basic, front line PCs.

We could toughen up our courts and put public protection ahead of rehabilitation.

Where criminals who deserve jail get the longer sentences I'd like to see, we could ensure they serve them, in full.

Of course, none of the above will happen, whatever noises we've recently heard coming out of various quarters.

We live in strange times, where headlines are more important than actions, and where pressure groups and media pundits and human rights lawyers and 'experts', self-appointed or otherwise, have more say in what happens on our streets and in our jails than do the taxpayers who actually cough up for their salaries.

The truth about modern British streets is this: some types of crime are coming down and, in some parts of the country, all crime is still extremely rare. But some areas are now virtual no-go zones and some offences – assaults and stabbings by hoodied youths, for instance – are getting worse. It's these areas and these crimes we should focus on.

Unfortunately, the people in a position to make the necessary changes don't really suffer from violent crime, because they don't live in council blocks with piss-stained stairwells and crackheads slumped on the landings. They don't trust the police, they don't really understand criminals and they don't believe things are as bad in some areas as ordinary people say they are.

So instead of putting time and money into combating actual problems, they divert it into measuring people's 'feelings', changing their perception, closing the 'reassurance gap' I mentioned earlier.

If we can keep telling people often enough that everything is fine, maybe they'll eventually believe us.

We now have the 'public reassurance agenda' thoroughly embedded in our 'tactical delivery plans' and 'control strategies'.

There's a major ongoing scheme called the 'Citizens' Focus Agenda', which involves a lot of cold-calling, often by agency staff or civilian call centres, with people being asked a number of questions for a variety of different surveys. Don't be fooled by the title – the 'agenda' is not one of actually 'focusing' on what 'citizens' want, it's about honing media responses and assessing the reassurance gap and producing justifications for things like PCSOs and Neighbourhood Policing – and making sure we stay one step ahead of Her Majesty's Inspectorate of Constabulary.

Some of the people we contact have recently been victims of crime. We will select a certain crime type and call everyone who has suffered from it 24 days after the report was logged.

I was given the job of overseeing this. A few things about it puzzled me.

'How do we decide which crimes we're going to call people about?' I said.

The answer was, we find out which crimes the HMIC are focusing on and follow their lead.

'Right… why 24 days?' I said.

Because HMIC phones victims at 30 days, and the first HMIC question is, 'Have you had any contact with the police in the last 30 days?'

So whoever they call on our patch, every single one of them will say, 'Funnily enough, yes I have. They phoned me just last week.'

Tick.

The next question we ask is, 'Do you know the name of your local officer?'

The victim says he doesn't.

'Well, it's PC so-and-so. And here's your local PCSO, too.' And then we send it to them in writing, just to make absolutely sure they've got the message.

'Why do we do that?' I asked, sort of knowing the answer already.

It's because the next question the *HMIC* ask is, 'Do you know the name of your local officer?'

Tick.

How cynical is this? Are we really focused on the victims, or is it just about making sure HMIC get the right responses when they ring up?

My view is that this time and money would be better spent on policing. But the worst thing is, it's OK ringing people up and asking how they got on with us – until they say, 'Ah, I'm glad you've called. I want to talk to you about the following issues to do with my burglary.'

And suddenly the agency worker making the call, who's reading from a script, is screwed. He can't say or do *anything* meaningful, so what he does is he promises to take it up with the officer, and sends him a long email: 'I spoke to a burglary victim, Mr Smith, today and he wanted X doing, he wanted Y doing and he wanted to know Z.'

Then, later, he has to phone Mr Smith back, to make sure he got what he wanted. And he didn't, because the officer was on rest days and the email got lost in the general blizzard of electronic rubbish that surrounds modern police officers (if I am off for three days, there are 150+ emails waiting for me when I get back), so the agency guy now has to find another officer, and call Mr Smith back *again* – and this time he is out, or has moved house, or has been burgled again and wants to talk about that one instead.

Bear in mind, Mr Smith has almost certainly *had* all the service we can realistically give him. The plan was for us to phone up and speak to a victim so the victim tells HMIC they've had a good service: suddenly, we're in a world of pain which takes hours, even days, to resolve (if it can be resolved at all).

We also make another, separate round of 'quality assurance' calls to people who've rung the police about something but are *not* victims.

Sergeants have to make 10 of these calls a month – it takes up hours of their time as police supervisors, and it's not like they haven't got lots of other stuff to do.

'Mr Harris? I understand you telephoned us because you saw a car accident – can I just take 10 minutes of your time to speak to you about your experience with us?'

Mr Harris thinks, *10 minutes? I wasn't even at the crash scene for that long.* But he agrees, and we go through this long checklist of questions as to whether he was happy with us or not.

Again, the devil is in the background detail. What we do with *this* set of calls is we only actually phone people who we already *know* were happy. You go through the Command and Control System for the previous 24 hours, and the first thing you look for is people whose lost children we've found, or whose missing cats we've returned, or who we gave a lift home late at night when they were drunk. You ring them up, and ask them what they think of Ruralshire Constabulary, and they give you an hour of how wonderful you are and you write it all down, and that's one down, nine to go. You end up with fantastic results, which mean absolutely nothing.

A further set of people also get called – people rung at random, who've had no contact with the police whatsoever but who we're just generally interested in chatting to. We ask them about their fear of crime, looking for data about the reassurance gap.

Do you feel safe at home at night?

Do you feel safe walking the streets where you live at night?

Do you feel safe at home during the day?

Do you feel safe walking the streets in the town where you live during the day?

You have to question how helpful the resulting data is, here. When you're dealing with intangibles like the fear of crime, as opposed to real events that have actually happened, an awful lot depends on who you ring and when you ring them. If you ring single women in East Anglia, late at night, while the Ipswich murderer is still on the loose, can you compare the answers you get with those from calls made to similar women the year before? Or calls made to single women living in rural Wiltshire villages where there hasn't been a serious crime in the last decade?

In court, we use the concept of 'reasonableness'. If I give you a ticket for careless driving and you say, no, you were being careful, we need an objective test to decide between us. You were driving with no lights on like a maniac in the middle of the night: would the reasonable person think that was careless, or not? It's the same with the 'person of reasonable firmness at the scene', for public order offences; matey boy is kicking off, Gladys might be scared, Johnny might think it's all a bit of a joke. So, to be fair to the prisoner, we need to get an objective view. Now, if we apply that test in court, why don't we apply it to our Fear of Crime Surveys, instead of just taking whatever anyone tells us and punching it into the computer?

And who *are* we ringing, anyway?

One of my friends, a Sergeant, collared me at work the other night. 'You're not going to believe this, Gadget,' he said. 'Just as I was leaving the house this evening I got a phone call from someone conducting a police appraisal.'

This particular cold call was part of our 'Public Satisfaction Survey' and it came from someone at an agency somewhere.

My friend told the caller that he was happy to answer her questions, but that he was a front line police Sergeant and that she might, therefore, not want to talk to him.

She shuffled through her papers for a moment or two and then said, 'That's not on my list, so I will ask you anyway.'

He said, 'Ask away, but I'm just going to say that we're brilliant.'

'Yes, you can say what you like. What do you think of your local police force?'

'They are brilliant.'

'Do they come quickly?'

'Yes.'

'Have you ever called them?'

'Yes, I call them for assistance all the time.'

'Did they respond well?'

'Yes.'

'Were they dressed well?'

'Yes.'

'Were they polite?'

'Superb.'

'Did they solve your crime?'

'Absolutely.'

'Were you told what was happening afterwards?'

'Yes.'

'Were you regularly updated?'

'Yes.'

'Were you happy with your experience?'

'Yes.'

'Did you feel valued as a member of the community?

'Yes.'

At the end of it all, the woman thanked him. 'You've given us a 100% score for your local police,' she said.

'Of course I have,' he said. 'I told you I would – I'm marking myself.'

She didn't really get this, and put the phone down.

How ludicrous is that?

My point is, they must *also* be phoning criminals, of whom there are a lot more than cops, and they *hate* us. You can bet *they* won't be scoring us very highly.

I thought this deserved a little research, so I called someone at Headquarters. 'This Public Satisfaction Survey,' I said. 'We've just got our score through. Can I ask how many people in our division would have been called for it?'

'Sixty.'

'Sixty?'

'Yes. Is there a problem?'

'No. Thanks. Bye.'

I had naively been labouring under the misapprehension that, in order to get meaningful feedback from an population of 300,000, they would have called a couple of thousand people. Hundreds, anyway. But sixty? Already, I know one's a cop. Maybe *three* were. Maybe 15 were criminals. And these days, you don't have to be a criminal to be anti-police, either. Sometimes this anti-police sentiment is entirely justified. Sometimes it isn't.

Say Mr Walsh was smacked in the face and robbed by Jones, in front of his kids. We arrest Jones, drag him off, return the property, and take him to court – where the kindly/idiotic old judge gives him a conditional discharge, despite the fact that Jones has dozens of previous convictions. Happens all the time.

Say, further, that Mr Walsh sees Jones in the High Street that very afternoon, and Jones gives him a load of foul abuse and threats of further violence in front of his family.

Mr Walsh is fuming. He storms down to the police station and demands to see the investigating officer. 'That Jones, who beat me up and took my wallet, I've just seen him in the High Street. He's threatened me again. My kids were scared. How the hell is he on the streets? He should be in jail. This *cannot* be right. You lot are useless.'

The policeman wrings his hands. 'We took him to court,' he says, 'and he pleaded guilty – that's why you didn't have to come. We told them what had happened and he produced the usual sob story. The CPS dropped it from robbery to theft, because he punched you *after* he took the wallet and not before, sorry about that, and they gave him a conditional discharge because his wife/partner has just had a new baby. I'm sorry.'

Mr Walsh goes home, furious, and a week later our agency girl happens upon him at random for her survey. No, that's too much of a coincidence – she rings up one of the ten *other* people he has told about this scandal in the pub, or one of the ten people *they* have told about it. What answer are they going to give to her questions? It doesn't matter that we did everything we could, and that it was the courts who let Mr Walsh down by releasing Jones: we ain't getting a 100% score off those people.

Suddenly, with such small numbers being called, this is really important. It's important because senior officers agonise over the results at our morning SMT meetings, and whole areas of police policy are based around them. Forces, and divisions within forces, are marked on the responses to surveys like these, and put in league tables – league tables that are likely to be every bit as important to a senior officer's chances of promotion or a knighthood as actually cutting crime. Because, note, what we're *not* asking people is how many times they've been burgled, or mugged. I can tell you now that in most areas of this country, the answer to those questions, from 99.9% of people, would be, 'Never'. In other areas – the areas we should be focusing on – the answer might be 'Five times', and those calls might not be a complete waste of time and money.

I suppose you might say, *Well, isn't it important how people feel?*

I suppose it is, but is it something the police should be spending money on when we can't afford enough stab vests, or Airwave radios, or PCs (real ones, not on-paper ones)? Because I thought the job of the police was to catch criminals, not to worry about feelings. If I'm tasked with actively working on making people *feel* better, OK, fine. But which part of the job that I *was* doing do you now want me to park? What aspect of *actually* stopping crime doesn't get done while I get on with worrying about public perceptions and theoretical issues? How much energy should I put into addressing their feelings about things that have no relevance to my job or are completely outwith my control, at the expense of things I *can* affect?

Our place on the production line is very clear cut. We investigate crime, we try to deter it, we arrest offenders and we put them in front of the court. At that point, our job is done. When they're set free 50 times or more to carry on their criminal careers – again, this happens all the time – *that's* what worries the public, and it's not down to us.

I can't see any sign of this reassurance stuff stopping, though. If anything, it will get worse. We haven't yet reached the point where we phone and ask people for their hypothetical views on how they think it *might* go if they ever called us, but now that I've put the idea in print don't bet against someone picking it up.

COMPLAINTS

THE first member of the public I dealt with on my return to work after a slice of annual leave was someone who wanted to complain about us.

We get a lot of complaints from disgruntled people who are annoyed with the service we have given them.

When I was a PC, it used to wind me up, hearing that my force was crap all the time. I'd think, *No, we're not... I go to fifteen calls a night and we do* really *well.* The trouble is that, as a PC, or even a Sergeant, your perspective is limited. You arrive at some drama, you sort out the callers' troubles and depart, leaving happy customers behind you. What you *don't* know is that there are another 45 people on hold for half an hour, listening to Brahms or the Sugababes and fuming while they wait to speak to someone about *their* problem.

So – to an extent – I've come round to the complainers' side. I don't think the police are all brilliant. We make mistakes, some cops are lazy, others cut corners. We're human beings. I also don't think the public are all moaners, or criminals, or idiots – though I *do* think too many of them believe what they see on *The Bill* and *Inspector Morse* and *CSI*, where a crime happens, a big team works on nothing else, gets an arrest and the guy is banged up forever, all in 40 minutes. You might think that the public are not so daft as to believe that that is what it's like, but unfortunately lots of them are.

I have spoken to so many people who have said, 'What's happening with my case?'

'What's your name please, sir?'

'John Smith. I was robbed. That bloody Jones, again.'

'Just hold the line would you sir? I'm just going to go and have a look at my cases.'

'Have a look at your *cases*? What do you mean?'

'Well, I've got a dozen others ongoing.'

'A *dozen*? I thought you were investigating my robbery.'

Why are they so surprised? Where do they get the idea that we sit and do one thing at a time?

But if the response we provide *is* sometimes rubbish, and some of these complaints are quite justified, they're often aimed at the wrong people.

The bobby who didn't catch your burglar is run absolutely ragged and doing his level best; the fact that his best isn't good enough is down to the ACPO ranks and Home Office types who have strewn his path with obstacles.

I don't even think that everything the Government or the pen-pushers does is bad, mind you; I just think that they are economical with the truth. The people who make the decisions and sign the cheques won't come clean and admit that, as things are, there are limits to what we can do. I can only imagine that the reason they don't do this is because they fear that the public response would be to demand a refocusing of the police away from their beloved targets and initiatives and diversity projects and back to catching criminals. So they fiddle the figures and say everyone else is lying.

Anyway, my post-leave complainant. The man's name was Jessop, and he was angry because the night before it had taken us four hours to get round to a criminal damage at his house.

'It's just not good enough,' he said, literally banging the desk. 'The youths were probably still nearby when I rang. By the time your lads got to the house they'd long gone. What the hell am I paying my taxes for? What the hell am I paying your *wages* for?'

This one always irritates cops, not least because we pay tax, too, whereas a lot of the people who say it to us don't, being (unlike Mr Jessop) heroin-addicted, layabout burglars.

'I'm sorry you feel you've had a bad service,' I said. 'Now, do you want to have a real conversation about it or do you just want to shout at me? You choose.'

He harrumphed for a moment, and then said, 'Go on.'

'I'll have to look into the specifics of the case,' I said. 'But I can tell you now that your call was put on a list of other calls and, not being a life-or-death sort of thing, would be dealt with as soon as we had officers available. That might have been within 15 minutes, it might have been within 15 hours.'

'Well, that's ridiculous,' he said.

'Do you have any idea how many police there are in the country?' I said.

'No.'

'The total police strength is about 140,000,' I said. 'How many of those do you think will be available at any time to come out to you if you call us?'

'I'm not sure.'

'If you take out annual leave and rest days, appearances in court, courses, illness, injury, traffic officers, CID, domestic violence and all the other squads, maternity leave, people off with stress, custody officers, front desk, Neighbourhood Teams, licensing officers, armed officers, schools liaison, community liaison, diplomatic protection, PSD, British Transport Police, all the office-bounds and senior ranks, and then you remember that we operate a shift system so we can work around the clock, 24 hours a day, seven days a week, it's actually not all that many people. No more than a few thousand. Covering a population of over 50 million in a fairly large geographical area.'

He nodded. 'OK, I understand that not all 140,000 of you are available.'

'Locally, across this whole division, it's a dozen or so. And did you know that as soon as one of those dozen officers arrests someone, that is them off the street for a minimum of four hours, doing all the paperwork and so on?'

'Really?'

'Really. Now, any idea how many calls we get every day?'

He shook his head.

'This force takes 3,000,' I said. 'All it takes is one big fight, or a nasty accident, or just two or three separate arrests, and everything else has to go on hold.'

'I suppose I hadn't thought all that through,' he said.

'I always look at it this way,' I said. 'If you break your arm and it's a Saturday evening, and I take you to casualty, you're going to have to wait three or four hours to get it seen to. It's the same with us, except that we have to come to you. Imagine if casualty had to come to you, too. *Now* how long do you think you'd have to wait? And there are more people on duty at casualty and in the hospital generally on a Saturday night than there are of us.'

He sighed – just a normal, frustrated customer of the police service who was thoroughly fed up with life. 'It just seems like I pay my tax and I get nothing for it,' he said.

'You say that,' I said, 'but do you know how much of your council tax actually goes to fund your local plod?'

He didn't.

'The average household in Ruralshire pays £1.79 a week to the policing budget,' I said. I reached down into a drawer and pulled out a leaflet on which there was a pie chart showing how the cash is divvied up. 'That tiny little yellow sliver there is the police.' I reached back into the drawer, and picked out a couple of ballpoint pens, a little plastic helicopter toy someone had left in there and a ruler and a rubber in a set from the Post Office, and pushed them across the table. 'That is what your £1.79 can buy you, instead of policing, which covers everything from major international terrorist actions, right down to vandalism, serious road accidents, all the custody business, buying our cars and uniforms, training, the whole lot. We spent more than that in petrol just coming out to your criminal damage – eventually.'

He stood there, looking at the plastic helicopter.

I said, 'What I am *not* saying, Mr Jessop, is that I am *happy* about this. I really am not. I am really, really *un*happy about it, and I am sincerely sorry that we didn't get to you while these idiots were there. Me and my officers love nothing more than arresting people like that. It's why we joined the job. Unfortunately, there are a lot of other demands on our time. You might think some of those demands are silly, but that's not for me to say. I hope you at least understand now why things happened the way they did.'

'Thanks Inspector,' he said. 'Thanks for your time. I'm not happy, either, but at least I've got it off my chest and learned a few things I didn't know.'

We shook hands, and he left the police station.

Nothing that I told him was top secret or controversial or even hard to discover for oneself but, as I say, no-one at the top seems to explain stuff like this to people. Taking the time to point out how powerless and annoyed we are about it too can only help.

CONTROL STRATEGY CRIME, AND OTHER JARGON THAT WINDS PEOPLE UP

TWO other things I explain to people who complain, if they still have the will to live, are Control Strategy Crime and Volume Crime. They're separate but intertwined, like much of the semi-impenetrable undergrowth of police bureaucracy.

I was at a dinner party the other night. As the only policeman there, I was obviously cornered for most of the evening by people who wanted to ask how many criminals I had shot (none)/ask if it's true that you can drink three pints on a full stomach and still drive (it's not)/complain about the police.

One chap, Steve, was quite persistent. He'd been the victim of a criminal damage: his garage door had been sprayed with the word 'Tosser' and the window in the side of the garage had been smashed.

'I phoned your lot,' said Steve. 'All they were interested in was giving me a crime number to claim on my insurance. What about coming out to look for the buggers that did it?'

I couldn't speak for his specific case – different force – but it was a familiar story.

This is about Control Strategy Crime and Volume Crime.

CS Crime means types of crime that bureaucrats, our own and those in the Home Office hundreds of miles away, dictate to us as priorities. They will always include the really big stuff like rape and murder, plus domestic burglary and street robbery, but the other six or so will be things that will come onto and drop off our crime control strategy from time to time. I've just looked, and today they are:

Commercial premises burglary
Burglary non-dwelling (sheds)
Criminal damage
Theft from motor vehicles
Theft of motor vehicles
Assaults

Shed burglaries just came onto our list at the expense of class A drug use. That's not because people round our way aren't bothered about heroin addicts on the streets, and they really care about the theft of Strimmers, it's because our analysts say we've got Class A drugs under control for the time being, so we aren't worried about that any more. On the other hand, we've had a few shed breaks, so we need to get right on it. This means that everything we've got in terms of proactive resources – cameras, technical, scenes of crime, surveillance units – is diverted to the sheds. It means identifying offenders, looking into recent prison releases, leafleting homes, target-hardening and crime prevention. It means putting people out in plain clothes at night, focusing all the down time on those areas, targeting handlers. It means that every single person, when they are not doing a job, goes to those places where the sheds have been hit before, because it is not just a type of crime, it is an area too, a 'hot spot'.

'Volume Crime', meanwhile, is stuff exactly like that in the list above – the thefts from motor vehicles, minor criminal damages, shed burglaries, graffiti and all the attempts to do these sorts of things – but which is not at such a level, locally, as to have made it to the Control Strategy Crime list. The Home Office says, officially, that we need not investigate these crimes as long as they're not currently on our Control Strategy, and they fit certain criteria. These can be evidential (Did anyone witness the crime? Does anyone know who the offenders are? Did they leave anything behind? Is it on camera?) or value-based (If something was nicked or damaged, how much was it worth?)

The interplay between these two factors can, unsurprisingly, confuse and annoy our punters.

I assume Steve's force didn't have criminal damage on *its* list of Control Strategy Crime when he called, which is why they fobbed him off. If it is on the list the following week, after a spate of such incidents, and his neighbour's garage gets done over, the neighbour will get the full works.

I understand how bad this looks. I don't like not investigating crimes, however minor they might be. I would love it if every burglary victim got CSI and an investigating officer there within a reasonable time. I think it would be great if we could attend every criminal damage report, even if it turns out there is nothing there for us in the way of leads. Broken windows policing, pioneered in New York, where low-level crime is vigorously pursued, has a lot going for it (as long as the offenders get proper sanctions at court, which they wouldn't in the UK but do in the States). We *like* hassling petty criminals.

But we're back to our old friend reality again. What I would like, and you would like, is one thing: what we can deliver with current resources and ways of working is another.

Steve's garage is just the tip of the iceberg.

If you visit Google and type in the phrase 'police fail to investigate crimes' you come up with a stack of newspaper stories from November 2007.

A typical headline, from *The Sunday Telegraph*, is: 'Official: Police leave two million crimes uninvestigated'.

In the story, the reporter explains how we are 'refusing to investigate crimes including huge numbers of burglaries and thefts'.

The implication is that we are giving criminals an easy ride, and the story was widely commented upon, mostly by angry readers. The redoubtable Norman Brennan, the chairman of the Victims of Crime Trust and (then) a serving police officer, told the paper: 'The public are our masters and have a right to know why we don't turn up to every call and investigate every crime.'

There are two elements to this. The first is about solving crimes. The second is doing all we can to *try* to solve them.

There are some crimes we have no chance of ever clearing up. I'm sorry if that sounds defeatist, but it's the truth. Often, there just are no lines of enquiry – people smash up a bus stop at 2am and run off, there's no CCTV and no-one sees them. There's not much we can really do about that.

However, in many cases, as Steve would confirm, we don't even turn up to have a look. This is because, if we attended the scene and carried out an investigation every time anyone threw a brick through a window, or scratched a car, or wrote 'Tosser' on a garage, the whole law enforcement system as it currently stands, with existing resources, would grind to a halt and we would not be able to deal with more serious things.

If *Sunday Telegraph* readers really want us to investigate *every one* of those two million volume crimes, they need to understand that this will require a sizeable hike in the tax levy to pay for even more police. A practical example. We regularly get people calling to complain that their neighbour's burglar alarm has been ringing for hours and we haven't turned up. I've read research suggesting that something like 13 million burglar alarms go off every year. If we attended them all, we'd need a police force twice the size of the US Army. So what we do is ask the caller to go and have a quick look and see if he can see anything suspicious, at which point he gets outraged, and starts asking what he pays his taxes for. (Of course, if we cut back on our paperwork and got more of us out on the streets, we could certainly cover much more than we do with our current numbers.)

Most reasonable people understand this – even if they don't like it – when you explain it to them. It would help if police forces and the Government took that line, instead of making dreamworld promises about how they're going to deal with minor crime through Neighbourhood Policing and Citizen Focus and whatever follows next. It would also help if Norman Brennan's suggestion that 'the public have a right to know why we don't turn up to every call and investigate every crime' was accompanied by an explanation from Norman as to why this is the case.

The truth is, the only people who can really deal with much of this stuff are the public themselves. Indeed, they used to deal with it without us and, in many parts of the country, they still do. In the village where I live, for instance, we don't have problems with kids smashing up the phone box because our local parents control their kids. No-one else does that for us. It's not because of the massive police presence in the area, because there isn't one. In a lot of places, people now look to the police to do that kind of job, but we just can't do it, however much we might like to.

In the absence of 200,000 new bobbies or a radical change in working practices, I suppose we do have to have *some* method of getting crime down to a manageable heap.

Personally, I don't think it should be done on how much of it there is; I think it should be done on the moral equivalence of it.

If 90-year-old Gladys has had some scumbag in her house nicking her life savings, that should be of greater priority than some drug dealer who gets boshed over the head when a deal goes wrong. But it won't be, because his is a 'street crime' and hers is just a theft.

Sorry, Gladys.

THE OSPRE WAY

UNFORTUNATELY, no matter how carefully you make your case, some people – mostly, the aforementioned heroin-addicted layabouts – don't care and won't listen.

My final approach when dealing with complainers like this is to fall back on my OSPRE training.

OSPRE – Objective Structured Performance Related Examination – is the acronym for the two-part exams we take to become Sergeants and Inspectors. The first part is a multiple choice test; the second consists of a series of wholly unrealistic 'realistic scenarios' played out by actors and delivered to you in quick time. The issues are very predictable and bear no resemblance to anything you will ever deal with in real life in the role. For instance, you will be given five minutes to address something like a race riot on a housing estate – something which would actually be commanded at Assistant Chief Constable level at least. There has always seemed little point to Part II of the exam until recently, when I saw the light.

Now, when I've been through all the talk about budgets and calls and manning levels and tried to explain how we just cannot be in five places at once, being merely mortal, and have got nowhere, my last tactic is to employ the OSPRE-approved conflict resolution model, to the letter.

This means giving the irate complainer the full treatment – all the officially-endorsed patronising, politically correct, jargon-loaded nonsense I can dredge up.

I care passionately how they feel about the issue.

I offer short, medium and long term solutions.

I use the 'problem-solving clock' (don't ask).

I engage them.

I offer membership of community groups, participation in schemes, visits from PCSOs.

I record it all and check their understanding.

By this stage, I am usually on my own in the front counter office, even the most hard-core of recidivist complainants having fled at about the 'problem-solving clock' phase.

The beauty of this approach is that if you do things the OSPRE way, you can't be criticised.

You can be punched by an irate member of the public who just wanted to tell you that police didn't attend an incident for three days, but being punched by members of the public isn't covered in OSPRE because it smacks a bit too much of real police work.

SOCIAL SERVICES (AGAIN)

HERE'S another vignette involving horrific violence, family breakdown and bureaucratic intransigence.

It's few weeks back, it's a busy night and I am Duty Inspector.

I am trying to control and command everything that's going on on the streets. Because the Detective Inspectors are on-call, I'm also responsible for all the initial investigations into all the crimes that are going on in CID. Plus I'm in charge of custody, all the PACE compliance stuff I oversee and I am Bronze commander for any serious incidents in my half of the county. So I am reasonably busy.

I'm out and about when I hear of an incident going on in A&E in one of our big towns.

A teenage girl has turned up with some mates after putting her fist through the window of the council's housing office.

They've put her on a drip and told her that the doctor will be with her as soon as possible. After about five minutes, when she has not received the immediate service to which she thinks she is entitled, she has smashed the hospital reception up and run off, dripping in blood, with a cannula hanging out of her arm.

Our CCTV operators have located her in High Street. Now she has a knife, which she's waving around at passers-by.

It turns out to be Kelly.

Kelly's well-known to us. One of our regular MISPERs, her mother is an alcoholic whose children are all on the at-risk register. She's violent and nasty, this kid. Yes, she's only 14, but she's not like any 14-year-old girl you know, trust me.

We send two young female officers over to confront this blade-wielding maniac. (It's relentless, this sort of danger. It's not as bad as being surrounded by the Taliban, say, but it presents a serious amount of risk – of injury, of blood contamination, of bogus complaints being made about you later on – and our young officers get next to no credit for dealing with it.)

The two PCs manage to get control of her and the knife. It's not easy. By the time I get there, she is lying on the ground going absolutely bananas. There is blood everywhere – on Kelly, on the officers, in the gutter. In fact, I've rarely seen so much claret around, other than at the scene of a major accident or during my military service.

She's screaming. She's spitting. Her face is contorted with rage and hatred. She is issuing all sorts of threats about what she's going to do to these two coppers if she gets her hands on the knife again. A big semi-circle of punters is gathering around, watching this amazing scene develop, like a small herd of drunken bullocks. Half of them are egging her on, or telling the police to leave her alone, she ain't done nothing. Just another day at the office for Response policing, to be honest.

An ambulance arrives. He's single-crewed.

He says to me, 'I shouldn't be here… we're not supposed to answer these calls single-crewed because we get assaulted and our drugs get nicked. But when I heard your officers calling for assistance I decided to come.'

The ambulance service are heroes. We seriously love them.

'Thanks for that, mate,' I say. 'We owe you one. Can you take her to hospital for us?'

'Yeah,' he says. 'I'm not supposed to, but I'll do it.'

We get Kelly in the back of the ambulance; she's still wriggling and struggling and shouting and kicking out, so we strap her to the bed with restraints. Have we got the legal authority to do that? I don't know. When she makes a complaint next week, some human rights lawyer somewhere down the line will say we haven't, but right now that's a bridge we're going to have to cross when we come to it.

She gets back to hospital, and this time she tries to attack the doctor and the nurses. We handcuff her to the bed and the medics patch her up – she needs stitches to nasty, but essentially superficial, lacerations to her hands, feet and scalp.

Soon afterwards, a gang of friends and assorted hangers-on turn up at the A&E department, drunk. They kick off, and we now have to deal with them, too. Two of them end up in custody.

As does Kelly, after spending three hours at hospital with a couple of my officers sitting with her, helpfully taking them out of the game.

By now, it's the early hours of the following morning and she is completely calm. She's sitting on her cell bed, bandaged up, a blanket wrapped around her. The cell door is open – she is on constant supervision, with another officer sitting in the corridor, watching her. Sorry to bang on about this, but that's *another* of the on-paper shift strength taken off the streets.

So what have we got here, then? Several counts of criminal damage, numerous threats to kill, affray, assault, possession of a knife... it's a long list.

The Custody Sergeant says to me, 'We need to deal with her, guv.'

I say, 'Yep, I've reviewed her, she's alright.' This means I think she is fit to be interviewed. 'CID is coming down to see her now.'

With that, I go off to join the troops outside the local nightclubs.

Ten minutes later, two Detective Constables take her into an interview room, sit her down and make a bit of introductory small talk. Cup of tea, how are you, that sort of thing. Everything's going fine until they say, 'Right, enough of this, Kelly... let's talk about your possession of a knife and all this criminal damage.'

At this point, she goes mad and leaps over the desk, trying to scratch the nearest DC's eyes out. He presses the custody alarm, everyone piles in there and she's bundled back into her cell. I'm called back in off the streets. I go into see her. 'What was that all about?' I say.

She says, 'That f**king copper wound me up.'

Like that's a fair enough reason – even if it were true, which it isn't. 'He didn't wind you up,' I say. 'I've just listened to the tape. All he did was ask you what happened.'

She starts to go off on one again. I decide I want a Mental Health Assessment done. I need to see if she is, for want of a better word, mad. If she is, we need to get her the treatment she needs. If she's not, and she's just an aggressive little madam, we need to have experts establish that, too; if we don't, the first thing her lawyer will do when she reaches court is try to have our case chucked out on the basis that she is (or was) nuts and we didn't bother to find this out.

The Custody Sergeant goes off to get hold of a Mental Health Assessment Team (a doctor and two social workers) for me.

After half an hour or so, he puts one of the social workers through on the phone.

'Ah, hello,' I say. 'It's Inspector Gadget, here. I've got this young lady in the police station and I just want to have her assessed.'

There's a silence. Then he says, 'Has she been drinking?'

They won't assess people who have been drinking.

'We don't know,' I say. I haven't smelled any booze on her.

'That's a *Yes*, then.'

'No, that's not a *Yes*, it's a *We don't know*.'

'Yes, but under our rules if you don't know, we classify it as a *Yes*. We can't see her because she has been drinking.'

'OK, she *hasn't* been drinking,' I say.

'But you said she had.'

'No, I didn't. She hasn't been drinking.'

'OK. You mentioned that she was in hospital. Why was that?'

'She's injured.'

'Oh, we don't see them if they're injured.'

'The injuries are minor and they have been dealt with, so there's nothing there for you to be concerned about.'

There's a brief pause. 'Why is she in custody?'

'There are criminal offences.'

'Oh, we don't deal with them if they have committed criminal offences.'

I'm on the verge of tearing my hair out. We always get this. Often, we require Mental Health Assessments on people who are not

213

criminals – just folks who are suicidal, or running down the road naked, or howling at the moon, and whom we have collected on the street and brought into custody for their own safety under S136 of the Mental Health Act. But the moment you mention there's an assault involved, or drugs, or a weapon, the Mental Health Assessment Teams back off. Why they back off, I really don't know. There must be a reason, but I don't know it.

'But look,' I say, almost pleading. 'She needs assessing.'

'Well, we're not coming.'

With that, the phone goes down.

I go back through to the Custody Sergeant.

It's absolute mayhem in there by now: there are people throwing up, there are people fighting, there are solicitors wanting to talk to you, there are 'appropriate adults' hassling you, there are people doing fingerprints, talking, shouting, writing... In the middle of all this lunacy, one of my skippers, Dan, says to me, 'You know what, guv, there's actually a Mental Health Assessment Team here now. They're here to deal with the bloke in cell 10.'

The bloke in cell 10 tried to drive a screwdriver through his own eye when our patrol got to him; personally, I think that's just about all the assessment of his mental health that you need.

'Fantastic,' I say. 'Are they seeing him now?'

'Not yet.'

'Great. Where are they?'

'In the medical room.'

I pound on the door and go in. Inside are two social workers and a doctor. Just sitting there reading dog-eared copies of *Heat* and *Top Gear*. What a result! Getting that combination of professionals in one room together just when you need them... well, it's like stumbling across the Kohinoor (diamond, not takeaway).

Immediately I enter, the social workers are like hawks, looking at me with hard, beady eyes full of suspicion.

One says, 'You're not the Inspector for our case.'

I can see I'm going to get nowhere with them. I turn to the doctor.

'Doctor, I've got a real problem. I wonder if you can help me?'

'Yes,' he says. 'What is it?'

I explain about the girl and how I need to establish her state of mind. 'If she is mad,' I say, 'I want her treated. If she's not mad, I

214

want her to go to court. What I can't do is just put her out on the street, because if she then stabs you in the car park where does that leave me? Let alone you? I need a Mental Health Assessment as part of my strategy for this person.'

The doctor nods. He's a reasonable human being: why wouldn't he? 'OK,' he says. 'I'll see her. Lead the way.'

I hear a sharp intake of breath from the social workers.

'What's the problem?' I say.

'Well, we can't see her.'

'Why not?'

One of them holds out a piece of paper. 'Because we came here for this job number.'

The other starts to look really ill. She is shaking, and she pulls out a notepad and starts writing things.

'Don't worry,' I say. 'I'll have officers in with you if you're frightened.'

'I'm not scared of her.'

'What's the problem, then?'

'It's just not our job. We came out to *this* job. The police are *always* doing this to us. They ask us to come for one job and when we get here we have to do two.'

'Well, are you doing anything else just now?'

'No.'

'Sorry, I thought you were a social worker who deals with mad people?'

'I am.'

'So what's the problem, then?'

A minor hissy fit breaks out so I leave them to discuss it between themselves for a few moments. After all, it's not like I haven't got the rest of Saturday night going on in my other ear.

Just then, Kelly's mum arrives and – hallelujah! – she is both reasonably sober and accommodating. She joins up a few of the dots for me.

'It's all about Noah,' she says. 'He came round our house today and beat me up.'

Noah is Kelly's ex. He had been in prison on remand, awaiting trial for a variety of offences including a nasty assault on one of my constables, but he's just been given bail on appeal by a helpful and enlightened judge. He's supposed to be staying at a bail address in a town 70 miles away, but what self-respecting 18-year-old adheres to his bail conditions these days? He came straight back to Ruraltown looking for Kelly and blacked her mum's eye when she told him to clear off. It was hearing about the assault on mum that made Kelly go loopy earlier tonight. Confused? It's run-of-the-mill stuff, this.

'Look, Mrs Smith,' I say, eventually. 'I'd like to get Kelly assessed. Would you mind speaking to the Mental Health team about what she's going through? Will you do that?'

She agrees. I grab Sergeant Dan and we nip back in to the medical room with her.

'Good news,' I say. 'Kelly's mum's here – she's happy to talk to you.'

The social workers look at me. One of them says, brusquely, 'Oh, we don't deal with relatives.'

'Who are you going to deal with, then?' I say.

'We deal with the police.'

'But she's her mum – she knows the history.'

'What history?'

'Kelly has a psychiatric history.'

'Where?'

'In Oldtown.'

'Oh, that's not our division.'

I ask mum to leave the room for a minute. Then I turn to the social worker. 'Have you no heart?' I say. 'Have you no compassion?'

'It is not about that.'

'It is exactly about that.' There's a pause. 'Right,' I say, 'it's like this. You are a Mental Health Assessment Team. I have a young girl here whose mental health needs assessing. I am not letting you leave this custody area until you see her, because you have a duty of care to her.' This sounds authoritative, though I'm not sure if it's strictly true. 'Now, I've got to go because I have other prisoners, a very nasty double stabbing and a bad car accident to deal with. I'm going to leave you in the capable hands of Sergeant Dan.'

Off I go, to crack on with all the other nightmares and deal with everyone who's screaming at me to sign this, review that, decide on such-and-such.

It isn't until a couple of days later that I get to see Dan.

'What happened with Kelly the other night?' I say.

'The doctor persuaded them to carry out the Mental Health Assessment in the end,' he says. 'They decided she was OK and fit to be interviewed. Then the Custody Sergeant refused to keep her in because in his eyes she wasn't fit to be detained, so we had to give her bail.'

'How long did that take?'

'She was out within an hour after you left.'

'What happened then?'

'She went straight back to the hospital and attacked the original staff nurse who'd called us in the first place. She smashed her over the head with one of those stands they hang blood bags off. We nicked her again and this time we got CPS to agree to remand her.'

And so it goes.

IT'S NOT HIS FAULT

I HAPPENED to be in the Crown Court a while back, and while I was waiting for my case to come up I took the opportunity to sit in and listen to one or two others.

In every case, when it came to sentencing, the defence barristers stood up and made almost identical speeches.

One man of 22 had pleaded guilty to a nasty wounding outside a pub. The victim's jaw had been broken and a rib cracked when he was kicked as he lay on the ground.

The defendant's counsel pulled back his robe, thumbed the lapel of his £1,000 suit and began to make his plea in mitigation; this is the part where a rich, BMW-driving brief who lives nowhere near the thug he's representing uses the oiliest language he can find to try to keep his man out of jail and on the streets.

'Your Honour,' said the lawyer, 'as you will see from the pre-sentence reports, my client had an exceptionally difficult childhood. His own father had a history of criminality and his mother was an alcoholic. Given his chaotic and disordered early life...'

Having heard this twice already, and lots of times before that, I got up and left.

Before I joined the police, and probably even afterwards for a while, I used to believe that a very difficult upbringing actually did mitigate behaviour – in other words, because your home life is crap, you really can't be expected to know right from wrong.

I no longer believe this to be the case. There are a number of reasons why.

Firstly, if it *were* the case, how do we explain the many thousands of people who grow up in poverty, or come from broken homes, or have 'poor role models', who *don't* turn to crime? For instance, I have a PC at my nick who grew up in care and had a very rough time of it as a child: why is this person working hard for a living and not out robbing and stealing every night?

Secondly, if a deprived childhood *did* leave one unable to understand the concept of – say – theft or assault being crimes, how come our local thieves and muggers are the first people on the phone to us, shouting *I want him done! Get him nicked!*, when *they* are the victims? If they know to call the police when their mobile is half-inched, why don't they know it's wrong to steal old ladies' pension money?

Thirdly, any youngster from any home knows not to touch a red-hot stove top. He might be more likely to do it in the first place if his parents are semi-comatose heroin-addled alcoholics than if they are members of the church choir and the PTA, but if he does it once he won't do it again. Why is this? It's because there are serious, non-negotiable, immutable and immediate consequences to his action. What his home life is like is an utter irrelevance.

BOUNDARIES

YESTERDAY we had James in.

James is one of our prolific burglars/muggers. A ball of bile and greed covered in bruises and scars from his chaotic, violent life, with scabbed knuckles and tattoos on his neck, he'd be reasonably intimidating to most people not in the business (and a few who are).

He's been breaking into people's houses and robbing them in the street for 10 years and has a list of convictions as long as your arms and mine put together.

Funnily enough, I had personally served ID papers on him twice last week for two separate robberies. Now here he was again, nicked for yet another burglary dwelling.

When I walked into custody, he was standing at the desk and complaining loudly. The problem was that he had been in custody for twelve hours and he had now been told that he was going to stay in custody overnight. As is almost always the case, this was entirely his own fault: he was wanted on a warrant because he hadn't turned up for the ID papers that I had served on him. Again as is always the case, he blamed everyone but himself.

To up the ante a bit more, he hadn't had his methadone or his heroin. He wanted a fag, but of course we're not allowed to smoke in police stations any more.

The longer he stood there, the more jittery, aggressive, angry and threatening he became.

'I want a cigarette!' he yelled. 'AAAARRRRRGGGGHHH!'

The Custody Sergeant started explaining how cigarettes were verboten but James just screwed up his face and began banging his head on the custody desk. I don't mean tapping it in frustration, I mean smashing it, as hard as he could.

Although this was on video, and was therefore not magically going to mutate into an assault in custody, we obviously can't allow prisoners to do this sort of thing to themselves.

At this point, all there was in custody was me, one young female officer from CID (with an armful of files), a civilian gaoler (who was scared) and the Custody Sergeant. The DC dropped her files and she, the Sergeant and I wrestled James back into his cell. It wasn't easy to do, but after a couple of minutes we had him inside. Then I called the doctor, who came down to have a look at him.

As soon as the doctor left, James started screaming and banging his head against the brick walls of the cell.

This was crying out for a 'cell entry'. We carry out a fair few of these, because a certain sort of man simply cannot just behave once he has been arrested. The procedure usually involves a team of seven 'Level Two' officers led by a Sergeant, all kitted out in overalls, body armour, helmets, thick gloves and long shields. They rush into the cell and use the shields to pin the man to the wall or floor. Then he is sprayed with CS or held by force of numbers, and wrapped up in restraint belts – one tied just below the knees, one around the ankles and one around the torso pinning the arms to the chest. He stays like that, under constant supervision, until he calms down. Then he is released, whereupon he kicks off, the team go back in and the process begins again. This can sometimes continue all night, or until the guy is exhausted. (Often, people like this are charged through the cell hatch with CPS agreement, without an interview but with their lawyer present outside the door.)

By now, we had a few more bodies in the area so a cell entry it was. Once he was restrained, I looked at him. 'I'm sorry James,' I said. 'I'd love to let you have a cigarette, I really would, but I can't. It's the law. There is nothing I can do about it. You are not going to get a cigarette, so stop hurting yourself and yelling, eh?'

Eventually, he accepted this and calmed down.

If James had been brought up from a young age to understand that there were some things he wanted but couldn't have… well, he wouldn't have been here in the first place, would he? Unfortunately, that's not how he was brought up. In fact, we are just about the only people who have ever provided James with firm, non-negotiable boundaries.

If you look at James and his situation, he represents a decade of failed interventions by pretty much every agency who he has come into contact with.

Of those agencies, the one group of people you *can't* blame for his situation is the police: we've nicked him and put him before the courts more times than we can remember, so we've done our bit.

The courts, though, have handed down a series of weak and meaningless sentences which haven't been enforced, mirroring and reinforcing the attitudes of his parents and all the other adults he came into contact with in his early years.

His record will show that he has been sentenced to years and years and years in jail, but if you take a moment to peer below the surface you will find that he's never done more than three months, thanks to electronic tags and early release schemes and time off for pleading guilty and good behaviour and completing anger management courses and drug rehabilitation programmes that have no effect whatsoever on either his anger or his drug use.

Three months in jail might be fine – if the sentence *was* three months. But when the sentence was *12* months, what sort of message does it send when you only make James serve a quarter of it? What sort of message does it send out when he's allowed to breach his bail conditions time and again, or not to pay his fines, or when suspended prison sentences are not activated upon re-offending?

James is someone who is trapped in the revolving door of sociological and criminological ideas of how to prevent people from offending, when what he *needs* are boundaries: if you burgle another house, you *will* go to prison for five years.

A BAD NIGHT ON THE ROADS

IF YOU'VE worked on Response for any length of time, and you have any imagination, it changes your attitude to driving forever.

I almost died on my first day in the job, when someone pulled out in front of our car. We were doing about 50mph, and a woman in a 4x4 turned onto the road 20ft from us. We hit her head-on and bounced into the oncoming traffic, missing a scaffolding lorry by a matter of inches and ploughing into some trees. We ended up smashed into a huge oak tree, about two feet from a thick branch which lay across the bonnet: it would have taken our heads off if we'd been going any quicker.

As we sat there, senses scrambled, the front end caught fire. The driver's door was wedged shut by the tree and my side was buckled, and the flames were getting hotter and higher. We managed to kick the passenger door open and, somehow, walked away from it. Someone put the fire out with an extinguisher. No real harm done, except to my nerves, and I was back at work the next day.

The front wing of that car was squashed to about the size of a cushion: a triangular piece of metal with a jam sandwich stripe on it. For a long time, I kept that triangle in my front garden, just by the gate, so that when I left for work I saw it and it reminded me not to drive too fast.

Unfortunately, others are not so lucky.

It's a really busy Saturday night, there's mayhem kicking off all over the place. I'm Duty Inspector and I'm driving along a main road which cuts our area in half, east to west. I hear my skipper calling me to a fatal. It's 10 minutes from where I am, on a stretch of motorway that intersects the road I'm on now.

I get there and find Sergeant Dan and a deserted motorway: both sides have been closed off while we recover a car and the bloke who was driving it half an hour ago.

It's weird. The car is *here*, smashed to bits after smacking into the central reservation at very high speed and then rolling down the asphalt for 200 metres. But the only body in sight is *there* – another 50 metres or more down the road.

He must be the driver, but we need to be sure; the incident has happened close to a bridge, and it's not unknown for people to take their final journey off there, straight down into the fast lane.

Identification won't be easy. His body's in pretty good shape, all things considered, but his face… well, his face looks like yours would if you'd exited a car through the windscreen at 100 miles an hour and then bounced down the Tarmac for a while.

We walk down the road to look at him. He's really not a pretty sight. No shoes on, which sounds odd but isn't – for some reason, when people get thrown from fast-moving vehicles they often leave their shoes behind.

We stand there for a moment or two, in the flickering blue strobe light from our cars. It's very eerie, here in the dark on a closed motorway, with a body at your feet. There's no sound, save for the wind tugging at our jackets and the radio chatter. Somewhere, a family has lost a dad, a son, a brother. They just don't know it, yet.

'I'd better get going, Dan,' I say, and leave him to contemplate the body and work out how to ID it. I walk back to my vehicle, thinking about what a closed road and a tied-up Sergeant means for the mundane chaos of a normal Saturday night. Just then, a guy arrives from the Serious Road Incident Enquiry Team. This is a specialist unit which – surprise, surprise – investigates serious road traffic incidents, usually fatals. I'm sure they're very professional officers, and good at their jobs, but their attitude stinks. They swan about with clipboards a lot, and seem to think the world owes them a living. They're not my favourite people, but I try to maintain good relations with them because we're always bumping into each other.

I watch as this guy gets out of his car and starts striding about, looking important. While he's doing this, a call comes in.

A sports car has left the road and ploughed into a hill on the outskirts of a village not far from here. Dead and injured people, the caller says.

S**t. It never rains but it pours.

I look at my map. It's only two miles away from where I'm sitting, maybe less.

Who is there to go to it? No-one. *Right*, I think, *I'll go*. Hoping I'll get there after the ambo and Trumpton.

I get back out of my car and hurry over to the guy from SRIET. He's looking at the damage to the central reservation.

'Listen, mate,' I say. 'When you've finished here can you get over to X location, because we've got another fatal there?'

He straightens up and looks at me. 'No,' he says. 'No, you'll have to call me out again.'

'Do what?' I say.

'I'll have to go home, book off and then you can call me out again.'

'Why?'

'Because I get an overtime call out fee every time I get, er, called out.'

This is a badged officer, here. I can't believe my ears. I look at the skipper and he looks at me. We're both thinking, *Holy s**t... we must be on different planets.*

I look at the Accident bloke. 'No,' I say. 'No, you're a police constable, this is a lawful order, I am telling you to come from here to there when you finish.'

I get in my car, stick the blue lights on and race off.

Within three or four minutes, I am at the second scene.

It's a country lane, with a steep hill rising off to the right. It's also pitch black: a mile from a village, there are no street lights and what starlight there might be is hidden behind the overhanging trees. I can't see a damn thing, so I turn my car and shine the headlights onto the hillock.

I'm looking into a field and what I see looks, literally, like something out of a war zone: a BMW M3, in bits, as though it's been hit by a missile from an Apache helicopter. I look back at the lane. I can see a lot of mud and debris where the car has come screaming round the bend and clipped the verge. It's then been launched into the air and has corkscrewed through the top of the thick hawthorn hedge before impacting 30 metres away.

There are several bodies – either dead or very seriously injured people – scattered around the grass. I have a horrible feeling that I'm going to have to get into the field and see what I can do for them.

Just then, thank goodness, the ambulance and the fire brigade turn up.

I spend the next few minutes trying to close the road while the fire crews take chainsaws to the hedge so that they can get to the car with their cutting gear.

We get a helicopter up, a real luxury, to light up the scene. The paramedics do what they can for the people – two in the front, three in the back. Some of them are dead. I don't need to know how many.

More relief, now. It's very close to our force border, and four units from the next door force turn up. Nothing much going on for them. A big help.

Their skipper organises her people, then sidles over to me and we have one of those incongruous conversations. Dead people and paramedics on that side of the hedge, on this side she's going, 'So, guv… while we're here, I live in Roundhouses. Don't suppose there's any jobs for patrol Sergeants going down there?'

'Yes,' I say. 'Actually, there are. Do you want an application form?' Then, 'Hang on a minute… let's do this some other time?'

The Air Ambulance comes and they get the people out, one by one. SRIET turns up. It's not the guy I ordered to come. I leave, because life goes on: custody is full of drunks, and I'm needed there.

GAY HORSES, CHIP ASSAULTS
AND HANNAH'S NAILS

I KNOW I've said modern policing is mad, but I can tell you still don't believe me.

Try this one on for size.

One of my colleagues was serving an attachment on the Beat Crime Unit, a team set up to deal with low level assaults and criminal damages. One day he was sent to see the victim, offender and witnesses of an assault on the previous Saturday night outside a kebab shop.

One man had thrown a bag of chips at another man after an argument over the queue.

That was it. No violence, no injury – just chips.

Unfortunately, the CCTV operator had seen it happen and had broadcast the fact that a disturbance was happening in the High Street.

A patrol arrived. One of the drunks accused the other of the chip throwing and the other admitted it. In a normal world, the thrower would have been told to put the chips in a bin, grow up and clear off home. But because the incident had been called in by CCTV as a 'violent disturbance between two men' they couldn't leave without a crime report. Under the Home Office Counting Rules, the patrol was left with no alternative but to gather information for a report and deal with the assailant. The officers seized the soggy and now cold bag of chips and placed them in an evidence bag in the property store as an 'exhibit'. I think they were having a laugh.

The crime report was then sent to the Beat Crime Unit and my colleague there had to visit and interview all the different people involved. It mattered not that the so-called 'victim' was now sober, and didn't want anything to do with it; once an assault is reported, and especially where you have an offender who has admitted it to officers, it simply can't be made to go away. That is a 'detection' and every single one of those is gold dust; after a time-consuming and expensive process, during which the officer was unable to deal with any real crime, the 'offender' was cautioned. (We had a very similar case recently, where a kid threw a dead pigeon at someone else.)

This sort of rubbish is happening everywhere, more and more often. Ask the police in Kent, where three officers were sent to Boots the Chemist to deal with 12-year-old Hannah Gilbert. Hannah had put a tiny stripe of nail varnish on her fingernail to see if she liked the colour. A security guard pounced, because it wasn't a tester bottle (there wasn't one in the colour she liked) and three cops were sent. *Three* – for a 12-year-old nail varnish 'thief'! In the event, they left one officer to 'mediate' with Boots, and the whole thing eventually went away, but the truth is that if the store manager had been insistent, they would have had to 'crime' this. (Imagine the detections we could get if we did this everywhere, every time anyone sprayed a little perfume or anti-perspirant to see if they liked the smell, or checked the shade of lippy.)

Hannah turned out to be a member of a Christian Fellowship group, on her second-ever solo visit to town – just the kind of people we ought to be banging up. Her mum said: 'Hannah was scared and crying. The whole approach was very heavy handed. I find it incredibly hard to believe this was the most serious incident going on for the police. Frankly, this country has gone crazy. This is the sort of thing that just makes me want to pack our bags and leave as soon as Hannah's finishing her schooling.'

A lot of people will be nodding at this. Actually, in this case, it seems to me that the police handled it about right. They attended, realised it wasn't really a criminal matter and agreed this with the store.

Some cops, though, are fully on board with this nonsense, to their eternal shame. Perhaps the most famous case of recent times was that of the Homosexual Horse of Oxford.

On a night out in the city of dreaming spires, student Sam Brown said to a Thames Valley mounted officer, 'Mate, you realise your horse is gay?'

He was arrested under section 5 of the Public Order Act for making homophobic remarks, spent a night in the cells and was then given an £80 PND. He refused to pay this and ended up in court where the case was eventually dismissed for lack of evidence.

How did we ever move from arresting burglars and drug dealers to locking people up for equine homophobia?

IT'S NOT EASY BEING GREEN

IN MOST walks of life, the further up the chain you go, the more detached you become from what's actually happening at ground level.

In our job, that's truer than in most others. There are, of course, some excellent senior officers around, and I've been fortunate enough to work with one or two. But even the best of them no longer spend time rolling around in the gutter fighting with drunks, or finding dead kids in smashed-up cars, or going through the sheer pointless, monotonous, bureaucratic grind of day-to-day policing. Instead, they are dreaming up strategies and policies and systems to 'help' us on the front line.

How 'helpful' these ideas actually are will generally depend on how grounded in some sort of reality the originator is.

One of the deep joys of working for Ruralshire Constabulary is 'new policy day'.

This is usually Wednesday, and it consists of the Chief Constable sending out a blanket email to all staff explaining a new policy and couching it in all the usual politically-correct guff in which all public sector announcements must, apparently, now be made.

These new policy announcements are always about some abstract, tangential issue which, at first sight, seems to have little to do with catching criminals. Then you scratch the surface and find that, yep, it's an abstract issue which has little to do with catching criminals.

Last week we had a new 'Single Crew Policy' delivered to us.

Over at Headquarters they had worked out that if the Response Teams deployed as *single* officers, on their own, we would get twice as much exposure on the ground.

More yellow jacket bang for your buck, so to speak.

As usual, there were a few issues with this that they hadn't considered.

Firstly, it means we need twice the number of vehicles to cover the patch (F Division is 200 square miles in size, remember).

Secondly, there is now twice the amount of traffic on the radio channel.

Thirdly, we now send two single-crewed cars to all violence calls, because we can't send one officer alone.

Fourthly, if we make an arrest that means we have to leave one car parked in the street while we convey our prisoner(s) to Central Custody. Central Custody can be 25 miles away or more. After we've booked in, we have to convey the driver of the car we left behind back again to collect it. If it's still there, and in one piece.

I'm not at all sure that those who learned their street skills in former days understand that, here in 2008, not everyone in Ruralshire is pleased to see the police when we show up. Of course, in the 'old days', if you needed assistance there were always plenty of bobbies around to provide it (or you took care of things yourself and the magistrates turned a judicious blind eye).

The people who will really suffer as a result of this policy are the taxpaying local residents who are waiting patiently at home for a police response to their burglaries. Can you please wait a few hours more, while we run about trying to sort out the SCP?

This week brought another new policy. This one was about our 'Green Footprint'.

Here's the Ruralshire Constabulary preamble:

'As a service, we care deeply about the global environment. Ruralshire Police Authority is committed to providing a clean and efficient police service to the citizens of this county. We are also aware of our wider responsibilities to provide emission reductions as part of the Government's global strategy.'

OK. Now here's the actual policy itself:

All Ruralshire Constabulary staff who travel long distances to work are encouraged to take part in the Ruralshire County Council car-share scheme.

Neighbourhood Officers will use public transport or bicycles (where possible) to travel to calls for assistance from the public.

Video conferencing will replace face-to-face meetings as part of our daily business.

Here's the Inspector Gadget explanation of the new policy:

'We have run out of money to pay for petrol.'

This has happened for a variety of reasons. Not least among them is the Single Crew policy, which now sees us drive two cars to each serious incident and then pootle around the county dropping off prisoners and returning to pick up the cars we've left at various scenes. Then there are the huge and completely impractical promises we have made to attend every little call, which has doubled our mileage. There are also the hundreds of PCSOs driving or being driven miles every day to walk around empty villages for a few minutes. Lastly, there has been (you may have noticed) an increase in the cost of fuel.

Let's break the new policy down a bit further.

The Ruralshire County Council 'car-share scheme' – how's that going to work? Strangely enough, when I entered my details into the on-line database (designed to find me a 'buddy' to share my home-to-work-to-home journeys) I couldn't find anyone from the whole RCC workforce who wanted to travel from Ruraltown to my village at 3am after a Late Turn. Neither could I find anyone who wanted to report to work at 8pm and return at 6am. I guess this policy might work for office-based, 9-5 type people, who will never be late due to a difficult prisoner or a last-minute warrant or up at A&E having a fat lip stitched up – which may explain how the suggestion came to emanate from Headquarters, not the streets.

How about 'Neighbourhood officers using public transport'. I like this idea, this works. Except for one minor point. There is no public transport in rural areas. And – spookily – Ruralshire Constabulary is a rural police force.

Video Conferencing? No one reading this who works for a public service employer will be surprised to hear that the technology doesn't work. So we all sit staring at several vacant screens, while some poor PC scurries around trying to fix wires and plugs, until we eventually lose interest and do it all by telephone.

Sometimes, when we're sitting in the van outside the Copacabana on Saturday night, waiting for someone to glass someone else in the face and cause a mini riot, I wonder what next Wednesday's new policy will be.

(By the way, the reason we're sitting in the van, and not waiting outside the club to prevent these glassings happening in the first place, is because on another Wednesday the Diversity Monitoring Unit suggested that police officers standing near the entrance to such places might make ethnic minority youths feel threatened. This is especially stupid if you bear in mind that we have a tiny ethnic minority population in Ruraltown, most of whom are supportive of the police and none of whom would go to a dump like the Copacabana anyway.)

CHECKING OUT

LAST week, I saw someone hanging from a lamp post, I saw a man who had tried to shoot himself with a shotgun and failed but died later and I saw a woman who had jumped off a car park who died while we were there waiting for the ambulance.

Hanging and jumping off bridges are the most common methods of killing yourself in our area, though we also have a fair share of shootings in our more rural parts, where more people own shotguns. This is controversial – and I stress that I'm not a doctor, this is just what *I've* seen – but in my experience, people who take overdoses of tablets are *usually* not all that serious about it. Call it a 'cry for help', but most of our overdosers have a history of it and, self-evidently, they haven't succeeded. I *have* come across a lot of very poorly people, who have landed themselves in comas but who survive; not a single death, though.

Often, we'll take a MISPER call, where the family talk about the person's history of depression and how they haven't been seen for 24 hours. Usually, we find the missing person alive and well – they've just felt the need to get away for a while for whatever reason – and then I get to knock on the door and tell the relatives that everything is OK. That's a great feeling: you get a lump in your throat, and find it very difficult to speak with all the emotion around you.

Sadly, some calls don't end happily.

An accountant, a married man with two grown-up daughters, had gone missing. He'd left a note and we eventually found his car parked not far from a bridge over a deep and fast-flowing river.

By then, a week or so had gone by, and I got an underwater search team down. It was really a question of what state he would be in when we found him, but the family refused to give up hope; somehow, they discovered where we were and came down to watch the search. I managed to persuade them to leave. Thank goodness, because not long after that his body was found, trapped and entangled in some underwater tree roots at the side of the river bank.

I went to the house to tell his family. As I pulled on to the drive, I could see all of them sitting inside – wife, daughters and their husbands – waiting, and hoping.

I was about to destroy that hope and it felt horrible; I knew that some of them would fall apart.

I knocked on the door and one of the sons-in-law answered.

'I'm sorry,' I said, quietly. 'We've found him, and I'm afraid he *is* dead. I'm going to need your help.'

I went through, everyone else looking at me. My face obviously gave it away immediately, and they started crying. I knelt down next to the wife – widow, now – to be at her eye level. 'I'm sorry,' I said. 'We have found your husband and he has passed away. The paramedics have told me that he didn't suffer at all and I just thought I would come and tell you personally. I am very sorry and would like to offer you my sincere condolences.'

Her face was wet with tears and all around me were the sounds of people sobbing quietly.

I found that very difficult, and it was hard not to break down myself. It wasn't as if I'd known the dead man; I think it was the sheer amount of emotion in the room, and the fact that I had delivered the news which had kicked that emotion one way instead of the other.

In many ways, suicides are the most traumatic jobs that we go to – the people involved can often be young, they can have killed themselves violently, their bodies may have been undiscovered for some time, and the families are always utterly distraught.

I think the saddest case I've ever dealt with was that of a teenaged girl who hanged herself just before her A level results were published because she felt that she wasn't going to get the grades she needed for a place at university.

What made a very sad event even worse was that she actually did get the grades. I'm sure that her A level results were only one part of the story, but, for me, that was horrendous. You leave a house like that, and you carry a weight with you that you can never quite put down.

Some officers take the view that suicide is an extremely selfish act, but in cases like the A level girl, or where it's to end an objectively miserable life, or is an action taken in a moment of extreme anguish, I think that's a very harsh call. Sometimes, I think you can *quite* see why people do it, though you may not condone their act. A man threw himself in front of a train in one of our towns. British Transport Police – who will talk at length about the traumatic effects these deaths have on train drivers – usually deal with such incidents, but we were first there, and it was a nightmare, extremely messy. The leaper carrying plenty of identification and a note that he had laminated, almost to the point of indestructibility, because he had foreseen what was going to happen to him when he jumped.

The note said he had a terminal brain tumour, and was in huge amounts of pain which could not be managed. *Life is terrible for me now*, was the gist, *and I want to die*. At the bottom was an apology to the fire brigade, who he thought would have to pick him up off the track, details of his next of kin and a declaration that he wanted to leave his house to his brother.

We spend a lot of time searching for people who have called us, threatened suicide and hung up the phone. This guy hadn't called or told anyone: he just thought it through, planned carefully, went to the railway station with a timetable in his hand, waited for an intercity express and jumped in front of it.

There was a bizarre postscript to this sad job. The only other person who was on the platform at the time was a student, who was sitting on a bench with his iPod in, his woolly hat pulled down low over his brow and his eyes shut, head nodding in time to the music. The man who committed suicide chose to jump off the platform close to where this teenager sat. When he was hit by the train, lumps of his torso and limbs flew back across the platform at around 90mph and could quite easily have killed the boy. Instead, he sat there, utterly oblivious, until we arrived five or six minutes later.

A female officer went over to him and shook him on the shoulder. He looked up. 'Hey, man, what's going on?' he said.

She said, 'Take your headphones out please.'

He did, and she said, 'Did you see anything?'

'See what?'

She led him off the platform. I don't think he ever found out what had happened.

HAIR AND TEETH ON THE SWAMP

NO-ONE was stabbed to death (or even stabbed) in Ruraltown last night.

But there was a nasty altercation in Mugabe Road on the edge of The Swamp. Sharon Baylis pulled Kylie Mahon's hair over an allegation that she was sleeping with Brandon Smith (Sharon's last 'partner', and the father of at least one of her children).

Kylie then ran off and texted Sharon's brother to say that Sharon was a slag and would... ahem... meet an untimely end in the not too distant future.

Thirty years ago, before everyone had a mobile phone and when fewer of us looked to the State to regulate our lives, threats to kill were very rare. Now we get loads and loads of people ringing us to report this 'offence' every day, and it presents us with the perfect modern problem.

On the one hand, if we hit the red button for every idiot who says they're going to knife their ex/ex's new partner/neighbour/stepfather we would (honestly) do nothing else all day.

On the other hand, the one time in 100,000 that they actually go ahead and do it, there will be enquiries and media outrage and lots of people sucking their teeth and asking why the police didn't 'do something' to prevent it happening.

This supposes we *can* actually do something.

I often feel like saying to the journalists and agitators who demand the heads of cops when these 'preventable' tragedies occur, what would you have us do?

Do you want us to nick everyone who texts a death threat? Do you realise that there are thousands of them? Where shall we put them all? What do we do when they are released on bail almost immediately? Are we supposed to start tailing them all from the nick or the court, and watching them, 24/7? Are you prepared to foot the bill for this huge exercise in pointlessness? Will you also foot their legal bills when they sue us for harassment or invasion of privacy or something else under the new human rights laws? Will you absolve us from blame for all the other crime that happens while we're dealing with all these Kylies?

We're stuck in an impossible position, here. MPs, judges, those who write newspaper columns – they don't threaten to kill people, and they imagine that anyone who does must be serious and motivated and mean it. Actual murderers rarely give their victims advance warning; those who threaten it are usually just drunk, stupid fools with low self-control, few social inhibitions and a 500-texts-a-month-deal with Vodafone.

Having made the threats to Sharon, Kylie thought about it for a while. Sharon comes from a big family of local criminals, and has a wide, though loose, network of friends and associates. Any one of these might decide to come after Kylie and give her a good hiding on Sharon's behalf. So Kylie had an attack of what you might call, *I hate the gavers (police) but I've done something stupid and now I might actually need their help*, and called us to confess what she'd done.

When Kylie and Brandon lived together they used to get drunk every night and beat each other up. This means that someone in a suit who never leaves the office has declared Kylie as a 'High Risk Domestic Violence Victim', which means that we have to take her call seriously.

Hence, we sent a police van and an Inspector (me) to Mugabe Road to sort this problem out.

After we arrived, various members of the Smith, Mahon and Baylis families dragged themselves away from their plasma tellies and wandered up to stand outside Sharon's, eying each other suspiciously and throwing the odd insult or bottle at us and each other.

Sergeant Dan and I ended up arguing with some drunken bloke who had no front teeth from a previous incident. I decided that the best way to calm him down was to chat about the lack of NHS dentists in Ruralshire. He told me to f**k off, which I thought was harsh but probably fair in the circumstances.

Meanwhile, Response officers arrested Sharon for criminal damage, having discovered that Kylie has hair extensions. Hair extensions are 'property' and, believe me, they were damaged.

No-one got killed, but we picked up another 'detected crime' for the pot – happy days.

KIDS THAT CAN'T READ GOOD

ROLAND is all alone. Well, actually, Roland is far from alone at this precise time, but this precise time will not last long and he knows it.

Roland's mother is disinterested and his father is absent. He has various foster parents and a social worker. Roland has no friends because he is 'fat' and 'thick'. So the kids in his class tell him.

The armoured youngsters from Response stand around looking knowingly at each other. They are glad I have arrived.

'The Boss has arrived,' they say.

'Who is the Boss tonight?'

'It's Gadget.'

'Oh yeah, we know him. He eats kebabs.'

As usual, the scene is illuminated by the blue flashing strobes mixed with the dead orange of the street lights. It's not raining now but it has been. It's dead quiet, and there's no-one around except us and the firefighters.

Roland has a fuel can and a lighter. The lid is off. He is twenty feet away in the middle of the road.

'Hello Gadget,' says the Fire Brigade Sub Officer.

'What can you do for me, fella?' I ask him.

'I can give him half a ton of water before he can blink.' He nods over to his crew, who are struggling to keep a high pressure hose at 'off'.

I ask him to give me a minute. I walk over to Roland. Control are going on about a trained negotiator but there isn't time for that.

'Hello, Roland,' I say. 'Please don't do anything with that.'

'I'm not going to, Mr Gadget.'

We look at each other for a while, and eventually he puts the lighter down.

'You're a good kid, Roland. Shall we go now?'

We walk away, leaving the gas can in the street.

Before he gets into the Response car, he asks me if I think he's 'thick'.

I look at him, deep in his eyes, and grab his shoulders. 'You're not thick Roland, you're a good kid.'

Then he's away, sectioned again.

Time to 'resume', as we call it. The Sub Officer comes up to me in the silent, musty street.

'You OK, Gadget?' he asks.

'No.'

'No,' he says. 'Me neither. Still…' He smiles as he tosses the can over to me. 'It would have been alright.'

The can has a small red logo on it, which reads 'DIESEL'.

Roland can't read. No one has taught him.

I sit on my own in the car, with my head on the steering wheel. I think of my own kids and I can't breathe for a moment. But Control need me for a firearms job in town. This job is starting to get very lonely. I drive away leaving another small piece of me on the street.

ALSO OUT NOW FROM
MONDAY BOOKS

DIARY OF AN ON-CALL GIRL
True Stories From The Front Line
WPC EE Bloggs (£7.99)

IF CRIME is the sickness, WPC Ellie Bloggs is the cure... Well, she is when she's not inside the nick, flirting with male officers, buying doughnuts for the sergeant and hacking her way through a jungle of emails, forms and government targets.

Of course, in amongst the tea-making, gossip and boyfriend trouble, real work sometimes intrudes. Luckily, as a woman, she can multi-task... switching effortlessly between gobby drunks, angry chavs and the merely bonkers. WPC Bloggs is a real-life policewoman, who occasionally arrests some very naughty people. *Diary of an On-Call Girl* is her hilarious, despairing dispatch from the front line of modern British lunacy.

WARNING: Contains satire, irony and traces of sarcasm.

"Think Belle de Jour meets The Bill... sarky sarges, missing panda cars and wayward MOPS (members of the public)."
- The Guardian

"Modern policing is part Orwell, part Kafka ... and part Trisha." – **The Mail on Sunday**

£7.99 – and read her at **www.pcbloggs.blogspot.com**

Available from all good bookshops, or direct from the publishers at www.mondaybooks.com or 01455 221752.

IN FOREIGN FIELDS: TRUE STORIES OF AMAZING BRAVERY FROM IRAQ AND AFGHANISTAN

Dan Collins

OUT IN SEPTEMBER 2008 IN PAPERBACK, PRICED £7.99

In Foreign Fields features 25 medal winners from Iraq and Afghanistan talking, in their own words, about the actions which led to their awards.

Modestly, often reluctantly, they explain what it's like at the very sharp end, in the heat of battle with death staring you in the face.

If you support our armed forces, you will want to read this modern classic of war reportage.

"Awe-inspiring untold stories... enthralling"
- **The Daily Mail**

"Excellent...simply unputdownable. Buy this book"
- **Jon Gaunt, The Sun**

"The book everyone is talking about... a gripping account of life on the frontlines of Iraq and Afghanistan... inspiring"
- **News of the World**

"Riveting and unique... magnificent. A book to savour"
- **Dr Richard North, Defence of the Realm**

'Modesty and courage go hand-in-hand if these personal accounts of heroism are a measure... an outstanding read.'
- **Soldier Magazine**

'Astonishing feats of bravery... in laconic, first-person prose'
- **Independent on Sunday**

'Incredible courage and leadership in the face of almost certain death... amazing stories.'
- **The Western Mail**

PICKING UP THE BRASS

Eddy Nugent (Paperback, £7.99)

IT'S 1985, The Smiths are in the charts and Maggie Thatcher is in No10. Eddy Nugent's in Manchester, he's 16 and he's slowly going out of his mind with boredom. Almost by accident, he goes and joins the British Army. Overnight, he leaves the relative sanity of civvie street and falls headlong into the lunatic parallel universe of basic training: a terrifying (and accidentally hilarious) life of press ups, boot polish and drill at the hands of a bunch of right bastards.

Picking Up The Brass is a riotous and affectionate look at life as an ordinary young recruit – the kind of lad who doesn't end up in the SAS or become an underwater knife-fighting instructor.

'Eddy Nugent' is the nom de plume of two former soldiers, Ian Deacon and Charlie Bell. Closely based on their own experiences, it's a must-read for anyone who has served, anyone who is planning to join up or anyone who's ever thought, 'Surely not every soldier in the Army is trained to kill people with a toothpick?'

'Laugh-out loud funny' – **Soldier Magazine**
'Hilarious' – **The Big Issue**
'FHM- approved' – **FHM**

Available from all good bookshops, or direct from the publishers at <u>www.mondaybooks.com</u> or 01455 221752.

A PARAMEDIC'S DIARY
LIFE AND DEATH ON THE STREETS:

Stuart Gray (Paperback £7.99)

STUART GRAY is a paramedic dealing with the worst life can throw at him. *A Paramedic's Diary* is his gripping, blow-by-blow account of a year on the streets – 12 rollercoaster months of enormous highs and tragic lows. One day he'll save a young mother's life as she gives birth, the next he might watch a young girl die on the tarmac in front of him after a hit-and-run. A gripping, entertaining and often amusing read by a talented new writer.

IT'S YOUR TIME YOU'RE WASTING
- A TEACHER'S TALES OF CLASSROOM HELL
Frank Chalk (Paperback £7.99)

THE BLACKLY humorous diary of a year in a teacher's working life. Chalk confiscates porn, booze and trainers, fends off angry parents and worries about the few conscientious pupils he comes across, recording his experiences in a dry and very readable manner.

"Does for education what PC David Copperfield did for the police"

"Addictive and ghastly"
– The Times

Available from all good bookshops, or direct from the publishers at <u>www.mondaybooks.com</u> or 01455 221752.

WATCHING MEN BURN
A SOLDIER'S STORY

Tony McNally (Paperback, £7.99)

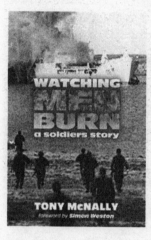

++ The Falklands ++ 1982 ++ TONY MCNALLY is a Rapier missile operator, shooting down Argentinean planes attacking British troops and ships. And it's a tough job – the enemy pilots are fearless and they arrive at supersonic speed and breathtakingly low altitude.

But Tony's war is going well...

Until they bomb the Sir Galahad – a troop ship he is supposed to be protecting. His Rapier fails and he watches, helpless, as bombs rain down on the defenceless soldiers. Fifty men die, and many are left terribly injured.

Tortured by guilt and the horror of the bombing, Tony has relived the events of that day over and over again in his mind.

Watching Men Burn is his true story of the Falklands War – and its awful, lingering aftermath.

Available from all good bookshops, or direct from the publishers at <u>www.mondaybooks.com</u> or 01455 221752.